Live Methods

The Sociological Review Monographs

Since 1958, *The Sociological Review* has established a tradition of publishing one or two Monographs a year on issues of general sociological interest. The Monograph is an edited book length collection of refereed research papers which is published and distributed in association with Wiley-Blackwell. We are keen to receive innovative collections of work in sociology and related disciplines with a particular emphasis on exploring empirical materials and theoretical frameworks which are currently under-developed.

If you wish to discuss ideas for a Monograph then please contact the Monographs Editor, Chris Shilling, School of Social Policy, Sociology and Social Research, Cornwallis North East, University of Kent, Canterbury, Kent CT2 7NF, C.Shilling@kent.ac.uk

Our latest Monographs include:

Measure and Value (edited by Lisa Adkins and Celia Lury)
Norbert Elias and Figurational Research: Processual Thinking in Sociology (edited by Norman Gabriel and Stephen Mennell)
Sociological Routes and Political Roots (edited by Michaela Benson and Rolland Munro)
Nature, Society and Environmental Crisis (edited by Bob Carter and Nickie Charles)
Space Travel & Culture: From Apollo to Space Tourism (edited by David Bell and Martin Parker)
Un/Knowing Bodies (edited by Joanna Latimer and Michael Schillmeier)
Remembering Elites (edited by Mike Savage and Karel Williams)
Market Devices (edited by Michel Callon, Yuval Millo and Fabian Muniesa)
Embodying Sociology: Retrospect, Progress and Prospects (edited by Chris Shilling)
Sports Mega-Events: Social Scientific Analyses of a Global Phenomenon (edited by John Horne and Wolfram Manzenreiter)
Against Automobility (edited by Steffen Böhm, Campbell Jones, Chris Land and Matthew Paterson)
A New Sociology of Work (edited by Lynne Pettinger, Jane Parry, Rebecca Taylor and Miriam Glucksmann)
Contemporary Organization Theory (edited by Campbell Jones and Rolland Munro)
Feminism after Bourdieu (edited by Lisa Adkins and Beverley Skeggs)

Other Monographs have been published on consumption; museums; culture and computing; death; gender and bureaucracy; sport plus many other areas. For further information on Monograph Series, please visit: http://www.wiley.com/WileyCDA/Section/id-324292.html

Live Methods

edited by Les Back and Nirmal Puwar

Wiley-Blackwell/The Sociological Review

BLACKWELL PUBLISHING
350 Main Street, Malden, MA 02148–5020, USA
9600 Garsington Road, Oxford OX4 2DQ, UK
550 Swanston Street, Carlton, Victoria 3053, Australia

First published in 2012 by Blackwell Publishing Ltd

Library of Congress Cataloging-in-Publication Data

Live methods / edited by Les Back and Nirmal Puwar.
    pages cm. – (The sociological review monographs, ISSN 0038-0261)
    Includes bibliographical references and index.
    ISBN 978-1-4443-3959-8 (pbk. : alk. paper)
    1. Sociology–Research.   2. Sociology–Methodology.   I. Back, Les,
    1962–   II. Puwar, Nirmal.
    HM571.L58 2012
    301–dc23

                                                              2012043404

A catalogue record for this title is available from the British Library

Set by Toppan Best-set Premedia Limited

by Page Brothers, Norwich

ISSN 0038-0261 (Print)
ISSN 1467-954X (Online)

All articles published within this monograph are included within the ISI Journal
Citation Reports® Social Science Citation Index. Please quote the article DOI when
citing monograph content

The publisher's policy is to use permanent paper from mills that operate a sustainable
forestry policy, and which has been manufactured from pulp processed using acid-free
and elementary chlorine-free practices. Furthermore, the publisher ensures that the
text paper and cover board used have met acceptable environmental accreditation
standards.

Contents

Series editor's introduction

Chris Shilling

This is the second successive *Sociological Review Monograph* to address the value to sociology of research methods. The choice of topic reflects a growing concern about the purpose, relevance and distinctiveness of the discipline at a time when sociologists in the UK and elsewhere face questions regarding their contribution to the study of social life and threats to their intellectual autonomy. These challenges are manifest in various forms, but are related centrally to (1) the apparent transformation of sociology's traditional subject matter (as an unprecedented profusion of data from new media and a proliferation of associated life-worlds raises fresh questions about the nature of 'the social'), and (2) contemporary systems of governance that are seeking to manage intellectual production on the basis of 'impact' agendas directed towards economic growth, national security and a narrow range of other utilitarian measures. Against this background, Les Back and Nirmal Puwar have assembled together in *Live Methods* a set of original and stimulating articles that, in reflecting upon the history of methods and in interrogating the sociological potential of new tools of investigation, map important dimensions of the difficulties facing the discipline and invite us to think again about 'what sociology was, is and might be'.

In probing these questions further, it is worth recalling what was specific about the project of sociology as it emerged in the West out of an Enlightenment context characterized by a decline in Christian notions of divine order and the rise of the idea that human life was amenable to rational reflection and intervention. Philosophy addressed this situation by seeking to identify variously the limits of what could be known, transcendent principles against which could be assessed existing institutions, and the creative and nihilistic potentialities of the human will. The later emergence of sociology, in contrast, tended to encourage the combination of theoretical construction, substantive analyses and empirical investigations, explorations that required the development of methodologies and the design and deployment of research methods in order to assist human understanding of the modern world. This was evident in the emphasis Durkheim (1982 [1895], 1951 [1897]) placed upon social facts and the use of statistical data

The Sociological Review, 60:S1, pp. 1–5 (2012), DOI: 10.1111/j.1467-954X.2012.02113.x

to explain variations in suicide rates, for example, and in Weber's (1991 [1904–1905]) development of hermeneutics within sociology via his concern to identify through a variety of data and inference the meanings, emotional parameters and motivations associated with the Protestant ethic.

If the origins and early development of sociology brought together theory, analysis and research in an attempt to illuminate social life and provide the potential for people to achieve a degree of control over their surroundings, the mid-twentieth century witnessed a degree of disciplinary specialization that was judged by critics to be a narrowing of vision that dislocated sociology from its founding ambitions (Shilling and Mellor, 2001). There was no more sweeping or perhaps powerful indictment of this tendency for sociology to become divided into either Parsonian style 'grand theory', concerned with 'the associating and dissociating of concepts', or 'abstract empiricism', in which there is fetishism for the 'how' of research that results in confusion between the methods and object of study, than that contained within C. Wright Mills' 1959 *The Sociological Imagination* (Mills, 2000 [1959]: 26, 51).

The importance of Mills' assessment and agenda for sociology echoes throughout the contributions to Back's and Puwar's *Live Methods*. There are good reasons for this. Mills detailed how disciplinary specialization and fragmentation had detracted from sociology's capacity to understand 'problems of biography, of history and of their intersections within social structures', and to ascertain those structural changes required to help people understand their lives and enlarge the sphere in which explicit decision-making is possible (Mills, 2000 [1959]: 143, 174). If sociology had abdicated its founding mission, moreover, the imagination that was once central to it seemed for Mills increasingly to be practised *outside* the discipline. These tendencies appeared to be compounded by growing evidence that the turn to abstract empiricism, identified by Mills as the dominant orientation within American sociology, was facilitating bureaucratic control and marginalizing 'the great social problems and human issues of our time', by harnessing research to 'the direct service' of state and commercial interests (Mills, 2000 [1959]: 73, 80, 85).

Mills' challenge to sociology may have been of its time but it has found strong resonance amongst present generations of sociologists concerned with what has become of their vocation. As evident in Back and Puwar's introduction to this collection of articles, *Live Methods* does not just highlight concerns about the current state of the discipline. It is also very much concerned to engage with possible futures for sociological research and the manner in which potentially new methods might be developed that would enable the discipline to gain an emboldened sense of mission and purpose. Each article in this contribution addresses from its own vantage point the question of sociology's value in a potentially new 'information age', in which the distribution and redistribution of social research have become important issues. Each displays a keen sensitivity for what Back in his own contribution refers to as a sociology, 'able to attend to the fleeting, distributed, multiple and sensory aspects of sociality through research techniques that are mobile, sensuous and operate from multiple vantage points'.

In this context, and without pre-empting the editors' introduction, I want to highlight some of the major questions and debates raised by the contributors to *Live Methods*. These can be framed within Noortje Marres' explication in this volume of optimistic and pessimistic visions of where current developments in digital social research may lead us in years to come. However, they also reach beyond this distinction in questioning the novelty of these developments and in returning to issues that have been recurrent within sociological debate. In so doing, they demonstrate how contemporary 'big data' (research occurring under such banners as the 'digital economy', 'e science', and 'transactional data') can be conducted sociologically at the very time that governments and commercial organizations are employing this information to assess current levels of economic activity and to monitor and control people's online activities. We have in these contributions fascinating analyses of the uses to which such research has been put (eg Back, Lury and Uprichard), and debates about whether centralizing tendencies within current research methods can be responded to critically via an 'amphibious sociology' in which 'there can be no single centre but only a middle, or rather many middles to be worked in, worked up and worked out' (Lury), or through cross-disciplinary and cross-practice attempts to 'map social and economic power as a whole' (Toscano). Uprichard returns to C. Wright Mills' analysis of the importance, but also the historical relativity, of history in interpreting contemporary developments. Michael's 'idiotic' objects and methods proposes a way of interrupting our taken-for-granted knowledge of the technological world in a kind of revised Garfinkelian experiment with the (material) rules by which we live. Motamedi Fraser explores the potential of research to 'provoke experience' among the audiences and also the practitioners of research, while Gunaratnam highlights the outer parameters of the concern with data by exploring the practical import of inter-corporeal understanding at the borders of life's end when biographical, historical and structural issues intermesh at the point of pain and finality. Puwar and Sharma address another theme that pervades this collection and is key to C. Wright Mills' work, the distribution of sociological research both within and outside of sociology and amongst the public at large. Noting the significance of the Mass Observation studies in Britain, from their founding in 1937, Puwar and Sharma highlight the potential of 'curating sociology' as a means of extending and stimulating the sociological imagination through creative collaborations, publicness and exhibiting; activities which for them involve a degree of *mutation* within the craft of sociology.

If C. Wright Mills' concern with addressing the distinctiveness of the discipline through questions regarding the sociological imagination echoes throughout these contributions, so too does the interest that he and other sociologists have long displayed in the practical outcomes and purposes to which sociological research is put. This is not, it is important to re-emphasize, a matter of endorsing the type of impact agendas that have become common among governmentally funded sponsors of research, developments that appear to signify a realization of at least some of Mills' fears regarding the bureaucratization of social research. It does involve a concern with helping to both build and strengthen self-educating and 'self-strengthening' publics (Mills, 2000 [1959]: 186); a theme that possesses certain resonances with the concern manifest in the US, the UK and beyond over the last decade to promote a 'public sociology' (eg Burawoy, 2005).

Mills' discussion about sociology's potential contribution to self-strengthening publics builds on a central ambition in sociology to utilize the discipline to enhance society's capacities for 'intelligent self-direction' (Levine, 1995: 267). Of particular relevance to the debates in this volume is Dewey's (1989 [1927]) suggestion that improved communications technology could help create an informed, open and self-educating public through the circulation of information. The contributors to *Live Methods* add their own voices to this debate, even if they are sometimes sceptical of the type of body that is being constituted by addressing 'the public' and are concerned with the power implications of such a move. They also seek to address an additional strand of this debate, however, by considering the potential of a dialogue and collaboration that is driven not simply by discursive debate but which is sensory and immersed within a recognition of the multiple embodied capacities of the producers and audiences for research. This is evident in the inter-corporeal understanding suggested in Gunaratnam's work, for example, and in the programme for curating sociology reported on by Puwar and Sharma.

In widening our conception of how sociological research can be conducted, *Live Methods* asks us to reconsider and make more nuanced and differentiated the sociological distinction between the crowd that is characterized by emotion and the public that is characterized by discussion of a specific issue (Park, 1972). It also returns us to those issues that were central to the foundations of the discipline itself: how can and how should sociology combine theoretical construction with methodological approaches and research methods that can assist our understanding of the increasingly complex world in which we live? Given the dominance of instrumentalism in the current era, there is much to be said for returning here to Mills' (2000 [1959]: 211) reminder that it is the 'imagination . . . that sets off the social scientist from the mere technician', an imagination that goes beyond arid technical programmes of training in methods, but that requires its own apprenticeship in learning and understanding.

The Sociological Review Monograph series consists of collections of refereed papers and could not continue without the goodwill, advice and guidance of members of the Board of *The Sociological Review*, and of those anonymous referees who assess and report on each of the papers submitted for these special editions. I would like to thank all of those involved in this process, especially Jennifer Mason, Gordon Fyfe, Rolland Munro, Larry Ray, Tim Strangleman and also the editors of *Live Methods* for having produced such an engaging and timely volume.

References

Burawoy, M., (2005), 'For public sociology', *American Sociological Review*, 70 (1): 4–28.
Dewey, J., (1989 [1927]), *The Public and its Problems*. Athens: Ohio University Press.

The Sociological Review, 60:S1, pp. 1–5 (2012), DOI: 10.1111/j.1467-954X.2012.02113.x

Durkheim, E., (1982 [1895]), *The Rules of Sociological Method*. S. Lukes (ed.), Basingstoke: Macmillan.

Durkheim, E., (1951 [1897]), *Suicide: A Study in Sociology*, New York: Free Press.

Levine, D., (1995), *Visions of the Sociological Tradition*, Chicago: University of Chicago Press.

Mills, C. W., (2000 [1959]), *The Sociological Imagination*, New York: Oxford University Press.

Park, R., (1972), *The Crowd and the Public, and Other Essays*, ed. Henry Elsner, Jr, Chicago: University of Chicago Press.

Shilling, C. and Mellor, P. A., (2001), *The Sociological Ambition*, London: Sage/TCS.

Weber, M., (1991 [1904–1905]), *The Protestant Ethic and the Spirit of Capitalism*, London: Harper Collins.

A manifesto for live methods: provocations and capacities

Les Back and Nirmal Puwar

Abstract: In this manifesto for live methods the key arguments of the volume are summarized in eleven propositions. We offer eleven provocations to highlight potential new capacities for how we do sociology. The argument for a more artful and crafty approach to sociological research embraces new technological opportunities while expanding the attentiveness of researchers. We identify a set of practices available to us as sociologists from the heterodox histories of the tradition as well as from current collaborations and cross-disciplinary exchanges. The question of value is not set apart from the eleven points we raise in the manifesto. Additionally, we are concerned with how the culture of audit and assessment within universities is impacting on sociological research. Despite the institutional threats to sociology we emphasize the discipline is well placed in our current moment to develop creative, public and novel modes of doing imaginative and critical sociological research.

Keywords: live sociology, methods, politics, collaboration, art, stories, design, digital

Sociology is facing an unprecedented challenge and opportunity. Historian Chris Renwick has pointed out that sociology was a radical movement in the 19th century because it was a new way of inquiring into society and thinking about it (Renwick, 2012). The history of methods helps us to think about what sociology was, is and might be. The early sociology of Lancelot Hogben, Patrick Geddes and Francis Galton signalled a move from the armchair to the field. Research methods became both tools of investigation and vehicles for thought. However, in the early 21st century, sociology can no longer claim exclusive jurisdiction over empirical techniques of investigation (Savage, 2009, 2010; Savage and Burrows, 2007). So, what might be sociology's value in the midst of a society that is producing more information at a greater frequency than at any other point in human history? What are the opportunities afforded to researchers where our primary tools are no longer confined to the survey or the tape recorder?

This volume brings together a range of writers and researchers who all share a commitment to re-thinking sociological craft and forms of representation.

The Sociological Review, 60:S1, pp. 6–17 (2012), DOI: 10.1111/j.1467-954X.2012.02114.x
© 2012 The Authors. Editorial organisation © 2012 The Editorial Board of the Sociological Review. Published by Wiley-Blackwell Publishing Ltd, 9600 Garsington Road, Oxford OX4 2DQ, UK and 350 Main Street, Malden, MA 02148, USA

Despite the wide range of theoretical investments and significant differences, each of these articles combines a sense of liveliness to the present with critical reflections on the state of sociological research. Our starting point is an aspiration to cultivate a 'live sociology' (Back, 2007) equal to the new coordinated forms of social reality manifest in the contemporary social world (Adkins and Lury, 2009). We were unsure initially how we might approach this introduction. Should it be a user's manual and provide a guide to new methodological possibilities? Or should we think of it as a manifesto for live methods? In the end we settled on focusing on the provocations and capacities that reverberate throughout the entire volume.

We are not, however, arguing that live sociology is one thing. It is an idea that resonates differently across the papers in the collection. As editors we have composed the manifesto by drawing out key aspects from the articles themselves and in addition invited the contributors to convey their own investments and priorities. From these we have put together a composite that provokes specific directions and highlights the capacities for the sociological craft. At the same time we do not want to suppress the intellectual differences, tensions and dissonances between individual papers across the volume as a whole. Our intention is not to flatten the intellectual distinctiveness of each piece of work included here and in this respect what follows is our own attempt to draw together the implications of what we have learned rather than produce a statement that reflects the common thoughts of all of our contributors.

Live methods aspire to:

1. Develop new tools for 'real-time' and 'live' investigation

The tools and devices for research craft are being extended by digital culture in a hyper-connected world, affording new possibilities to re-imagine observation and the generation of alternative forms of research data. Part of the promise of live methods is the potential for simultaneity in research and the possibility of re-ordering the relationship between data gathering, analysis and circulation (Marres). This can be done collaboratively in real time to produce a pluralization of observers, which opens up new possibilities for 'crowd sourced' or transactional data. However, technological enchantment should not cloud critical judgement. New devices cannot fix longstanding epistemological problems with regard to how the social world is constituted through the methods and techniques we use to make data and enact social life (Law and Urry, 2004). We may be moving to a situation where the pencil and notebook is being replaced by the iPhone and iPad but these devices produce new kinds of methodological problems as well as opportunities (Back). Researchers now have to be adept in technological and intellectual skills that enable them to engage with the mediated nature of social life in information-based societies. What constitutes engagement remains open to debate. In a piece by Edward Said on *The Public Role of Writers and Intellectuals* he notes that with the greater distribution of digital networks, while we reach wider audiences than before, still 'the chances of retaining that audience are by the same token quite chancy' (2002: 28).

2. Avoid the 'trap of the now' and be attentive to the larger scale and longer historical time frame

Wanting to move away from the mole-like behaviour of sub-specialisms, Emma Uprichard suspects that today our 'case studies are not sufficiently ambitious enough to generate the kinds of descriptions and/or theories that enable us to radically re-think, re-describe, re-imagine social dynamics'. With reference to temporality this requires that one is not lost in the short time frame of the now, captured in real time digital methods, for instance. Lost in the 'latest', 'newest' and 'most recent' 'plastic present', caught up in the nets of a relatively small time horizon. In this genre of digital research 'people remain stuck in the traps of now', and are quashing the development of sociology and its ability to iden- tify historical trends. If we remain stuck in the short time frame of the now we are also likely to 'become bereft in the imagination of futures' (Uprichard). There is a need to see the larger picture, temporally but also geo-politically, without which it becomes difficult to undertake the epistemic work of develop- ing a sociological imagination that moves between personal anxieties to large, impersonal social conditions. After all, even the most intimate experience of dying (transnationally) is part of an ecology of pain in a world 'marked by crea- tive and brutal geo-social networks and divisions' (Gunaratnam).

3. Develop capacities to see the whole, without a totalizing perspective

Bruno Latour's (Latour and Hermant, 1998; Latour, 2002) critique of the pano- rama as a totalizing device is contrasted with activist spatial methodologies and experiments. Based in the arts, touched by critical theory, live methods offer oppositional levers that valuably, in the confused mess of private troubles, provide aids to identify the 'sensitive nerve-centres' of contemporary capitalism. Herein Alberto Toscano finds, outside the academy, the qualities of mind identi- fied by Mills for the making of the sociological imagination. Within mapping techniques there is a combined playfulness of aesthetics with the serious drive to make sense of 'power's fulcrums, structures and devices'. Sociologists are urged to work with critical forms of cartography – as artistic narratives, models and diagrams – which offer the potential to think and experience the world beyond our private traps, precisely because they provide forms of counter 'reconnaissance and spying' which don't give up the strategic practice of 'seeing it whole'.

4. Make sociological craft more artful and crafty

Live methods seek to enhance our capacities towards an engaged 'artful craftiness to the craft of sociological methods' (Back). So, for instance, in the context of digital research, they encourage us to be aware but not inhibited by the expansion of corporate and state digital data sets. To intervene in this process and to develop alternative tools that institute 'method as intervention – online' (Marres). This alerts us not only to the challenges of reading digital data but also of assessing critically the way digital tools themselves shape our understanding of contemporary social life. The massive accumulation of digital data in the hands of corporations to generate (largely market driven) predictions is not approached as a threat which displaces the methodological edge of the sociologist, who faces an 'empirical crisis' (Savage and Burrows, 2007) and is left behind in the wake of digitally accelerated forms of observation and construction. Rather, these contemporary developments are a provocation to the sociologist to collaboratively invent devices which adapt, re-purpose and 'take advantage of the analytic and empirical capacities that are embedded in online media'. By developing research tools such as Issue Crawler (a web-based platform for hyperlink analysis) and Co-Word Machine (an online mechanism for textual analysis), Marres 'accords to these devices the capacity to generate potentially new methods of social research'. This also means that sociological craft is extended into technical realms that require us to care about new skills and techniques. Being more artful in our practice means learning to take an interest not only in photography or in creating an installation but also in how to make a data visualization tool like Gephi display word labels or create word clouds from wordpress sites. Caring about these practical problems of craft can lead to a deeper engagement with internal mechanisms and social realities of technology and informational cultures. Contrary to being dazzled by the profusion of data sets and reduced to a state of 'data envy' (Back), the emphasis is on adapting and remaking 'research tools that run on top of web devices, like Google' (Marres).

5. Develop empirical devices and probes that produce affects and reactions that re-invent relations to the social and environmental

The conversation between sociology and design expands the capacity to build new kinds of research devices or probes: this also is an invitation to encourage a playfulness that undermines and interrogates prevailing research conventions. On the basis that an object is part of the empirical process of engagement Mike Michael advocates 'proactive idiocy'. Influenced by speculative design, he reminds us that in this field 'probes proactively seek the idiotic'. This introduces a live sociology which 'actively seeks out' empirical objects and events that are 'idiotic' (Stengers, 2005). The 'idiotic' is 'possessed of an incommensurable difference that enables us to slow down and reflect on what we (as social scientists) are busy doing'.

We need to take our research tools and devices for a walk. Michel de Certeau's (1984) idle walker is identified as a precedent for designing sociological accounts. This draws on Charles Baudelaire's image of the 'flâneur', which has been appropriated in a range of ways from the gothic Marxism of Walter Benjamin (2006) to sexual politics and queer theory (Munt, 1998). As the idle walker evades the disciplinary grids of being in the city, they present us with a prototype that prompts unexpected relationalities with the environment, the body and the senses. Presented with strange encounters, alternative ways of categorizing and knowing the world emerge. Within this 'idiotic-methodology' we as researchers become exposed to openness and the liveliness of the events we try to get close to. The idea here is to generate better questions rather than fixed answers.

Speculative idiotic prototypes carry the open-ended potential to re-imagine future inhabitations and relationships. Given that the relation of subject to object is one which is in 'perpetual animation' we could, arguably, be led towards a frog's eye rather than a bird's eye view (Lury). Celia Lury makes a case for an 'amphibious sociology', on the basis that this is a categorization which references animals that live both in water and on land, living in two media. Taking this further she says that 'we live in (at least) two media'. We exist 'in a dynamic or live space that is the product of artificial, para-textual forces', an insight that prompts us to re-conceptualize how specific properties of our humanity are incorporated into and divested from the methods we use in the craft of thinking sociologically.

6. Curating sociology within new public platforms

Explicit research questions can be critically transformed into aesthetic practices. Thus in our craft we consider 'learning new strategies for telling society and for affecting and persuading audiences' (Puwar and Sharma). The curation of public performances and exhibitions, for instance, involves morphing and becoming 'apprentices in the craft of curatorship through practice' (Puwar and Sharma). Tools are developed for sharing, adapting and absorption. Experiments are conducted to generate prototypes for collaborative working practices across disciplines. According to Bruno Latour scholars and researchers have a limited capacity to make things because they are inhibited by the modes of cultural critique that they were schooled in. He writes provocatively 'what performs a critique cannot also compose' (Latour, 2010: 475). The challenge for live sociology is how to undertake making and critical thinking in equal measure. Puwar and Sharma, for instance, use the notion of *call-and-response* drawn from oral and musical traditions and reinvent it as a method that allows for both autonomy and exchange for collaborations between academics, film-makers, artists and musicians. Without bearing the impossible weight of becoming 'Jack of all trades' and the 'master of none' [*sic*], dialogue and collaboration is instituted across disciplines and creative movements. Working with artists, designers, musicians and film-makers enables new modes of sociology to be developed and performed. The approach remains alert to regimes that direct collaboration towards measures of social impact or other criteria (Strathern, 2004). We open ourselves to collaborative relations wherein these specialists do not simply service sociologists. Rather we induce capacities for a respectful exchange, with both partners open to mutation and becoming otherwise.

7. Utilize our senses equally in attending to the social world

The attentiveness that heightens our capacities as researchers needs to be in touch with the full range of the senses and the 'multiple registers' within which social life is realized. Pushing further the already emergent multi-modal forms of sociological methods, as researchers we learn to embody movement so that 'ethnography becomes a kind of social ballet' (Back). In this process the very 'quality of data makes other kinds of critical imagination possible'. Thus, the sociologist becomes not only attentive to what people say but also to the *doing* of social life. We become mindful of tacit co-existence, the fleeting, the emotional and sensory. The challenge is to do this without falling into an 'intrusive empiricism' that carves up the life of life. As sociologists are in the middle of the process of recovering the senses in relatively new methodological directions, let us not forget that the sensory has always been constitutive of the social texture of life. Sociological attentiveness and listening has been put to use in warfare through enlisting academic researchers in the Human Terrain Teams operating within the US Military. Commercial organizations are continuously re-calibrating their products and our senses for new markets; market research consultancy firms specialize in being attentive to the senses. We have to train ourselves to be alert to what uses the sensory has been put already, as well as where else we can take it. Thus we not only argue for an alternative future but we also have to 'craft one into existence' (Back). *Noise of the Past* acknowledged the very production of war, memory and nation as a sensory set of encounters and resonances. At the same time this creative public production sought to reroute current resonances into new moments (Puwar and Sharma). We launch these pieces as kinaesthetic provocations in the social world.

8. Foster the liveliness of words

Fostering the liveliness of words requires that we provoke ourselves as writers to recognize that what we do is 'closer to sculpting (something material) than writing (something discursive)' (Motamedi Fraser). It requires that we develop capacities for recognizing how the 'make believe' might be an aid to the sociological imagination: if, for a moment, we slow down to consider what sociology 'does with its materials and methods', we may better grasp the kinds of relations we are in and could be in (Motamedi Fraser). Sociology need not lose its disciplinary distinctiveness within the 'make believe', as we craft 'patterns of relations' between facts, fictions and truths.

Storying can thus be a provocation, as it has been to Motamedi Fraser who has sculpted the 'vitality of words' from an uncatalogued archive which she has found and started to care for in the Bodleian library. In the *'Irradiant Archive'*, the very liveliness of 'words as forces in the field of research' has led her to imaginatively explore Iranian and British relations. Myth, affect and historical fact come together in her novel, which has been written outside the confines of sociological chronicles. The 'make-believe' does not sit comfortably in the inventory of methods. Nevertheless, widening the parameters of what counts as sociological research will strengthen rather than weaken the discipline.

There is, for instance, the relationship between surrealism and mass observation studies (Hubble, 2012) or the *cinéma vérité* forged between the film-maker Jean Rouch and the sociologist Edgar Morin in the making of their 1960s documentary *Chronique d'un été* (Chronicle of a Summer).[1] Today, technical innovations have further enhanced the researcher's capacity to work with the 'make-believe', to develop multimodal forms of analysis which incite the researcher to do the craft differently. Using multimedia and new devices we can produce pieces of work that are 'compounds of word, image, sound and text' (Back).

9. Recover sociology's history of inventive craft

Within sociology's past, tendencies can be recovered that provide the historical foundation for live sociology. Invention and methodological innovation were very much part of the early days of sociology. Nowadays, there is also a yearning for researchers to achieve proximity to social phenomenon and this includes scientific techniques along with forms of artistic experimentation. It is relatively well established that Francis Galton (1822–1911) invented the statistical questionnaire; for him society was a statistical phenomenon and statistics provided a means to question what was known, seen and heard. There was a profound search at the London School of Economics (LSE) through the work of Lancelot Hogben for scientific methods that were equivalent to the scientist's laboratory. Until recently it was little known that Patrick Geddes (1854–1932) created innovative, site-specific sociological experiments like the 'Outlook Tower' in Edinburgh to foster a sociological attention and reconfigure looking and listening (Bates, 2011; see also Scott, 2007). L. T. Hobhouse, who beat Galton and Geddes to the prize of the first chair of sociology at the LSE, was preoccupied with first principles and theory that steered sociology away from inventive craft. Returning to this history and recovering in it the experimental combination of art and science provides a licence for methodological experimentation today.

We argue for a re-examination of the history of sociological craft and the need to exhume the full range of methodological experiments to be found there (Puwar and Sharma). We also remain sceptical of the cultish compulsion for innovation for its own sake or hollow and showy inventiveness. Paul Connerton, in *How Modernity Forgets*, reminds us of two corollaries – the cultish memorialization of specific pasts and the need for newness and the erasure of memory in the market (Connerton, 2009). While we excavate creative practices, which have largely remained off the radar of the textbook version of sociological methods, we do not want to do this in a manner that becomes embroiled in the parochial history of British and North American sociology. At the same time, as we invent new future oriented methods, we do not want the institutional (career) imperative to merely display inventiveness like the emperor's new clothes. Thus it is important to look back over sociology's history and tease out lessons for developing live sociology now (Puwar, 2012).

10. Take time, think carefully and slowly

We need to rethink the relationship between time and scholarship. The governmental regimes of audit and measuring produce a frenzied rhythm of research assessment exercises in the UK. The imperative to publish fast threatens both the attention that social researchers can apply and the quality of our writing. Fostering alternative ethical and political reasons for being 'there' in the context of research offers a counter-weight to the forces of instrumentalism and timidity within academic sociology. The long-term intellectual future of the discipline is best served by participating in modes of knowledge that are beyond the instrumentalism of the audit culture and what is referred to in the United Kingdom as the 'impact agenda', that is, the need to demonstrate the value of sociological research and writing through providing evidence of its impact on the economy or social policy.

Live methods involve immersion, time and 'unpredictable attentiveness', allowing for a 'transformation of perspectives that moves slowly over time, between fieldwork sites and the academy' (Gunaratnam). For instance, the transformative experience of switching modes from researcher to archivist requires the long immersion of attentiveness (Motamedi Fraser). The patience of long-term studies rather than the 'quick encounter' meant it took Veena Das 20 years to write her book *Life of Words* (2006), which has subsequently been used by critical theorists as well as artists. From working with the terminally ill, Yasmin Gunaratnam notes that just as 'attentiveness to the situation' of total pain requires 'experimental care' from the carers, researchers also have to attend to 'improvisations of methodology'. She notes the circuits of 'inter-dependency between learning to be affected and being affected'. Some forms of connection and understanding cannot be resolved in short time-spans. They require time. She reminds us of how it took Pierre Bourdieu a decade of repeated listening to tape-recorded interviews with two farmers to appreciate the precarious nature of their existence.

Yet in the academy outputs are speeded up and 'time is short', leaving very little room for failure or open-ended research (Motamedi Fraser). Research and the outputs of research have to be decided in advance of funding applications and sabbaticals. We need to provoke ways of interrupting this rushed temporality because it works against good quality immersive and attentive research. Or, as Emma Uprichard puts it, we need to find ways to destabilize our bureaucratic modes of measure and value. Yet she fears that sociologists have lost the confidence in our discipline and are not 'brave enough or confident enough to stand up and refuse to accept some of the conditions that increasingly obstruct our own work and knowledge systems'.

It is not a matter of refusing or moving away from the use of 'metrics' but rather subjecting them to a critical investigation of their deployment within the audit culture that has taken hold in academic life. Along with Roger Burrows (2012), we argue for the need to subject the metrics like the 'H Index', used to create a single measure of a scholar's value, to serious sociological investigation.[2] The usefulness of metrics should not be reduced to the perverse means by which they serve the audit institutional market culture. This includes measurements of research and teaching including university admissions figures in the neo-liberal era of education. Metrics have the capacity to make complex social processes legible and empirical sociology needs to keep open the possibility that they may be re-purposed to 'disclose and enact social liveliness' (Marres).

11. Engage political and ethical issues without arrogance or the drum roll of political piety

In 1895, in the opening essay of the first issue of the *American Sociological Journal*, Albion Small stressed the importance of the discipline's capacity to intervene in public issues (Small, 1895). More recently, the American Sociology Association has rallied to the promise of a public sociology (Burawoy, 2005). Notwithstanding the contentious issue of what constitutes a public aversion to connecting the craft of the sociologist to politics continues (see Bourdieu, 2003). We are not proposing a commitment to a programmatic or party political manifesto (Latour, 2010), neither do we want to play God in saving the wretched of the earth (Chow, 1998). Bearing in mind these potential traps and pitfalls, Back argues that politics cannot be put on hold and in fact a 'renewed political purpose' is what the sociological craft requires. There is potentially the 'underlying drive of methodology as a disposition and imperative to care about and to ameliorate suffering' (Gunaratnam). What we choose to be concerned with, or focus on and listen to, involves making judgements not only about what is valuable but also what is important. Sociology has a public responsibility to pay attention to vulnerable and precarious lives and to seek to establish the conditions that offer them a 'livable and breathable "home"' (Latour, 2010: 488). To this end the discipline has the capacity to 'develop strategic knowledge in the public practice of social science' (Toscano).

The Sociological Review, 60:S1, pp. 6–17 (2012), DOI: 10.1111/j.1467-954X.2012.02114.x

Turning our backs on sociology as an ethical vocation is tantamount to what Toscano graphically describes as a 'lobotomy of the relation between social research and political action'. Let us not forget that the power of sociology can precisely be its performative capacity as a subject. Speaking of Marx, Weber, Durkheim and Merton, Uprichard notes that their 'detailed multi-dimensional and historical descriptions . . . effectively produced theoretical and empirical descriptions that were causally influential in thinking change and continuity in the social world'. The exercise of reflexivity in knowledge production has productively situated the claims that scholars in sociology can make. However, within an increasingly regulated university context the preoccupation with 'ethical approval' and 'risk assessments' results in anxiety among researchers producing something close to a kind of 'ethical hypochondria' (Back). Adjoining the medical analogy with the spirit of a manifesto, Uprichard urges us to consider the ways in which sociology is 'rotting from the inside out and not empowering anybody anymore, as a way of going some way towards trying to create desired changes both to the discipline and the world in which it is situated.'

* * *

In the 20th century, sociology's distinctive position relied on its research methods (survey, interview and focus group), which gave it a special capacity to produce empirical data that formed the basis for new forms of social understanding. Today we are less confident about articulating the sensibilities that make up the researcher's craft. Government agencies and the corporate world have incorporated these empirical methods, from statistical analysis to ethnography, into the statecraft of market research. For sociologists, this should not produce methodological defeatism or inhibit using technological possibilities to create new tools for investigation.

We are arguing for the cultivation of a sociological sensibility not confined to the predominant lines of sight, the focal points of public concern. Rather, we are arguing for paying attention to the social world within a wider range of senses and placing critical evaluation and ethical judgement at the centre of research craft. Sociology's authority is not only based on its capacity to develop novel empirical techniques of inquiry. The researcher's craft is now to measure and weigh data and to evaluate the unprecedented volume of information being produced by humankind. Amid these changes, it is a timely moment for conducting a contemporary *Homo Academicus* (Bourdieu, 1988), and to debate the forms of work we are doing, the kinds of academics we are producing, and the institutional and life worlds we occupy as well as make.

Notes

1 *Chronique d'un été* is a documentary film made during the summer of 1960. It begins with Rouch and Morin discussing whether it is possible for those filmed to act honestly. The director camera-

man Michel Brault in large part shaped the visual style of the film. A cast of ordinary people from Paris and Saint-Tropez discuss a wide range of issues relating to French society and at the end the participants watch the recorded footage. The film was released in 1961.

2 This figure aims to capture both the number of publications and how often the work is cited by other scholars. It is arrived at by ranking an author's papers by number of citations. The metric is the number of papers with an H number of citations or more. In other words a scholar will have an H Index of 11 if he or she has published 11 academic papers that have been cited in other academic papers 11 times.

References

Adkins, L. and Lury, L., (2009), 'What is the empirical', *European Journal of Social Theory*, 12: 5–20.

Back, L., (2007), *The Art of Listening*, Oxford: Berg.

Bates, C., (2011), 'Experimenting with sociology: a view from the outlook tower', *Sociological Research Online*, 16 (3) 9, http://www.socresonline.org.uk/16/3/9.html

Benjamin, W., (2006), *The Writer of Modern Life: Essays on Charles Baudelaire*, Boston: Harvard University Press.

Bourdieu, P., (1988), *Homo Academicus*, Cambridge: Polity Press.

Bourdieu, P., (2003), *Firing Back: Against the Tyranny of the Market*, London: Verso.

Burawoy, M., (2005), 'For public sociology, *American Sociological Review*, 70 (1): 4–28.

Burrows, R., (2012), 'Living with the h-index? Metrics assemblages in the contemporary academy', *The Sociological Review*, 60 (2): 355–372.

Chow, R., (1998), *Ethics after Idealism*, Bloomington, IN: Indiana University Press.

Connerton, P., (2009), *How Modernity Forgets*, Cambridge: University of Cambridge Press.

de Certeau, M., (1984), *The Practice of Everyday Life*, Berkeley, CA: University of California Press.

Das, V., (2006), *Life and Words*, Berkeley, CA: University of California Press.

Hubble, N., (2012), 'Imagism, surrealism, realism: middlebrow transformations in the mass-observation movement', in E. Brown and M. Grover (eds), *Middlebrow Literary Cultures: The Battle of the Brows, 1920–1960*, 202–217, London: Palgrave Macmillan.

Latour, B., (2010), 'An attempt at a "compositionist manifesto"', *New Literary History*, 41: 471–490.

Latour, B. (ed.), (2002), *Iconoclash: Beyond the Image Wars in Science, Religion and Art*, Cambridge, MA: MIT Press.

Latour, B. and Hermant, E., (1998), *Paris Ville Invisible*, Paris: La Découverte/Les Empêcheurs de danser en rond.

Law, J. and Urry, J., (2004), 'Enacting the social', *Economy and Society*, 33 (3): 390–410.

Munt, S., (1998), *Heroic Desire: Lesbian Identity and Cultural Space*, New York: New York University Press.

Puwar, N., (2012), 'Mediations on the making of Aaj Kaal', *Feminist Review*, 100: 124–141.

Renwick, C., (2012), *British Sociology's Lost Biological Roots: A History of Futures Past*, Basingstoke: Palgrave Macmillan.

Said, E., (2002), 'The public role of writers and intellectuals', in H. Small (ed.), *The Public Intellectual*, 19–39, Oxford: Blackwell.

Savage, M., (2009), 'Contemporary sociology and the challenge of descriptive assemblage', *European Journal of Social Theory*, 12: 155–174.

Savage, M., (2010), *Identities and Social Change in Britain since 1940: The Politics of Method*, Oxford: Oxford University Press.

Savage, M. and Burrows, R., (2007), 'The coming crisis of empirical sociology', *Sociology*, 41, 5: 885–899.

The Sociological Review, 60:S1, pp. 6–17 (2012), DOI: 10.1111/j.1467-954X.2012.02114.x

Scott, J., (2007), *The Edinburgh School of Sociology*, http://sites.google.com/site/sociologysource/
   thebranfordproject2
Small, A., (1895), 'The era of sociology', *The American Journal of Sociology*, 1 (1): 1–15.
Stengers, I., (2005), 'The cosmopolitical proposal', in B. Latour and P. Webel (eds), *Making Things
   Public*, 994–1003, Cambridge, MA: MIT Press.
Strathern, M., (2004), *Commons and Borderlands*, Wantage: Sean Kingston.

Live sociology: social research and its futures

Les Back

Abstract: The article draws on recent debates about empirical sociology's methodological crisis that results from the emergence of sophisticated information-based capitalism and digital culture. Researchers face the challenge of 'newly coordinated social reality' in which social relations and interconnections exist across time and space. However, this challenge co-exists with an unprecedented opportunity to use digital multimedia to reimagine social research. In the face of these developments it is argued that the sociological craft needs to be invigorated by a renewed focus on its political purpose. Digital culture offers researchers the opportunity to develop new methodological devices. This vision is contrasted with a critique of dead sociology that is characterized as objectifying, comfortable, disengaged and parochial. The article argues for a live sociology, able to attend to the fleeting, distributed, multiple and sensory aspects of sociality through research techniques that are mobile, sensuous and operate from multiple vantage points. If researchers enact reality rather than simply reflect it, there is an opportunity to create sociological forms of representation that are more knowing and innovative than their antecedents.

Keywords: digital culture, research methods, politics of knowledge, ethics, sociology of the senses, methodological innovation

Introduction: crisis and opportunity

There is more opportunity to reimagine sociological craft now than at any other point in the discipline's history. Twenty-first century human society is producing information at an unprecedented level and scale. It is not merely that people today can communicate with great ease through information technologies like mobile phones and social networking websites. Rather people are increasingly observers of their own lives, or, in the words of YouTube, 'broadcasting themselves'. As a result social enquiry and analysis is no longer simply the province of researchers. This contains an opportunity for sociologists to think about how we can add new techniques to our empirical toolbox. It also poses a challenge

The Sociological Review, 60:S1, pp. 18–39 (2012), DOI: 10.1111/j.1467-954X.2012.02115.x
© 2012 The Author. Editorial organisation © 2012 The Editorial Board of the Sociological Review. Published by Wiley-Blackwell Publishing Ltd, 9600 Garsington Road, Oxford OX4 2DQ, UK and 350 Main Street, Malden, MA 02148, USA

as to how we assess analytically this 'spontaneous sociology'. The opportunity offered to social researchers in the 21st century is a potential to train our socio-logical attentiveness differently and to reflect on the analytical problems posed by the digitization of social life and the emergence of a global information culture (Lash, 2002). However, regardless of the potential mentioned here there is – from a variety of angles – a concern that empirical sociology is facing a crisis.

Academic research in a digital age has been out-manoeuvred by freelance fact-makers in policy think tanks and corporate research. Mike Savage and Roger Burrows argue that empirical sociology is overshadowed by the capacity of industry and commerce to know patterns of behaviour and taste in more sophisticated ways than sociologists and social researchers. They cite the example of the capacity of Amazon.com to almost automatically anticipate what we like and want to buy next (Savage and Burrows, 2007: 891). Mike Savage has also pointed out how the digitization of social relations enables government agencies and the security services, as well as commerce, to map descriptive assemblages which pose an empirical challenge to sociology but which should also themselves be the 'subject of social science inquiry' (Savage, 2009: 171). The dazzle of this profusion of data sets might induce in social researchers something close to 'data envy'. The corporations have so many more resources, the think tanks have much larger access. For Savage and Burrows, evoking the idea that 'theory gives us a special quality' is a mistake. We might be better placed to focus on our ability to describe that which is not paid attention to: 'through a radical mixture of methods coupled with renewed critical reflection' (Savage and Burrows, 2007: 894). The accounts of the social life produced in the data machines of 'knowing capitalism' (Thrift, 2004) are not concerned with thick description or sustained critical attention. It is here in the nature of sociological attention that we suggest we can begin to make a case for the worth of sociology.

The different imperatives of academic and corporate research were revealed at a 'data analysis session' held at Goldsmiths a few years ago, where academic sociologists were collaborating with a group of commercial qualitative research-ers. Just as the analytical discussion seemed to be getting going it was called to a sudden halt. One corporate ethnographer announced: 'I've got enough for a PowerPoint presentation!' It was very telling. The threshold of 'enough knowl-edge' in these worlds is passed when they can predict your next Amazon pur-chase, or have enough ideas to furnish a PowerPoint presentation. This is not to diminish the productive power of some of these modes of corporate research. Something really significant is at stake when a supermarket like Sainsbury's is attempting to model the consumer habits of its customers within a database of 1,000,000 people. However, we have to be more strident about the value of the kinds of critical attentiveness, a compound of dialogue and critique, which I will return to, yet not fall into a scholastic arrogance.

Sociologists, anthropologists or those from any number of disciplines in the humanities have never had the monopoly on social analysis. Howard Becker's book entitled *Telling about Society* makes exactly this point; in fact he goes further to suggest that an attention to the ways in which artists, playwrights and novelists go about the process of telling might contain new ideas for social researchers in terms of the ways in which we convey not only the content of our research but also moral and political commitments (Becker, 2007). Most notably, how might we make sociological texts that are open and invite users and readers to conclude the argument or participate in the project of making a political judgement?

It is not simply that freelance and corporate fact-makers are doing it so much better with more resources and larger samples. Lisa Adkins and Celia Lury have pointed out that the 'crisis and return to the empirical' is one that has to reckon with a fundamental break with social research's modes of representation. Rather, they suggest that we are confronted with 'a newly coordinated reality, one that is open, processual, non-linear and constantly on the move' (Adkins and Lury, 2009: 16). The complexity of social relations and the interconnections across time and space have also led some commentators to question whether social research is even possible. John Urry writes: 'One could hypothesize that current phenomena have outrun the capacity of the social sciences to investigate' (Urry, 2003: 38). Is this sociology's death knell? The problem is not just a matter of method, but suggests that our intellectual architecture is not adequate in attending to the scope and scale of global social processes. Regardless, I argue in the face of these challenges that there are some aspects of sociological practice that we need to bury in order to embrace new opportunities.

The article is structured around four key themes. First, it will conduct an autopsy on *dead sociology,* pointing to the aspects of sociological practice that in our current moment are no longer vital. Secondly, it will discuss the ethical and political questions raised by the ways in which social science techniques and languages have spread and proliferated beyond the academic within the human terrain. Thirdly, it will offer an argument and a characterization of the elements and key principles of a live sociology that give detail to opportunities mentioned at the beginning. Finally, the article will argue for a more artful form of sociology that is engaged but also brings a bit of craftiness to the craft. I will argue that the current pressures on the empirical sociological imagination need not lead to epistemological defeat but perhaps a greater humility about the truth we might touch but not grasp fully, while contesting the realities that others claim with such certainty.

Dead sociology

In July 1895 Albion Small published an essay entitled *The Era of Sociology*. It was the opening article in the first edition of the *American Journal of Sociology*, the first sociological periodical of its kind ever to be published. Small claimed that sociology would occupy a foremost place in modern thought because modernity had brought humankind into more intense contact, producing

The Sociological Review, 60:S1, pp. 18–39 (2012), DOI: 10.1111/j.1467-954X.2012.02115.x

complex human tangles of social relatedness. For Small the task was to understand these relationships but also to intervene in public issues and reflect on the nature of the times. He wrote: 'the Journal will attempt to translate sociology into the language of ordinary life, so that it will not appear to be merely a classification and explanation of *fossil facts*' (1895: 13, emphasis added). Small's warning is not merely relevant to the danger that academicism leads to social disengagement but also to the potential for sociological literature itself to turn the diversity of modern experience into lifeless relics. How many of the articles published in the *American Journal of Sociology* after his would fit this description? More than enough to make Professor Small turn in his grave.

The question remains how to account for the social world without assassinating the life contained within it. My intention here is not an exercise in sociological iconoclasm but a playful provocation, as my own research and writing contain traces of what I will call dead sociology. Rather, I argue that there are four syndromes that result in *fossil facts* and lifeless conceptions. The first of these is the rendering of live things to dead objects. Tim Ingold has argued convincingly that the social inspection of objects tends to render them as complete surfaces that through our inspection will yield their meanings. The result is that the object is plucked from the relations and vitality that circulate in and through it. Ingold, drawing on Heidegger, prefers the idea of a *thing* that is vitalized by its bundle of connections and threads rather than an *object* that has a single designation. Ingold comments: 'Life is open-ended: its impulse is not to reach a terminus but to keep on going . . . The thing, however, is not just one thread but a certain gathering together of the threads of life' (Ingold, 2010: 10). The observations here have a wider application beyond the current discussions in sociology regarding the material world. One might also point to the way that transcribed talk is made into an object in the sense Ingold uses it. Quotations are extracted for meaningful inspection from the live contexts from which they emerge in the first place. They become epitaphs to a life passed in living. The challenge is how to find ways to represent such lives and objects that sustain rather than foreclose their vitality and ongoing life.

Secondly, dead sociology takes intellectual comfort in 'zombie concepts'. Ulrich Beck commented controversially that residual dead theoretical ideas inhibit the sociological imagination and are ill-fitted to the task of understanding the contemporary shape of global society. For Beck, the late 20th century constitutes a break, or the emergence of a second modernity that necessitates the embrace of otherness and a cosmopolitan vision for sociology (Beck, 2000; Beck and Sznaider, 2006). This point is developed and extended by Scott Lash in his argument for an empirical sensibility that is *a posteriori* rather than *a priori* (Lash, 2009). He argues that at the heart of the work of the classical social theory of Durkheim, Tönnies, Simmel and Parsons is a key question: 'how is society possible?' However, the question itself presupposes a conception of society itself, what Lash refers to as a 'symbolic a priori' (Lash, 2009: 177), grounded in a mode of reasoning that operated from a preceding understanding of society's elementary forms. Lash concludes: 'Sociologists at the beginning of the 21st century are faced with a social reality of global flows, mobilities, and uncertainties. It is no longer a question of finding the conditions of security of the social but being attentive to and describing this uncertainty' (Lash, 2009: 185). I would add to this a need to question the comforts of *a priori* reasoning and an embrace of discomfort, of what is surprising and disconcerting. For Lash *a posteriori* reasoning involves profound engagement with emerging forms and social phenomena that contain incipiently the concept within the form that the empirical takes.

Thirdly, dead sociology refuses to face the consequences of the digitization of social life. There is a strong current of technophobia in the sociological research community manifested either in the refusal to carry a mobile phone or aversion to the dubious magic of PowerPoint presentations. As digital natives, younger researchers are less prone to this than the professoriate but social life can no longer be understood apart from its technological mediations. The iPod has transformed the social experience of urban life (Bull, 2007) and mobile phones not only change the relationship between private and public but also the experience of place and time. In John Berger's extraordinary study of migration, *A Seventh Man*, the immigrant's sense of missing home is described as the 'double pain of absence'. Berger explains: 'He misses everything he feels to be absent. At the same time, that which is absent, continues without him' (Berger and Mohr, 1975: 178). This study was conducted in the 1970s. The migrant experience of this kind of absence today has been radically transformed. Through the mobile phone and virtual social networking migrants can be technologically connected to the life 'back home' that is unfolding without them. They sit in a cafe in London and keep track of the lives of loved ones left behind and even participate remotely through text messaging and email. However, the technological connection does not lessen the pain of absence: quite the contrary, it can exacerbate it. This was demonstrated by the case of a young asylum seeker called Clifford who participated in a study of young adult migrants with my colleague Shamser Sinha. Clifford's life was effectively on hold while his immigration case was being processed – he could not work legally or plan for his future. Every day he kept up with his friends in Ghana who were working, falling in and out of love and building a life. The fact that through his iPhone he was in contact with the unfolding lives of friends and loved ones – in real time – exacerbated his own sense of being trapped in the present. His immigration status meant he was unable to move forward or back. Clifford's experience shows how the digitization of social life has transformed the relationship between here and there without lessening the negative consequences of being caught between.

Lastly, the scale of dead sociology's imagination is parochial both geographically and in relationship to the past. Beck argues that sociology is inhibited by equating societies with nation-states. He calls this 'methodological nationalism' which 'assumes that humanity is naturally divided into a limited number of nations' (Beck and Sznaider, 2006: 3). For Beck, the sociological challenge is to transcend such parochial concerns and develop a cosmopolitan and global sociology. However, Gurminder Bhambra comments that Beck's conception of the cosmopolitan and global is itself a Eurocentric formulation that 'takes Western perspectives as the truth of global processes'. Bhambra continues 'A cosmopolitan sociology that was open to different voices would, I suggest, be one that provincialised European understandings' (Bhambra, 2007: 154). This argument resonates with other theorists like Dipesh Chakrabarty and Walter Mignolo who argue that European social thought is limited by occidentalist perspectives that are in fact local and particular (Chakrabarty, 2000; Mignolo, 2000). Sociological practice is not only parochial in its lack of appreciation of the transnational scale of contemporary globalized forms of social life but also, in its self-consciousness, its particularity is 'effaced within a false universalism' (Bhambra, 2007: 155). Parochialism also limits our understanding of the history of sociology itself. This point is demonstrated by George Steinmetz's work on the imperial entanglements of sociology in the United States, Britain and France. He suggests that sociologists have rarely acknowledged both our discipline's contributions to understanding empire or the sociological complicity in imperial politics and the intellectual architecture of empire and racism. Steinmetz not only documents the involvement of social researchers in supporting imperial and Nazi projects but also offers examples where sociologists were explicit critics or, more ambiguously, impartial analysts. He concludes that recovering this history offers lessons for today's researchers: 'Research on the way sociologists have dealt with threats to their scientific autonomy in past imperial episodes may help them ward off such threats in the present' (Steinmetz, 2009: 78). This issue will be picked up in the following section that deals with the presence of social research methods within the wider human terrain. In summary, dead sociology is objectifying, comfortable, disengaged and parochial.

Before moving on to argue for a more vital sociological future I want first to explore the ethical and political issues raised by the problem of parochialism. It will be argued that current challenges and opportunities require researchers to face and reflect on our ethical commitments and the political implications of our craft.

In the human terrain

The doubt cast across social scientific authority is not just a matter of the difficulties of scale, surface and speed of movement. The arrogant claim that science could know the 'whole truth' and legislate for solutions in order to perfect society led to complicity in the brutal and banal exercises of power. Commenting on the implication of 20th-century intellectuals in this perfidy, Paul Rabinow concluded: 'The industries and sciences of Thanatos have had a glorious century' (2003: 103). We have our own examples today. There is a direct link between interrogation techniques such as hooding and noise bombardment trained on the 'unlawful combatants' in Guantanamo Bay, Cuba and psychological research on sensory deprivation (Harper, 2004). The betrayal and perversion of knowledge is not a lesson from the past but a condition of the present. I am also thinking about the controversy concerning the use of anthropologists and sociologists within the so-called 'human terrain teams' in Afghanistan where, as Colonel Martin Switzer commented, 'the centre of gravity becomes the population' (Grant, 2008: 1). In an article published in the *New York Times* it was claimed that the advent of social researchers in Eastern Afghanistan had cut military operations by 60 per cent and had also mediated in the settlement of tribal land disputes (Rohde, 2007). As *Newsweek* put it: 'A gun in one hand, a pen in the other' (*Newsweek*, 2008). The militarization of research is part of our present, as it moves towards the future. In May 2008 Michael Bhatia, an American doctoral candidate from Oxford University, was killed in Afghanistan while assisting 82nd Airbourne Division to understand tribal customs (Glenn, 2008). James Der Derian, Director of the Global Security Programme at Brown University, said his former student had: 'a unique ability to really listen and see and that came out in his research' (Vaznis, 2008). The death of this young scholar is tragic but it raises a wider question of the uses to which social science is being put and what social research is for. The involvement of researchers in military human terrain teams replays anthropology's relationship to the colonial encounters of the past, in the name of cultural translation and understanding.

This is not just happening in relation to military operations abroad but also in struggles happening at home. In our time a surprising number of intellectuals from Robert Putnam (2007) to Anthony Giddens (2007) worry that political correctness is hindering the social science imagination. Being complicit with racism, as in the case of the praise given by the British National Party in their magazine *Identity* to the Young Foundation's study *The New East End* which suggested that the white working classes had been adversely affected by Tower Hamlet's housing policy (Dench *et al.*, 2006) seems less of a danger (Mayhew, 2007; see Back, 2009b for a fuller discussion). Our work is not needed to dictate how people ought to live, or for that matter to be a torturer's accomplice. It is for this reason that the certainty to which social science is prone needs to be laid to rest in the graveyard of 20th-century conceits. Perhaps the challenge is to navigate between the arrogance of such forms of certainty on the one hand and the timidity about what we can claim to know or judge critically on the other.

The call for attentiveness or listening is no necessary protection from violations of another kind. Carolyn Steedman's brilliant discussion of what she called 'enforced narratives' is a case in point. Here, she argues, the stories of subaltern women and working-class stories are filched under the licence of sympathy and empathy. For the affluent listener: 'The possession of a terrible tale, a story of suffering, is desired, perhaps even envied, as a component of the other self' (Steedman, 2000: 36). This tension between give and take in research encounters, between portrayal and betrayal, is an ongoing problem that cannot be entirely settled by ethical guidelines or the pronouncements of ethics committees. As a result we might add another style of empiricism that works in the

The Sociological Review, 60:S1, pp. 18–39 (2012), DOI: 10.1111/j.1467-954X.2012.02115.x

opposite direction to what C. Wright Mills called abstract empiricism, the 'empty forms of ingenuity' of opinion poll research (Mills, 1959: 50). Rather than amalgamated patterns offered through numerical tables, *intrusive empiricism* claims to know and judge the very soul of its subjects. The most visceral portrayal of intrusive empiricism I have found is a sculpture by Juan Muñoz showing a human figure being suspended by its tongue (see Figure 1). Muñoz's artwork is extraordinary in its attention to issues of observation, incommensurability, proximity. Another of his works portrays a mute ventriloquist's dummy that looks out onto the floor while possessing the latent potentiality for us to manipulate it and make it speak (see Figure 2). Intrusive empiricism mines the secret failings of its subjects that in turn come to characterize the people prone to this kind of scrutiny. The journalistic exposé and reality TV ethnography are 'thick surfaces' that crackle with controversy, not careful evocation (Geertz, 1973). They occlude and hide what is at stake in the detail. They are, by definition, fast and produced with such swiftness, with one piled on another so quickly that each is soon smothered by a torrent of others. Intrusive empiricism is defined by revelation, occlusive detail, fast turnaround and a data surfeit. Although abstracted and intrusive empiricism is largely a non-academic style of fact-making, academic research can be coloured by these patterns. The work we do collectively needs to develop a kind of attentiveness that stands in contrast to this.

The point that I would emphasize is that the contents and techniques of social research travel, they develop lives of their own and, more than this, come to

Figure 1: *Juan Muñoz* Hanging Figures, *1997 (Photography by Kritien Daem courtesy of Juan Muñoz Estate and Marian Gallery, New York)*

Figure 2: *Juan Muñoz* The Wasteland, *1987 (Photography by Peter Cox courtesy of Juan Muñoz Estate and Marian Gallery, New York)*

populate the social itself. Mike Savage has argued that the success of social science in claiming jurisdiction over the social has proliferated ways of talking and thinking that furnish contemporary popular narratives (Savage, 2010). Through a close reading of mass observation accounts over a period of more than a half a century he argues that the late 20th century accounts are much fuller, individualized and placed within a larger frame and in a sense *more socio-logical*. He concludes: 'We cannot simply carry on interviewing or sampling as if the world is unchanged by fifty years of extensive social research' (Savage, 2010: 249). The implication is that what social researchers end up collecting – as 'interview data' – in fact are the frames of reference and social characterizations that sociology produced in the first place. In addition, Philip Gleason points out that social concerns themselves – like the notion of identity – are historically produced. Taking the case of US obsession in the social sciences and humanities with the question of 'identity' he argued that it emerges in the mid 20th-century American crisis over difference, continuity and sameness. However, as everything has become an issue of 'identity' the notion is increasingly loosely defined and diffuse. Identity has become a zombie concept that is 'little more than por-

The Sociological Review, 60:S1, pp. 18–39 (2012), DOI: 10.1111/j.1467-954X.2012.02115.x

tentous incoherence' (Gleason, 1983: 931). I would argue that the emergence of the interview as the prime method of generation of popular narratives suited perfectly the obsession with the kind of self captured through the notion of identity. We have reached a moment where interviews have a limited usefulness as a means of understanding and investigating social life.

The point emphasized here is the necessity to retain, as a core sociological value, ethical and political reflection on the place and impact of social research on social life. This critical sensibility is an essential part of the process of assessing the terms of future innovation. At the end of the first decade of the 21st century sociology is facing a profound threat but also an unprecedented opportunity. Renouncing scholastic arrogance and complicity with power, sociology can renew its values through the training of a critical attentiveness that is not mired in ethical hypochondria and timidity. In what follows the possibilities will be outlined for imagining our work differently. What kinds of data do we live with now? How is it different from the kinds of data we have produced, coded and catalogued in the past?

Live sociology

While it is a cliché to say that digital technologies and new media impact profoundly on our everyday lives, little attention has been paid to opportunities that digital photography, mobile sound technologies, CD ROMs and online publishing opportunities might offer the social researcher and the practice of research itself. It is still the case that most social scientists view the research encounter as an interface between an observer and the observed, producing either quantitative or qualitative data. Equally, the dissemination of research findings are confined to conventional paper forms of publishing, and research excellence is measured and audited through such forms, be it in monographs or academic journals. It remains the case that in social science the inclusion of audio or visual material in the context of ethnographic social research has been little more than 'eye candy' or 'background listening' to the main event on the page. The relatively inexpensive nature of these easy-to-use media offers researchers a new opportunity to develop innovative approaches to how we conduct and present social research. There are more opportunities than at any other moment to rethink the craft of social research beyond the dominance of the word and figure and to reconsider our reliance on 'the interview' (often taking place across a table in a particular place) as the prime technology for generating 'data'. Let me be clear: I am not arguing that interviews are bad or wrong. I have spent thousands of hours involved in such forms of sociality, where the outcomes of the words exchanged are complicated and cannot be simply reduced to a particular affect or correspondence with a reality beyond the telling (Back, 2010). Tom Harrisson, founder of the mass observation studies, commented 'What you say to a stranger may, on many matters, differ from what you say to a friend, to yourself, to your wife or lover; also it may, and often does, differ from what you think, or from matters of "fact" you are trying to remember or describe; or again from what you actually *do*' (Harrisson, 1947: 21). Interviewees can sometimes articulate a sense of gratitude after the recorder has been turned off that can be unnerving. This is not therapy but rather something else, akin to a kind of sociological sociability that allows people to be heard. However, what remains unspoken can be of even greater significance. Harrisson concludes: 'Words both assist and obscure the sociologist's understanding' (Harrisson, 1947: 21).

Our disciplines remain what Margaret Mead called 'disciplines of words' (Mead, 1995: 3). I am not suggesting that words are bad. Sociologists should think of themselves as the authors of representations but these representations need not be confined to the written word (see Puwar and Sharma, *Noise of the Past* project, in this volume). This is not to collapse the genres somehow but rather to extend the range, texture and quality of what passes as academic representational practice and writing. I want to argue for a more literary sensibility inside the research vocation but also for the extensions of sociological form through the embrace of multi-media (sound, image and text). More than at any point before we have the potential now to do the craft of research differently. I also want to suggest that the future holds out the possibility to animate social researchers through the use of other kinds of devices.

There are opportunities now to think about other ways to attend to the social world. John Law and John Urry have argued that social scientific methods have resulted in an extremely limited range of attentions.

> They deal, for instance, poorly with the *fleeting* – that which is here today and gone tomorrow, only to reappear the day after tomorrow. They deal poorly with the *distributed* – that is to be found here and there but not between – or that which slips and slides between one place and another. They deal poorly with the *multiple* – that which takes different shapes in different places. They deal poorly with the non-causal, the chaotic, the complex. And such methods have difficulty dealing with the *sensory* – that which is subject to vision, sound, taste, smell; with the *emotional* – time-space compressed outbursts of anger, pain, rage, pleasure, desire, or the spiritual; and the *kinaesthetic* – the pleasures and pains that follow movement and displacement of people, objects, information, and ideas. (Law and Urry, 2004: 403)

The challenge and opportunity that runs from this is to develop forms of attentiveness that can admit the fleeting, distributed, multiple, sensory, emotional and kinaesthetic aspects of sociality. The component elements of live sociology proposed here seek to expand the sensory dimensions of sociological attentiveness, to design methods that move with the social world and to develop multiple vantage points from which empirical accounts are generated.

Anita Wilson's ethnography of prison life points to how a sensory attentiveness expands the sociological imagination (Wilson, 2008). The title of her paper 'Is that Escape you're wearing Miss?' related to a question that a male prisoner asked her about the perfume she was wearing. For him the scent of *Escape* by Calvin Klein evoked memories of his girlfriend and his life outside. The sensorium of the prison was ingrained in the smell of polish used on the prison floors, the texture of the sheets and clothes that had been filled by other bodies and the taste of the metal of prison keys that clung to her hands. Inside, prisoners went to extraordinary lengths to keep the smell of the prison out. They washed their rooms down with radox, piled up 'Christmas tree shaped' air-fresheners on the radiators, put toothpaste around the door frames in order to change the sensation of 'being inside'. The first principle of live sociology is an *attention to how a wider range of the senses* changes the quality of data and makes other kinds of critical imagination possible. How quickly we want to say 'observation' when describing social research. In itself the notion automatically privileges the eye. This example also demonstrates the power of evocation and allusion in our modes of evidence. The challenge for the future is how to develop, based on an equality of the senses, attentiveness to the multiple registers of life.

A second point here is that live sociology requires researchers to *work on the move* in order to attend to the 'newly coordinated' nature of social reality. One of our current challenges is to re-invent forms of attentiveness that are mobile and can respond precisely to admit the fleeting, the tacit, the mobile, chaotic and complex. Anthropological film-maker Jean Roche anticipated this long ago. He wrote: 'For me, the only way to film is to walk with the camera, taking it to wherever it is the most effective, and improvising a ballet in which the camera itself becomes just as much alive as the people it's filming' (Rouch, 1995 [1973]: 89). Many researchers are experimenting with ambulant techniques of doing social research on the move, that do not simply try and reflect movement but which also embody movement and bring it to life. Today researchers have more opportunities than ever before to use digital media to rethink the nature of social observation using more multimedia and mobile forms. For example, Andrew Clark and Nick Emmel have explored the methodological potential of using walking tours and ambulant interviews in order to access hidden dimensions of community life (Emmel and Clark, 2007). The point here is the opportunity to take our devices (cameras, sound recorders, sensory instruments) for a walk, as ethnography becomes a kind of social ballet. Through using multimodality researchers develop a different kind of attentiveness to the embodied social world in motion. Not being limited to what people say explicitly enables us to train a kind of attentiveness to tacit forms of coexistence.

During 2006–2008 this approach was developed in the *Live Sociology* project funded by the Economic and Social Research Council within their Researcher Development Initiative.[1] The project trained researchers in the opportunities offered by the use of new media in ethnographic social research. The year long programme of five workshops combined theoretical and practical training, to develop skills in new multimedia techniques, collecting, analysing, archiving and curating ethnographic social research. The workshops aimed to bring sociology 'alive' by introducing interactivity and exploiting the possibilities of using new media for iterative analysis, the potential to extend reflexivity in the conduct of research and the potential to promote collaboration, integrative methods and secondary analysis. They explored how to use new media in social research: how

PDF (Acrobat) formats could be used to make simple interactive CD ROMs including sociological text and visual work, the possibilities for redesigning the relationship between the observer and observed using digital photography and how to use online interactivity to facilitate a relationship between researchers, research participants and users.

Twenty participants attended each of the five workshops and this annual cycle was repeated three times.[2] The workshops were over-subscribed and in all 75 researchers – encompassing a wide range of experiences from MA students to tenured professors – attended the scheme, some travelling from outside Britain. We wanted to take the methodological discussion out of the classroom and an integral initiative was to get researchers to work with digital photography and sound recording. The participants' enthusiasm and abundant imagination conveyed a yearning and impatience for alternative ways of conducting social research, as well as providing an exemplary case of the advantages of sociable scholarship. The project illustrates the third point I want to stress about live sociology as commitment to *pluralizing the vantage points from which sociological attentiveness is trained.*

As part of a workshop entitled *London Routes* we gave participants copies of the London A–Z guide marked up with suggestions of paths through the urban landscape and intellectual slogans to provoke ideas (see Figure 3). The participants took their cameras and sound recording equipment for a walk, and conducted listening experiments, not merely using the devices to conduct street interviews. Thinking with sound in this way invited a sociological sensibility close to George Perec's wonderfully eccentric experiments with cataloguing that which is all around us and yet unnoticed (Perec, 1997). For Perec the task is:

Figure 3: London Routes, *Live Sociology programme 2006 (Photograph by Sophie Back)*

The Sociological Review, 60:S1, pp. 18–39 (2012), DOI: 10.1111/j.1467-954X.2012.02115.x

to describe what's left: what isn't usually noted down, what isn't noticed, what has no importance: what happens when nothing is happening, just the weather, people, cars, clouds. (quoted in Becker, 2007: 266)

The varied nature of the sociological attention of the participants was striking even though they were often moving through the same social locations. It was constantly surprising what they trained their attention on (see Figure 4). Participants looking at the work later in the analysis sessions that followed were often surprised because they saw and heard things in the digital representations that they had missed when they were in the middle of the street. The devices enabled them to engage with the matter of things and things that mattered: social life in motion. The uses to which these digital representations might be put are more varied. It was not simply a matter of merely showing what the street looked or sounded like or simulating a sensory realism, that is, to 'see seeing' or 'hear hearing' etc. In the case of a digital photograph participants used them to pause the ebb and flow of social action in order to subject what was in the frame to close inspection (see Figures 5 and 6). Equally, blurred images took on representational value because they conveyed a sense of movement or flow even though as photographs they were 'technical failures'. Audio recording offered the possibility to tune into the voices in the foreground but

Figure 4: *Deptford Market, London (Live Sociology Programme 2006 courtesy of Grant McNulty)*

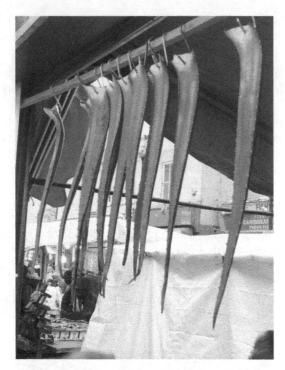

Figure 5: *Tails of Aloe Vera, Deptford Market, London (Live Sociology programme 2006 courtesy of Grant McNulty)*

also to listen to what was contained in the background soundscape that might be sociologically interesting. Conveying the vitality in the data required imaginative work. The best example of this came from a participant who made soundscape recordings of a street market as part of the exercise. Rather than playing the audio recording he made, he used it as a resource to write a truly remarkable description that contained a rich cultural texture, weaving emerging conceptual ideas into the empirical description.

My argument here is not simply confined to the relationship between research craft and digital culture. Additionally, there are examples of sociological representation that operate beyond text and in installation or curatorial practice. Nina Wakeford has been doing this for some time in her 'art-sociology' and 'studio-sociology' projects.[3] For example, her work *Trials of Strength* (2007) suspended unmarked thermometers by threads from large blue helium balloons above the heads of eminent sociologists as they lectured, like methodological swords of Damocles.[4] Each of these works provokes reflection on scholarly assumptions, practices and values. On a different scale Bruno Latour has developed a kind curatorial sociology through the *Making Things Public: Atmospheres of Democracy* (2005) exhibition.[5] The exhibition invited participants to engage with objects producing an assemblage of political views on current

Figure 6: *Taste of London's past, Peas Pudding, Deptford High Street, London (Live Sociology programme 2006 courtesy of Grant McNulty)*

debates that brought a new kind of public assembly into being. Equally, I am suggesting here that sociology might develop new ways of telling and showing its empirical evidence and arguments through using techniques established in sculpture, curatorial practice, theatre, music and television drama.[6]

There are tensions, perhaps with regard to the degree to which the boundary between art and social research can be blurred. Is it possible for artworks to argue in sociological ways? Should artworks – even sociologically inspired ones – be left to speak for themselves without explication? Some artists argue that it is unnecessary to explain their work. One of the first principles of social science is that nothing speaks for itself. It is impossible to settle these questions in general terms. We need to move from the arrogant convention in sociology to assimilate other practices on its own terms and within its own image (ie a 'sociology *of* art' or a 'sociology *of* computing') to a more collaborative practice that is mutually transformative (ie sociology *with* art or sociology *with* computing). As a consequence I am not suggesting that the boundary between sociology or ethnography can be collapsed with art but I am implying that research practice can be more artful. Here the issue of artfulness is not just about form. It is also about being mindful of the kinds of realities that are enacted and produced.

Artfulness in the sense it is being used here also involves being wily or bringing a *bit of craftiness into the craft*.

This is not argument for 'spin' or deception. Rather, craftiness, as it is used here, means reflecting on the choices we make about what is important for sociological investigation and what is valued as a consequence. It also means expanding the vantage point for social observation. Now that it is possible to redesign the observer and even the analyst there are new opportunities to democratize and expand access to sociological authorship and knowledge. However, pluralizing the locations from which observations are made also means not just thinking about what is portrayed but also how the representations themselves *betray* the conditions of their own production (see Back, 2009a). Lastly, craftiness also involves learning new strategies for telling society and affecting and persuading the audiences of sociological work.

To summarize, live sociology involves developing the methodological opportunities offered by digital culture *and* expanding the forms and modes telling sociology through collaborating with artists, designers, musicians and filmmakers and incorporating new modes and styles of sociological representation. The use of digital devices, like those used in the *Live Sociology Project*, offer the opportunity to augment sociological attentiveness and develop mobile methods that also enable the production of empirical data simultaneously from a plurality of vantages. Also, I am arguing that this invites a discussion about the analytical status we give the digital representations as data. Spontaneous sociology, often using the techniques described above, seems to be everywhere from Facebook to YouTube. This adds another dimension to the issue raised by Carolyn Steedman because today self-revelation and self-narrative are uploaded without invitation. Is there any longer, following Steedman's analysis, a 'silent other' that elicits such tales? Perhaps the injunction to personal revelation is now automated and automatic. Upload culture and online social networks produce a kind of vulnerability – particularly for the young – that results in self-exposure. Thinking sociologically now means navigating between the possibilities offered by digital culture while remaining cautious about the kinds of selves that are being produced through narcissistic articulation of online experience. One way to think about this is in relation to the potential for less violation, more democracy, deeper ethical commitment. I have argued here that we need to be committed in equal measure to innovation and critical reflection. If we accept that we do not simply reflect social reality but produce it, then there is an opportunity to do this in a more knowing and innovative way.

Conclusion: making some realities more real

For researchers the future holds an opportunity to rethink procedures and devices we use within social research. In addition there is a potential to expand our modes of writing and representation. We can contemplate the creation of new kinds of vital texts: curate sociology rather than just write it. In a piece called *The Public Role of Writers and Intellectuals* Edward Said contrasted today's global informational culture with the 18th-century pamphleteer Jonathan Swift, who brought down the Duke of Marlborough with just one publication. The 'oratorical machines', to use Swift's phrase, of the 21st century are fluid, fast and result in unpredictable consequences. Said, writing in New York for a British newspaper, has a good chance of reappearing on individual websites in the United States, Japan, Pakistan, the Middle East and South Africa as well as Australia. He concludes that 'All of us should therefore operate today with some notion of very probably reaching much larger audiences than any we could conceive of even a decade ago, although the chances of retaining that audience are by the same token quite chancy' (Said, 2001: 29). There is ever more potential and reach on the one hand but the attention of that audience is more fleeting.

It is not just that online formats have the potential of a global reach but that they provide an opportunity to think about how we conceive of the on-line format as a place to think the form of sociology differently, imagining 'texts' that are compounds of word, image, sound and text. It is possible to imagine forms of social research that are themselves animated and develop a life of their own within the spheres of the virtual, that produce and provoke further questions. In relation to sound it is possible to create books that we listen to and read simultaneously creating an acoustic environment for the act of reading itself.[7] Producing texts that can be read and listened to simultaneously also allows the potential for linear arguments to be combined with non-linear interconnections and routes.

I want to return to a passage from the Law and Urry text quoted earlier and a specific passage that others have also found suggestive (see Fraser, 2009). They write:

> If methods are not innocent then they are also political. They help make realities. But the question is: which realities? Which do we want to help make more real, and which less real? (Law and Urry, 2004: 404).

The idea that we enact the social world as we understand it is useful because it invites a discussion of the question of critical judgement. Which realities should be turned down or cut down to size and which others, through our sociological imagination, turned up and magnified? Bruno Latour cautions sociologists not to be drunk with political intent and to be 'sober with power' (Latour, 2005: 260). He argues that the moral commitments of critical sociology can inhibit the capacity to notice what is before us in any given state of affairs because what is important has already been defined *a priori* in political terms. However, it is also true to say that Actor Network Theorists, or any sociologist for that matter, can be blind to the consequences of their particular way of assembling the social.

Recently, I presented a paper on the young adult migrants research mentioned earlier at a conference in Oxford. The project attempts to practise live sociology, as participants become observers in their own lives, author their own representations (make art, keep scrapbooks, do creative writing, take photographs and keep diaries) and some have also participated in the process of writing. At the end of my presentation, which focused on photographs taken by one participant, a scholar, an Actor Network Theorist (ANT) of world renown asked: 'Why are you so interested in individuals?' The question was unnerving, not least because the young migrant's photographs had portrayed the personal consequences and violations produced by the immigration system. One of the key contributions of actor network theory has been its insistence on describing interactions between humans and the material world in ways that do not merely concentrate on agency in humans. ANT sees assemblages of human and non-human elements interacting in mutually connected fields of action and seeks to cut human hubris down to size. In the context of this I would argue there are human consequences for enacting the social in this way because the immigration police do not deport *assemblages of associations* but *individuals*.

Moral consequences follow from the way sociologists tell society. John Berger comments that traditionally stories are judged by their content, structure and plot. He suggests another way to assess their value is to ask where the story leaves those who have followed it. In what frame of mind are the readers as they close the book and continue on with their lives? Deciding on the moral of the story itself is only one way to approach this issue. Berger writes: 'In following a story, we follow a storyteller, or, more precisely, we follow the trajectory of a storyteller's attention, what it notices and what it ignores, what it lingers on, what it repeats, what it considers irrelevant, what it hurries towards, what it circles, what it brings together' (Berger, 2011: 72). Similarly I want to suggest that the value of sociological work is to be found then in the trajectory of the sociologist's attention and the quality of attentiveness we train on the world.

It seems likely that social research in future will be ever more closely tied to corporate interest and what Edward Said characterized as the 'organic intellectuals' of the 'knowledge industries' (Said, 1996: 9). Also, the Human Terrain Teams and the nostalgic apologists for racism provide a reminder of what is at stake in the judgement regarding which realities we choose to make more or less real. We need to argue for an alternative future but also craft one into existence. This is not just a methodological matter of bringing sociology to life but a way to live and sustain the life of things. C. Wright Mills commented in his essay on *The Social Role of the Intellectual*:

> The independent artist and intellectual are among the few remaining personalities equipped to resist and to fight the stereotyping and consequent death of genuinely lively things. Fresh perception now involves the capacity continually to unmask and to smash the stereotypes of vision and intellect with which modern communications swamp us. These worlds of mass-art and mass-thought are increasingly geared to the demands of politics. That is why it is in politics that intellectual solidarity and effort must be centred. If the thinker does not relate himself to the value of truth in political struggle, he cannot responsibly cope with the whole of live experience. (Mills, 1963: 299)

The Sociological Review, 60:S1, pp. 18–39 (2012), DOI: 10.1111/j.1467-954X.2012.02115.x

According to Mills, political commitments are not blinding but provide a means to make judgements about our relationship to live experience and the truths we enact through attempting to understand it. Our political and ethical commitments provide the only mechanism to answer Law and Urry's question. This kind of research training requires competence in digital technology alongside theoretical literacy. It fosters a different mode of attention, remarks upon what is otherwise ignored, renders explicit inequities that are passed over in silence and pluralizes the vantage points and jurisdictions for social commentary itself. Sociology, as a crafty science and artful sensibility, needs in the 21st century precisely to make these muted realities more real.

Acknowledgements

I am grateful to Emma Uprichard, Nirmal Puwar and Marcus Morgan for many conversations that helped shape the arguments discussed here along with the participant in the ESRC Research Development initiative *Live Sociology: Practising Social Research with New Media* (PTA-035-25-0017) January 2006–December 2008 particularly Grant McNulty. I would like to thank the ESRC for their support. Also, I would like to thank Catherine Belloy of the Juan Muñoz Estate and Marian Gallery, New York for permission to use images of Juan Muñoz's sculptural artwork. Last, but not least, thanks to Jane Offerman for casting her keen editorial eye over the article.

Notes

1 Economic and Social Research Council Researcher Development Initiative (with Celia Lury), *Live Sociology: Practising Social Research with New Media* (PTA-035-25-0017) January 2006–December 2008.
2 The detail of the sessions are outlined on the Live Sociology website http://www.gold.ac.uk/livesociology/
3 See Nina Wakeford's INCITE programme http://www.studioincite.com/people/nina.html and also her collaboration with Kat Jungnickel http://www.studioincite.com/73urbanjourneys/
4 See Trials of Strength (2007) http://www.ninawakeford.com/work8.html
5 See *Making Things Public: Atmospheres of Democracy* curated by Bruno Latour and Peter Weibel for Zentrum für Kunst und Medientechnologie, Karlsruhe, Germany http://on1.zkm.de/zkm/stories/storyReader$4581#
6 I am thinking of two examples here. First, a Princeton sociologist teaches an entire introductory course 'SOC 205 Sociology from East Street' using the music of Bruce Springsteen to introduce and evoke the experience of American social life that is then explored through sociological ideas and research (see Wallace, 2009). Secondly, David Simon's drama *The Wire* is an extraordinary example of combining sociological imagination with popular TV drama. Set around Baltimore, Maryland, it was made by the cable network HBO and it combined biographical accounts of urban life with an analysis of the structural failing of post-industrial life.
7 See, for example, *Academic Diary* at http://www.academic-diary.co.uk/

References

Adkins, L. and Lury, L., (2009), 'What is the empirical', *European Journal of Social Theory*, 12: 5–20.

Back, L., (2009a), 'Portrayal and betrayal: Bourdieu, photography and sociological life', *Sociological Review*, 57 (3): 471–491.

Back, L., (2009b), 'Researching community and its moral projects', *21st Century Society*, 4 (2): 2001–2014.

Back, L., (2010), *Broken Devices and New Opportunities: Re-Imagining the Tools of Qualitative Research*, ESRC National Centre for Research Methods, Working Papers Series 08/10, NCRM: Southampton.

Beck, U., (2000), 'The cosmopolitan perspective: sociology of the second age of modernity', *British Journal of Sociology*, 51 (1): 79–105.

Beck, U. and Sznaider, N., (2006), 'Unpacking cosmopolitanism for the social sciences: a research agenda', *British Journal of Sociology*, 57 (1): 1–23.

Becker, H., (2007), *Telling about Society,* Chicago: University of Chicago Press.

Berger, J., (2011), *Bento's Sketchbook,* London: Verso.

Berger, J. and Mohr, J., (1975), *A Seventh Man,* London: Penguin Books.

Bhambra, G., (2007), *Rethinking Modernity: Postcolonialism and the Sociological Imagination,* Oxford: Berg.

Bull, M., (2007), *Sound Moves: iPod Culture and Urban Experience*, London: Routledge.

Chakrabarty, D., (2000), *Provincializing Europe: Postcolonial Thought and Historical Difference,* Princeton, NJ: Princeton University Press.

Dench, G., Gavron, K. and Young, M., (2006), *The New East End: Kinship, Race and Conflict,* London: The Young Foundation.

Emmel, N. and Clark, A., (2007), 'We walk the walk, but can we talk the talk (with deference to John Lee Hooker): walkabouts to understand the lived environment of the community', Developing 'mobile' methods, 12 June 2007, Cardiff University at http://www.cardiff.ac.uk/socsi/qualiti/IntDisSem2007/rlmleeds.ppt (accessed January 2009).

Fraser, M., (2009), 'Experiencing sociology', *European Journal of Social Theory*, 12 (1): 63–82.

Geertz, C., (1973), *The Interpretation of Cultures: Selected Essays*, New York: Basic Books.

Giddens, A., (2007), 'Doubting diversity's value', *Foreign Policy*, November/December: 87–88.

Gleason, P., (1983), 'Identifying identity: a semantic history', *The Journal of American History*, 69 (4): 910–931.

Glenn, D., (2008), 'Social scientist in army's human terrain program dies in Afghanistan', *The Chronicle of Higher Education*, 9 May, http://chronicle.com/article/Social-Scientist-in-Armys/40946 (accessed 10 July 2011).

Grant, G., (2008), 'Anthropologists lend military insight into customs, values of foreign cultures', *GovernmentExecutive.com*, 25 April, http://www.govexec.com/dailyfed/0408/042508g1.htm (accessed 12 July 2011).

Harper, D., (2004), 'Psychology and the "war on terror"', *Journal of Critical Psychology, Counselling and Psychotherapy*, 4: 1–10.

Harrisson, T., (1947), 'The future of sociology', *Pilot Papers*, 2 (1): 10–25.

Ingold, T., (2010), *Bringing Things to Life: Creative Entanglements in a World of Materials*, ESRC National Centre for Research Methods Working Paper 15, Realities: Manchester.

Lash, S., (2002), *Critique of Information,* London: Sage.

Lash, S., (2009), 'Afterword: in praise of the a posteriori: sociology and the empirical', *European Journal of Social Theory*, 12: 175–187.

Law, J. and Urry, J., (2004), 'Enacting the social', *Economy and Society*, 33: 390–410.

Latour, B., (2005), *Reassembling the Social,* Oxford: Oxford University Press.

Mayhew, D., (2007), 'The new East End', *Identity*, April: 12–13.

Mead, M., (1995), 'Visual anthropology in a discipline of words', in P. Hocking (ed.), *Principles of Visual Anthropology*, 2nd edn, 3–10, Berlin and New York: Mouton de Gruyter.

Mignolo, W., (2000), *Local Histories/Global Designs: Coloniality, Subaltern Knowledges, and Border Thinking*, Princeton, NJ: Princeton University Press.

Mills, C. W., (1959), *The Sociological Imagination*, New York: Oxford University Press.

Mills, C. W., (1963), 'The social role of the intellectual', in I. L. Horowitz (ed.), *Power, Politics and People: The Collected Essays of C. Wright Mills*, 292–304, New York: Ballentine.

Newsweek, (2008), 'A gun in one hand, a pen in the other', *Newsweek*, 12 April, http://www.newsweek.com/2008/04/12/a-gun-in-one-hand-a-pen-in-the-other.html (accessed 4 July 2011).

Perec, G., (1997), *Species of Spaces and Other Pieces*, London: Penguin Books.

Putnam, R., (2007), 'U pluribus unum: diversity and community in the 21st century: The 2006 Johan Skyette Prize Lecture', *Scandinavian Political Studies*, 30 (2): 137–174.

Rabinow, P., (2003), *Anthropos Today: Reflections on Modern Equipment*, Princeton, NJ: Princeton University Press.

Rohde, D., (2007), 'Army enlists anthropology in war zones', *New York Times*, 7 October, http://www.nytimes.com/2007/10/05/world/asia/05afghan.html?pagewanted=print (accessed 12 July 2011).

Rouch, J., (1995 [1973]), 'The camera and man', in P. Hocking (ed.), *Principles of Visual Anthropology*, 2nd edn, Berlin and New York: Mouton de Gruyter.

Said, E., (1996), *Representations of the Intellectual*, New York: Vintage Books.

Said, E., (2001), 'The public role of writers and intellectuals', *Nation*, 17/24 September: 28.

Savage, M., (2009), 'Contemporary sociology and the challenge of descriptive assemblage', *European Journal of Social Theory*, 12: 155–174.

Savage, M., (2010), *Identities and Social Change in Britain since 1940: The Politics of Method*, Oxford: Oxford University Press.

Savage, M. and Burrows, R., (2007), 'The coming crisis of empirical sociology', *Sociology*, 41 (5): 885–899.

Small, A., (1895), 'The era of sociology', *The American Journal of Sociology*, 1 (1): 1–15.

Steedman, C., (2000), 'Enforced narratives', in T. Cosslett, P. Summerfield and C. Lury (eds), *Feminism and Autobiography: Texts, Theories, Methods*, 25–39, London: Routledge.

Steinmetz, G., (2009), 'The imperial entanglements of sociology in the United States, Britain, and France since the nineteenth century', *Ab Imperio*, 4: 23–78.

Thrift, N., (2004), *Knowing Capitalism*, London: Sage.

Urry, J., (2003), *Global Complexity*, Cambridge: Polity Press.

Vaznis, J., (2008), 'Afghan bomb kills scholar from Mass: Ex-Medway resident was aiding army's work', *The Boston Globe*, 12 May, http://www.boston.com/news/local/articles/2008/05/10/afghan_bomb_kills_scholar_from_mass/ (accessed 10 July 2011).

Wallace, S., (2009), 'Pop culture in the classroom', *Daily Princetonian*, http://www.dailyprincetonian.com/2009/12/03/24620/ (accessed 26 September 2011).

Wilson, A., (2008), ' "Is that Escape you're wearing Miss": a synaesthetic approach to research into everyday prison life', paper presented at Vital Signs: Researching Real Life conference, University of Manchester, 10 September.

Curating sociology

Nirmal Puwar and Sanjay Sharma

Abstract: Building on the range of methods available to the roaming sociological imagination, curating sociology is concerned with instituting 'live' public encounters. Contending that there are practices in the history of sociology that can be considered instances of curating sociology, this article makes a case for harnessing these to inventive research processes today. The discussion in this article draws attention to recent developments in curating before excavating a selection of practices within sociology upon which we can reflexively build live methods with consideration to creative collaborations, publicness and exhibiting as research. Each of these involves a degree of *mutation* within the craft of sociology. By way of illustration, the final section of the article explores an in-depth case study of curating sociology for the *Noise of the Past* project, which involved us, as sociologists, collaborating with creative practitioners and 'curating' a large-scale public event.

Keywords: method, curating, call-and-response, exhibition

Introduction

This article explores curating sociology – a practice both evident within yet obscured by conventional accounts of the discipline – as a series of sociological *mutations*, whereby researchers move with their questions into different fields of creative practice. Building on from the Latin term *cūrāre* to care, a curator is an overseer or carer of a collection, usually in a museum or gallery.[1] In the current era, the term 'curate' has morphed, not least of all because the role has expanded. So that now, in the art world, a curator is understood to be an active producer. A curator has become a catalyst who prompts dialogue by bringing artists, places and publics together. Curating sociology points to how sociological practice can engage with the academy and beyond, by turning to and deploying cross-disciplinary collaborations that engage in creative knowledge practices – as drama, event, exhibitions, installations, film production and music performance, for example.

The Sociological Review, 60:S1, pp. 40–63 (2012), DOI: 10.1111/j.1467-954X.2012.02116.x

In this article, we do not aim to provide an encyclopaedic coverage of all the episodes and moments in the history of sociology which could possibly be collected together under the rubric of curating sociology. A comprehensive overview is not the purpose of this article. Rather, we aim to call upon some aspects of heterodox practices in order to suggest the possibilities of a 'live sociology' built from curating sociology. It remains rare for students to be taught why and how sociologists might collaborate during or after their research with different types of creative practitioners to generate exhibitions, theatre productions, sound pieces or sculptures in places outside the academy. Marginal though these practices may be to methods curricula, textbooks and research proposals, nonetheless, they constitute fractured legacies which are certainly there to be found if we search for them.

At least three contexts are important to why sociologists might extend the methodological focus to curating sociology. First, the vast literature on public sociology has overlooked the potential of *creative* public engagements. Secondly, there has been a recent emergence of mixed methods in sociology, which could be challenged to innovate even further by paying attention to curating. Sociological encounters seek dialogue, not only in conventional forms such as notes in the press, but more so in productions that work *with* the arsenal of creative knowledge practices. Thirdly, as policy-led research directives in the UK instruct scholars to undertake social impact, knowledge transfer and dissemination activities, it becomes imperative to excavate and make use of long-standing critical traditions and practices on intervention from across subject disciplines.

The first part of this article outlines (at least) three key elements of curating sociology, focusing on publicness, creative collaboration and the research process of exhibiting. Here, the doing of sociology as a *curated* knowledge practice is elaborated with examples from across the history of sociology. This discussion makes it apparent that the sociological enterprise has been replete with (unruly) methodological multiplicities, both within and outside of its disciplinary boundaries, as has been noted by a number of recent historiographies of the discipline (Halsey, 2004; Osborne *et al.*, 2008; Savage, 2010; Scott and Bromley, 2012). We explore the rather neglected historical and contemporary assemblages of curating sociology in order to facilitate approaches that encourage us to do *more* with sociological research. The final part of the article examines our own endeavour as researchers to produce a public event-based practice of curating sociology, through the Arts and Humanities Research Council (AHRC) funded project we directed titled *Noise of the Past*. This initiative, as a methodological practice, has implications for how we can envisage and craft a collaborative, creative, public and event based sociology.

Part I: On curating

There is a long-standing interest in the sociology *of* art, institutions and curating (for an overview, see Tanner, 2003). But there has been little reflection on how sociologists can themselves participate in, or indeed have already undertaken, the practice of curating. Bruno Latour in a conversation on the occasion of his exhibition *Making Things Public: Atmospheres of Democracy* (2005), pointed to the limited forms which social scientists have called upon to assemble their research. Discussing what the exhibition can offer, he claimed:

> . . . here there are at least 20 scholars working hand-in-hand with artists to produce installations for the show. So it tries a little bit to wake up the social scientists: we are in 2005 still writing the same boring books. Wake up! There are lots of ways of presenting your data. There are lots of ways of collaborating with artists. Let's organize new connections . . . (Latour, 2007)

Since this statement by Latour, new methodological directions in the discipline have been increasingly attached to different outputs such as exhibitions. Some of these are now much more tied to research directives on social impact and knowledge transfer than critical notions of public intervention, although what is understood as the exhibition form remains restricted as a sociological craft. It is true, as noted by Latour, that creative collaborations with the arts have not been the mainstay of either sociological methods or of the historiography of the discipline. However, if we dig into the sociological archive, looking beyond standard methods textbooks, there is an array of creative and inventive practices which we can, in this respect, make use of today. A diverse range of fragments point towards how we can build on earlier ways in which sociologists have collaborated to 'curate' exhibitions, theatrical productions and music compositions. Working from contrasting theoretical and political episodes in the history of the discipline, no doubt the scholars would themselves be surprised to be grouped together. Nonetheless, there is a heterodoxy of sociological practices that can help us to devise a laboratory with which to build the craft of curating sociology. Together these existing practices offer us what Stuart Hall terms as a 'living archive' (2001), one that invites constant engagement, not for the sake of deference to the past, but one that provides a creative force for methods today. Thus, this archive of practices can be gathered and constituted to energize a 'live sociology'. Before moving on to highlight clusters of existing research practices which can be identified as ways of curating sociology, it is worth noting some key developments in curation more generally.

The field of curating is a constellation of forces, shaped by competition, distinctions and an enlargement of capital, as well as struggles for autonomy and inventive artisanship. Since the 19th century curators have administered, organized, selected, and used their specialist knowledge to collect and display objects (Bourdieu, 1993 [1987]). The curator's ideas and concepts would generate exhibitions, for which they raised funds, staked out and selected relevant pieces of work and published catalogues. In the art world, the role of the curator has expanded, and the practice of curating has proliferated in both professionalized and in the more autonomous zones (Farquharson, 2003; Greenberg *et al.*, 1996). The 1980s witnessed what Peter O'Neill (2007) has critically dubbed as the 'curatorial turn', whereby the stature and influence of the curator increased significantly. The role morphed into one of conceptual director, signalling the 'rise of the curator as creator' (Altshuler, cited in O'Neill, 2007: 20) and having the effect of producing what Ralph Rugoff (1999) referred to as the 'jet-set flaneur' curator of large-scale global exhibitions. In this context, curators have increasingly become mediators, operating between different agents and brokers, especially artists, funders and audiences (Andreasen and Larsen, 2010; Millard, 2001). Integral to the curatorial turn has been the growth in professional training programmes over the last two decades (Bryan-Wilson 2003; Tannert and Tischler, 2004). As the skill-base and reputation has widened, sociologists may be interested to know that curatorial education now involves practical aspects of funding and exhibiting, as well as cultural and social theory, including the sociology of the arts.

Alongside the expansion and exaltation of the curatorial role in professionalized established arts and cultural institutions, there has also been an increase in the number of self-fashioned curators, often working in an autonomous spirit (Vishmidt, 2006), as a part of the precarious, flexible creative labour force (Gielen, 2010; Velthuis, 2007). Amidst these recent developments it is important to keep in mind that since at least the 1960s there has been an emergence of curators influenced by avant-garde movements, who have been rethinking the exhibition space, questioning conventions and experimenting with critical practices and forms of media. Thus, over time, in these critical traditions new methodologies built on participatory and collective models of working collaboratively beyond traditional institutions of art have multiplied. A problematization of the gallery space and sensitivity to the shape of the physical environment has propelled an awareness of the performativity of the environment. Everyday spaces and online platforms have been reinvented and repurposed. At the same time, there has been a broadening of what is legitimated as art practice, even if official promotion is entangled with commercial endorsement. Both the independent and more institutionally supported developments have occurred in the context of an expansion of art markets, international exhibitions and the culture industries (Bauman, 1998; Bradley, 2003; Miller, 1996).

During the course of this article it will become apparent that curating sociology does not envision the researcher naively mimicking the role of the curator. Rather, the intention is to adapt some of the practices of the curator, and grasp 'curating as a research process' (Wells, 2007) that embraces creativity and experimentation in the production of public knowledge. O'Neill maintains that curating can involve processual participatory activities, engendering 'new practices, new meanings, values and relations between things' (2010: 6). Curating sociology therefore should not be reduced to a set of research techniques or methods. Rather, it is a methodological commitment to collaborative knowledge production for creative public intervention and engagement. Notably, methodologies from other disciplines are imputed, poached and mutated with sociological issues and concerns. The cross-disciplinary methods it deploys can be multiple; calling on statistics, drama, surveys, music, digital data, exhibitions, network analysis, film and site-based installations, to name just a few.

The sceptical reader may ask that if so much is borrowed from other disciplines, *'Is this still sociology?'* It is worth reminding ourselves of C. W. Mills' assertion that the sociological imagination was more likely to be found and developed *outside* the discipline of sociology. Remarking in the 1950s on the sociological imagination, he stated:

> Much of what the phrase means to me is not at all expressed by sociologists. In England, for example, sociology as an academic discipline is still somewhat marginal, yet in much English journalism, fiction and above all history, the sociological imagination is very well developed indeed. (Mills, 1959: 19)

It is usually noted that for Mills the sociological imagination has the capacity to consider historical social structures as 'urgent public issues and insistent human troubles' (Mills, 1959: 21); whereby private troubles are located as public problems. What is less emphasized in discussions is how Mills pointed to the sociological imagination as a 'quality of mind' which is also to be found elsewhere (1959: 19). Noting how the intellectual craftsmanship entailed in the sociological imagination can be 'cultivated', he observed that often the imagination roamed into other fields, not least of all because having embarked on a topic, 'once you are into it, it is everywhere'. For Mills, in the very development of the craft of analysis, there is a 'playfulness' of the mind combined with 'a truly fierce drive to make sense of the world.' Within the playfulness of the sociological imagination he identifies an 'unexpected quality about it, perhaps because its essence is the combination of ideas that no one expected were combinable . . .' (Mills, 1959: 211).

Thus, curating sociology is mindful to combinations and a roaming imagination. It is a set of practices that are alert to other ways of *telling* about society. As pointed out by Howard Becker, social scientists do not possess the only methods of telling. He contends that sociologists who seek to monopolize truth-telling are simply performing 'professional power garb' (Becker, 2007: 6). Photographers, novelists, visual artists, film-makers and 'lay people' all have ways of telling, often with analytic dimensions and possibilities ignored by social scientists. From the vantage point of curating sociology, by paying attention to the value of other ways of telling, we can, through unexpected combinations and collaborations, shift how the analysis can be put together, particularly in the process of placing it as a public issue.

The development of curating sociology as unexpected combinations, does not necessarily involve the researcher taking on the roles of other creative practitioners, such as dramatists, composers, artists, film-makers, photographers, musicians or computer programmers.[2] To presume so would be to deny the time, effort, skill and working routines integral to the development of specific crafts (Sennett, 2009). Creative practices are defined by specialisms, an indexicality of knowledge and tacit understandings (Becker, 1984). Nonetheless, for curating sociology, it is important to register that, consciously or not, this is a process where there is some degree of 'becoming otherwise' by working collaboratively. The degree of adaptation, absorption and transformation – for example, in encountering creative practices of music, drama or exhibiting – depends, of course, on the contours of the research project as well as the personnel involved.

On publicness

Among the swathe of debates on Burawoy's notion of 'public sociology' (2005), a notable critique has been made of what the *public* constitutes (see, for instance, debates in the *British Journal of Sociology*, 56 (3), 2005). A public cannot be assumed to either be on the side of the sociologist or be interested in what academics have to say. This is indeed a fraught field of intervention. Curating sociology is careful not to idealize the public sphere or the constituency of the 'public', however this amorphous collectivity is defined. Nor does it presume that the pervasiveness of the culture industries will lead to ready-made audiences engaging with creative research outputs (via for example, appealing data visualizations, aestheticized film or populist exhibitions). The manner in which publics are constituted and mobilized through creative practices is contingent on a range factors, including the modes of dialogic collaboration forged by research projects. Interestingly, Burawoy states that public sociology 'strikes up a dialogic relation between sociologist and public' (2005: 9). Yet the prototypes for how to enact the dialogic relation remain rather limited. Moreover, in the ASA mould of public sociology, creative modes for activating dialogic exchange of the kind suggested by curating sociology have thus far largely remained off the imaginative horizon.

If we look close enough within the archives of the discipline, however, sociologists have demonstrated a capacity to institute live events and situations, sometimes on a large scale which seek to both disrupt and embrace the collective public imagination. There have been modes of sociological practice that have not been confined to the conventions of presentation centred on writing, reading, lectures and public address. In 1912 for instance, Andrew Geddes wrote, directed and produced 'The Masque of Learning', a pageant of the history of civilization, with 650 participants. It was first performed to a huge audience of 2,500 children in Edinburgh University's Synod Hall (Boardman, 1978). In March 1913, the same performance attracted large audiences in the Great Hall of London University's Imperial Institute. Four editions of a booklet with directions and reflections written by Geddes were produced, and 9,000 copies were sold. In this process, Geddes, a botanist, geographer, sociologist of the city and town planner, reinvented himself into becoming director, choreographer and improviser.

Geddes, in partnership with Victor Brandford, further mutated the social sciences by bringing the arts as well as statistically and ethnographically based surveys together. At a time when sociology as a discipline was very much marked by struggles to define its field (Halliday, 1968; Scott and Bromley, 2012),[3] Geddes and Brandford bought 65 Belgrave Road in Chelsea, London where *Le Play House* was opened in April 1920. The building housed the Sociological Society (which was previously at LSE), and the journal *The Sociological Review* was founded there (Evans, 1986). Soon touring exhibitions, field trips, surveys, murals, glass work and sculpture became integral to the house. John Scott mentions that Geddes and Brandford sought to construct a 'civic sociology', one which 'envisaged a role for artists alongside sociologists, with the presentation of dramas and even carnivals as a means for enticing people into a deeper sociological understanding and involving them in the production of sociological knowledge' (Scott and Husbands, 2007; Scott and Bromley, 2012).

While Geddes and Brandford's ideas were far from accepted within the then emerging discipline of (British) Sociology (Halliday, 1968), it is important to note that when Geddes put together his ideas for exhibitions or drama, he was not simply a singular scholar ploughing a project on his own. He was embedded in the arts and craft movement, as well as the regional survey movement. Geddes was committed to improving the environment through educational, planning and housing initiatives (see Ferguson, 2011: 55). *Le Play House* has to be located in this context: influences, dialogue and collaboration with other disciplines and movements were vital to the curatorial practices.

On collaboration

Curating sociology is entangled with re-purposing methods from a cross-disciplinary standpoint. However, it is not a one-way exchange, as there may be much that is also shared and redistributed from within sociology. In this respect, it is useful to distinguish between at least three different types of cross-disciplinary collaborative practices. Andrew Barry *et al.* (2008) make the observation that (i) *multi-disciplinary* collaboration brings different disciplines into contact but does not lead to the altering of existing disciplinary framings. On the other hand, (ii) *inter-disciplinarity* attempts integration and synthesis of different disciplinary perspectives. And (iii) *trans-disciplinarity* differs further, by seeking to transcend existing disciplinary norms by collaboratively fusing disciplines. Curating sociology favours cross-disciplinary practices of (ii) and (iii), those that advance *dialogic* encounters between different formations of knowledge production and creativity.

Arguably, the most prolific medium deployed in creative collaborative inter- and trans-disciplinary methods has been through the use of photography and film. While visual methods in sociology are now becoming a growing area, there are plenty of antecedents from earlier sociological practice. Indeed both Geddes and Branford had intellectual and personal links with leaders in the field of documentary film and mass observation, including John Grierson and Humphrey Jennings, who were driven by an aesthetic to make films about 'real' people and 'real' things, which would contribute towards building a progressive socialism. Jennings was one of the co-founders of the mass observation studies started in the 1930s (archived at Sussex); an initiative built on a whole complex of mixed methods and modes of participation (Stanley, 2001; Hubble, 2006). Embedded in the arts movement, known as the Blackheath Group (London),

Jennings, for his own part, inflected surrealism into his 'real' documentaries (Logan, 2011). It is also worth recalling that as early as the turn of the twentieth century, the *American Journal of Sociology* (founded in 1895) included photographs which were influenced by realist documentary aesthetics (Shanas, 1945) and focused, for example, on exposing poverty and prompting reform (Becker, 2007: 189). Becker notes that these visual forms soon gave way to more positivist and traditional forms of knowledge presentation; a trend manifest within as well as outside of the *American* academy.

Sociologists have had a long-standing tradition of studying visual culture in its many manifestations, ranging from fine art to popular media forms. While not having a large body of visual methodological practice of their own, this did not prevent sociologists from poaching technologies and approaches from other disciplines. Historically speaking within visual sociology, partnerships with other disciplines, including anthropology, have often been vital to the formation of these sociological cross-disciplinary collaborations. The mutual influence of the arts and of anthropology upon sociology is apparent, for example, in Edgar Morin's creative practices.

The sociologist Morin collaborated with cine-ethnographer Jean Rouch, in order to analyse the urban environment utilizing more than the usual statistics and field notes of social science, which were the dominant social science modes of making sense of life in the city in post-war Europe.[4] Morin and Rouch made the documentary *Chronicle of a Summer* (1961). This film focused on a plural depiction of urban life in Paris, amid colonial struggles for independence in Algeria and Congo, and in the political moment of the 1960s. Methodologically, it was considered to pioneer *cinéma-vérité*; anticipating participatory documentary films, breaking down boundaries between the makers and spectators.[5] As opposed to *direct-cinema*, *cinéma-vérité* is based on creating artificial situations as prompts, provocations and catalysts – an interactive process.

Rouch and Morin stopped people on the street, asking broad questions such as 'Are you happy?' and 'How do you live?' In addition, over a six-month period they closely observed a small sample of people as they walked through the streets of Paris, in their homes, at work and over several dinners. This sample included students from the Ivory Coast, a Renault factory worker, holocaust survivors and a migrant from Italy. After editing 25 hours of rushes the film was composed of three parts, covering work, personal relations and present history, dominated by the war in Algeria. Of the twenty sequences in the film, some were spontaneous, others staged or provoked. For Morin the film was an experiment in cinematic interrogation. He considered it as a montage of images, during the course of which the leading question 'How do you live?' transformed, during the process of conversation and reflection, into 'How can one live?' and 'What can one do?' (Morin, 2003: 237).

Thus the film was a different kind of curation and artifice from 'fly-on-the-wall' observation studies: it acknowledged the dialogic and performative aspect of telling stories and being in front of the camera (Ungar, 2003). Launched in Cannes, the film circulated in leftist and avant-garde sites. It was criticized for being too invasive and 'psychoanalytical', rather than sociological. Interestingly, Morin did not label the film as sociology but he did see *A Chronicle of a Summer* as being sociologically inflected – as an interrogation of work and daily life, of job alienation, loneliness, the difficulties of living as well as the search for faith and political freedom.

What is useful for researchers and an aspect often glossed over in research accounts, is a set of recollections Morin provided, by way of a 'curatorial' working diary, of the tensions, mistakes, revelations, decisions and compromises during the course of filming (2003: 342–3). These were written from the seat of practising what we might today call visual sociology. We hear of the differences, of how far Morin wanted fiction to enter the film, with Rouch pushing for more surrealist tendencies. Nonetheless, between cuts, insertions and disappointments and 'from confrontation to confrontation' agreement was reached between the two through what Morin called a 'compromise schema' (2003: 253–4).

It would be naive to ignore the possibility that collaboration can incite tensions and differences among project partners. However, prematurely shying away from the difficulties that can arise fails to open up the sociological enterprise to different possibilities of engaging the world. The sociological imagination has after all produced some of the most inventive methods when practitioners from other disciplines have themselves roamed into sociology to fuse different directions together. John Berger's and Jean Mohr's text *A Seventh Man* (2010 [1975]) is one such exemplary case of trans-disciplinarity.[6] They combined statistics, photography, poetry, as well as theory, to consider the departure, work and return of migrants on the move to Western Europe in the postwar period. Berger and Mohr hoped the book would spark a political debate on the reliance of Western Europe on migrant labour. However, they found that the press and state-agencies ignored the book. But unexpectedly, it did capture the imagination of thousands who were themselves caught in the chains of global migration. Commenting on the public reception Berger stated: 'In the Global South there was another reaction. The book began to be translated into Turkish, Greek, Arabic, Portuguese, Spanish, and Punjabi. It began to be read by some of those whom it was about' (Berger and Mohr, 2010 [1975]: 8). In this process of linguistic and social-cultural exchange, the book became a series of public 'life stories' and 'lived moments', akin to a family photo album.

Developments in the 1980s and 1990s rethought the research relationship and the tools one deploys to record, see and hear. These were prompted by what was characterized as the 'crisis in representation' (Clifford and Marcus, 1986) as well as Bakhtinian influences to construct research as a 'dialogic' encounter (Cohen, 2009; Portelli, 1991, 1997, n.d.). There was a notable shift in the academic focus towards considerations of how research relationships are to be conducted, and how research subjects could be acknowledged as participants. This move enabled the sociologist to more readily engage with publics and present findings in new and unconventional forms. It also involved sharing the space of research so that participants could themselves deliver life-stories utilizing imaginative, creative methods. Educational pedagogy and performance theory and practice were strong components of these developments.

In view of the theatrical elements for example, at conferences researchers aimed to avoid delivering a traditional oral presentation, but instead asked members of the research team to perform the interview situation to an academic audience. Or, deploying the crafts of theatricality in pedagogic terms, interviewees were themselves encouraged to produce a public performance of the research exchanges and data collected. These non-standard formats became a genre in ethnographic presentation that Norman Denzin refers to as 'performance texts'.[7] Most projects were located at the borders of inter-disciplinary sociology. For example, the project *Finding the Way Home* (1996–8), considered multi-layered complex stories and visual landscapes of race, risk, identity and location in the lives of young people in different European locations (Back *et al.*, 1996; Rathzel and Cohen, 2008). The methods were designed as a learning process for the young people who participated in the project. Visual diaries, art projects, video, mapping and field-work diaries were co-produced, utilizing the creative expertise of artists in residence.

Working in the early 1990s, well before the current explosion of visual sociology and participatory media, Jasbir Panesar and Avtar Brah pulled together film and creative learning practices in ways that took the pedagogic impulse one step further, by working with the ethnographic imagination of South Asian elders from an adult education vantage point (see Puwar, 2012). They enabled Asian elders, who visited the Milap day centre in Southall, London to acquire the technical skills from community film trainers, to make a video film about migration, politics and life in the UK. The participants, who worked in languages and notations of their choice, directed a (rarely seen) movie of their journeys of life titled *Aaj Kaal* (1990, *Today and Yesterday*).[8]

These earlier examples of collaborative, cross-disciplinary sociological practice point to the innovation of the research process itself, rather than only being techniques of knowledge dissemination. So, it need not be the case that the arts or media are deployed in a 'service-subordination mode' (Barry *et al.*, 2008), for effecting more popular social engagement with conventional sociological research findings. In contrast, today, there is an emergent trend whereby the arts are used only in the final stages of research to produce an output for wider public dissemination and communication. Indeed, this is increasingly becoming the case in 'prescribed collaborations' (Strathern, 2004), driven by top-down research funding agendas keen to propagate directives that support inter-disciplinary engagements or 'knowledge transfer' and 'social impact'.

On exhibiting as research

It is becoming increasingly difficult to ascertain or disentangle the pursuit of a more public sociology from the governmental research council pursuit of 'social impact'. The valorization of social impact says little about the significance of curatorial practices in sociology, and their relatively under-developed status.

The Sociological Review, 60:S1, pp. 40–63 (2012), DOI: 10.1111/j.1467-954X.2012.02116.x
© 2012 The Authors. Editorial organisation © 2012 The Editorial Board of the Sociological Review

While the sociological imagination may roam, the conventions and disciplinary formations of sociology have often inhibited the development of experimental ways of imagining and presenting research.

Looking back at how Pierre Bourdieu developed his modes of research, he stated that his association with and crucial support from Raymond Aaron in the early part of his academic career steered him away from 'non-scientific' forms of expression (Bourdieu, 2003). Literary and novel forms of communication, which might have allowed more space for the affective qualities of his research were, at the outset, curtailed in favour of an academic style that offered authority and legitimacy via a form of sociology dominant at the time in North America. It was not until some 50 years after the critical event of being in Algeria (during the 1960s) that he had, as he stated in his own words, 'broken with the limits of scientism'. In *The Bachelors' Ball* (2007) for instance, which was written much later, we see the release of a very different writing style from Bourdieu.

Bourdieu took hundreds of photographs with his *Ikoflex* camera when he researched and taught in Algeria after being sent to do French colonial military service during the struggle for independence. He took these photographs in the process of being a disillusioned philosopher, and becoming an ethnographer, while in the thick of the field. Aside from publishing a small number of the photographs in his books, he did nothing more (publically) with them, at least not as a sociologist. And it was not until the late 1990s did Bourdieu elicit public engagement with the photographs, through collaboration with Franz Schultheis and Christine Frisinghelli from *Camera Austria*. This touring exhibition included an installation at Goldsmiths, University of London, of 150 photographs and text boards with excerpts from his own books, thematically organized as 'War and Social Change', 'Habitus', 'Work', 'Gender' and 'Blida' (see Back *et al.*, 2009).

Today, the increasing scale of experimentation in sociological methods – such as the use of research walks, collaborative mapping techniques, photo elicitation, event immersion, soundscapes, digital albums and diaries – has contributed to what may be identified as an emerging curatorial sociology. However, in the current context, sociologists perhaps too readily accept existing mainstream genres and forms of exhibiting and representation, and thus limit the possibility of experimentation. Nonetheless there are some signs that the innovation of exhibiting beyond the gallery format is starting to occur in sociology alongside an awareness of the performativity of the environment, within the specific context of curating sociology.[9]

Since the 1990s, sociologists located in the field of science and technologies have been more likely to rethink the exhibition form itself (arguably because art and science collaborations have been explicitly supported and funded for longer periods). Exhibitions are in themselves often constructed as sites of experimentation and observation. Taking the mutual exchange of disciplines one step further, methodological observations in science and medical settings are sometimes constructed using the tools and methods of exhibitions (Guggenheim, 2011). In this respect, the exhibitionary field becomes a *mode of research.* Noting the drama of the history of science and laboratories, rather like a 'thought experiment' (*Gedankenexperiement*), Latour (2007) sees himself partaking in a 'thought exhibition' (*Gedankenausstellung*). Thus, the exhibition becomes a place to dramatize facts, following the theatre of proof argument from science: 'A show where the conceptual and fun elements elide together' (Latour, 2005: 28). In his exhibitions *Iconclash* and *Making Things Public,* Latour envisages the exhibition form as 'giving flesh' to the political concepts such as the constitution of idols and public assemblies.

Notably, these kinds of high-profile exhibitions tend to be funded by large grants, supported by prestigious institutions, involving the participation of curators and artists who are already international names in the circuits of the art world. In contrast, the majority of curating sociology initiatives are likely to emerge under different conditions of production.[10] We are thus, slowly, witnessing developments similar to the arts, whereby there is the simultaneous expansion of the globe-trotting celebrity academic curator, as well as the more precarious autonomous curating activities of sociologists. The smaller-scale, less well-funded projects require different strategies and negotiations in an attempt to curate sociology. Many of these projects, especially those led by research students, are more localized and work with far fewer resources.

The increasing use of 'social computing' and 'digital methods' (Rogers, 2009) for both collection and dissemination in research contexts, may expand the possibilities beyond the local focus when curating. Notwithstanding inequalities in access to the Internet, digital methods can multiply the scope of both presenting research and in innovating the process of doing research (see Marres in this volume). Fields of research in sociology deploying statistics and patterns have, for some time, been able to produce visually accessible data from the results. Sometimes this has been deliberately utilized in order to communicate research beyond academic confines, as Otto Neurath did in the 1920s through pictorial statistics. Scholars working in the field of social network analysis, for instance, have always been adept at this, as they have utilized graph theory to identify societal links, relations and clusters.[11] For example, elite studies have produced illuminating graphs and maps of linkages between personnel from different sectors and organizations (see Scott, 2000). While these diagrams have appeared on the pages of academic texts, they are less likely to be exhibited on the walls and floors of public places. This is a largely untapped potential of research for sociologists to institute public conversations. There are, however, publics located at the edges of the academy who are utilizing these visual analytics. Network analysis has, for instance, recently migrated into the knowledge practices of social movements; at the European Social Forum in Paris in 2003, tents included exhibits with charts and flows of capital and surveillance. These activist practices are engaged in alter-cartographies via mapping techniques (see Toscano in this volume).

It is worth remembering that sometimes the analytical direction of the sociological imagination has been kept alive by the outsiders who have roamed into the discipline. Historically, creative practitioners have, for instance, mutated techniques of network patterns and connections, and exhibited them in arts institutions. Most famously, Hans Haacke is renowned for using sociological research techniques to deliver institutional critique via his installations.[13] He used his artwork to highlight the exchange of symbolic and economic capital between sponsors and galleries. His work *Shapolsky et al. Manhattan Real Estate Holdings, A Real Time Social System* (1971) considered networks and systems of exchange as a way of mapping the economic and legal transactions of one of New York's largest slum landlords. The work was banned from being exhibited at the Guggenheim Museum and the curator (Edward Fry) was also dismissed for supporting the work. Furthering the cross-disciplinary exchange with sociology, Haacke went on to analyse museums and institutional power as well as taste and state, with Bourdieu (1995).

Academics have also been exploring digital technologies for visualizing data analysis at exhibitions (de Nooy *et al.*, 2005). Different methods of representing and interpreting complex data sets and relationships have been innovated via sophisticated approaches to data visualization. These methods of data analysis *as* visualization have led to developing a range of practices of *doing and presenting* collaborative research. These developments continue to mutate the labour of academics: alongside writing academic papers, their work can involve developing software and visualizing techniques as a mode of curating sociological research.[12] However, Emma Uprichard (in this volume) points out that there is a danger of aggrandizing new technological tools, which focus on presentation at the expense of developing broader sociological comparative analysis. Linking back to Mills, this trend raises the question – is there a danger that in the playfulness of roaming into other fields we forget the analytical scope of the sociological imagination?

Part II: *Noise of the Past*

One of the challenges of curating sociology is that there is no methodological blueprint to follow or orthodoxy to reproduce. While its historical antecedents are replete with examples of practices that one can emulate, we contend that a curated project is principally constituted by the research problem it seeks to explore. Any experienced researcher will stress the point that methods – the tools and techniques available – should not define or drive a research project. In the real world however, the availability of resources, time constraints and the shared conventions of the personnel involved are often the determining factors of how a research activity is undertaken (cf. Becker, 1984).

The *Noise of the Past* project deployed a curatorial orientation built upon a collaborative process of working between academic researchers and creative practitioners. The project focused on making a public intervention through a large-scale cultural production of a site-specific event. *Noise of the Past* explored the vexed issue of postcoloniality, memory and belonging in relation to national(ist) commemoration ceremonies and proliferating 'global wars'. It is

The Sociological Review, 60:S1, pp. 40–63 (2012), DOI: 10.1111/j.1467-954X.2012.02116.x
© 2012 The Authors. Editorial organisation © 2012 The Editorial Board of the Sociological Review

notable that rituals of remembrance increasingly buttress the legacy of the British Empire while at the same time apparently recognizing the contributions of servicemen and women from the former colonies (Puwar and Sharma, 2011). Within the social sciences there is a rich tradition of scholarship on race, ethnicity and citizenship, and more specifically on how nations are engendered via calendric events on war and memory. Nonetheless, critical academic accounts of postcolonial national formation in relation to the World Wars have ostensibly remained confined to the journal article, monograph or conference paper. To publicly interrogate the sanctity of remembrance has increasingly become a fraught arena to navigate as modes of assimilatory nationalism are in their ascendency across Europe (Fortier, 2007). In contrast, the principal research aim of the *Noise of the Past* was to make a public intervention by asking:

How can we speak to the residual narratives of consecrated sites of memory and performative rites of British national remembrance by setting them into play with disavowed sounds and images of multicultural belonging?

The project intended to re-route existing forms of remembrance via the creation of two cultural productions – a film and a music performance – and to launch these at a public event in the historically laden site of Coventry Cathedral, before circulating them in wider international locations.

Our intention was to interrogate postcolonial narratives of war and memory, and disarticulate these from increasingly celebratory and militaristic forms of contemporary nationalism. However, there was a risk that the project could reductively propagate a didactic – *anti*-war, *anti*-imperialist, *anti*-racist – political tract. A key aim was to engage a diverse constitution of publics by offering a means to reflexively explore issues of memory and postcolonial belonging, rather than foreclose this possibility because of a predetermined political teleological stance. It was particularly a challenge for the project to connect with those ambivalent audiences with seemingly '*pro*-war' or '*pro*-British Empire' alliances. As academic researchers, we believed we possessed the conceptual resources for grasping traumas of war, deconstructing postcolonial entanglements and the politics of racialized national representation. But these did not readily appear to offer a means of productively intervening in public debates concerned with reimagining a British nation able to come to terms with its colonial past, in the present (contested) multicultural moment. In this respect, the project aimed to engage with existing currents of nationalist sentiment and remembrance, and *reroute* these towards more immersive, open-ended ways of belonging to a multicultural nation.

Influenced by our study of existing practices of what we identified as examples of curating sociology, collaboration with creative practitioners to realize *Noise of the Past* was pursued from the outset of the project. We recognized that contemporary state strategies of commemoration and assimilatory nation-building were operating both hegemonically and affectively (Sharma, 2011). To only offer audiences historical facts about the fraught relationship between Empire and its colonies during the World Wars was found to be wanting, especially if that was to wholly determine the pedagogy of the project. Moreover, *Noise of the Past* aimed to move beyond the limits of the realist testimonial (and documentary) modes of communication to speak of resident narratives within environments of national remembrance. Collaborating with creative practitioners offered the means to generate research work that did not present history in a palpable or didactic manner. Instead it offered both contemplative and visceral engagements with postcolonial migrant bodies, memories, sounds and affects that sat beyond the bounds of consecrated sites of remembrance. There has been much theoretical work on the affective and sensory dimensions of social life. At the same time academics are also rather fascinated in observing the play of intensities and forces in artistic assemblages. While we were informed by these debates, the project was not conceived as a practical instance to prove a theory, as is often the case when academics take their bodies and theories into the art world. The project was driven by methodological interventions which attempted to produce engagements by working with music, film, architecture and archives.

The project developed an iterative research process, which generated a series of cultural artefacts (oral, aural and visual) that mutually responded to the problem of postcolonial remembrance and representation. It was discovered that this problem required a multimodal approach because there is not necessarily a single response to how a multicultural nation can be re-routed and experienced otherwise. The project engendered a process of 'transmogrification' – a set of provocations were transformed and realized in the form of artistic/ cultural productions through a collaborative methodology of *call-and-response* which activated a chain of reflexive responses between the researchers, the creative practitioners and their cultural productions (cf. Minh-Ha, 1991). In this method, we as researchers were interlocutors more than directors with a one-way flow of direction and influence.

Call-and-response was a method that re-purposed both the dialogicism of Bakhtin and anti-phonal traditions of 'non-Western' cultures (Boone, 2003; Kochman, 1990). Interaction between different (and possibly contradictory) 'voices' is at the heart of the production of cultural meaning that has the possibility of 'transforming the democratic imaginary' (Hitchcock, 1993). And as Peterson (1993: 763) suggests, 'articulation is a primary act of cultural intervention . . . it orients itself toward an anticipated respondent'. In this respect, a call-and-response methodology was developed to enable a curatorial strategy to articulate how collaboration between academic researchers and creative practitioners could productively take place. It is important to register that within the call-and-response methodology of exchange, the dialogic form of communication is not confined to interpersonal linguistic utterances and responses, as is so often understood. Rather, the dialogic communication is stretched over durations of time and space; operating in stages and across different practitioners. Call-and-response is premised upon a process of exchange that involves stages whereby materials are passed and returned, transformed, only to be carried over to the next practitioner involved in the relay of co-production. So,

The Sociological Review, 60:S1, pp. 40–63 (2012), DOI: 10.1111/j.1467-954X.2012.02116.x

new responsive productions are not foreclosed, they can be a source of interaction at any time a new process of creation is generated. The way in which we re-purposed call-and-response was not pre-planned. It was a new found technique that emerged during the course of searching for a method of working that would enable multiple layers of exchange between sites, objects and especially interdisciplinary collaborators.[14]

The research process for *Noise of the Past* innovated a curatorial methodology that closely collaborated with practitioners from different creative fields. The practitioners participating in the project were a film-maker (Kuldip Powar), a poet (Sawarn Singh), a musician (Nitin Sawhney) and a composer (Francis Silkstone). The artistic forms of their productions evolved during the life of the project, principally resulting in the film *Unravelling* (Powar, 2008) and a musical composition *Post-Colonial War Requiem* (Silkstone, 2008). The *Noise of the Past* project and the process of making these works involved a number of 'stages' in the iterative generation of reflexive artistic responses, culminating in the production of an installation (which *Unravelling* and *Post-Colonial War Requiem* formed a part of). Both were launched at a large public event in Coventry Cathedral, a national site of war and reconciliation (for details, see Puwar, 2011). Each stage included workshops between the researchers and artists to expound and interrogate issues of the project *as they emerged*.

A key stage involved the researchers gathering and producing materials which mapped the terrain of national remembrance and postcolonial memory. These materials were generated from academic texts, colonial film and sound archives, migrant soldier documents, letters and photographs. A series of workshops between the researchers and the film-maker identified what was at stake in re-routing national belonging through collectively examining the academic and archival materials. These conversations facilitated a critical space of investigation exploring the aesthetics of migrant belonging. It led to the first tranche of the call-and-response methodology, which produced a cultural artefact, in the form of an oral Urdu poetic exchange between Powar and his grandfather (Sawarn Singh), a postcolonial war veteran residing in Britain. The poetic exchange was generated as a call-and-response. The poetry moved between the grandson (film-maker) and his grandfather (poet), as one asked and the other responded to participation in World War II under imperial powers and the subsequent arrival and inhabitation in Coventry (UK) for over 50 years. It became apparent that both generations were intimately connected to the Coventry Cathedral ruins, without necessarily feeling connected to the settled British narratives of war, trauma and reconciliation, which has over determined the site. Hence the site of the Cathedral, old and new, was to play a central part in how *Noise of the Past* was both developed and realized as a research project (Puwar, 2011). The embodied relation with the cathedral of the personnel in the project team, as well as the public more generally, shaped the project from start to finish. An awareness of the performativity of the environment was a key creative force.[15] The cathedral presented an architectural call in the making of the creative objects, as well as in the public interactions with the large-scale installation event in the cathedral, deliberately pitched during the official British national calendar Remembrance.

The poetry became a 'call' – an aesthetic object of dialogic meaning – which was responded to by the second artist, the musician Nitin Sawhney. At this stage, not only were the original research materials discussed with Sawhney, but the poetry became a central object of research inquiry, offering a means to interrogate war and memory beyond realist representation and national containment. In his subsequent creative response, Sawhney produced a second cultural artefact, in the form of a haunting 15-minute soundscape which ineffably integrated the original poetic dialogue.

In the relay of creative exchanges and impulses the soundtrack became another object of inquiry, another call to the researchers and the film-maker (Powar). Together, we explored how the soundtrack articulated migrant involvement in World War II, yet was allusive in seeking to represent Singh's memories of war. Powar responded by making the evocative film *Unravelling*, redolent with densely textured archival images of war, monuments and consecrated sites, and incorporated Sawhney's immersive soundscape (see Sharma, 2011).

The call-and-response methodology not only generated cultural artefacts, but was intimately tied to the research process. A unique element of the *Noise of the Past* was the development of a dialogic and performative methodology that worked with creative practitioners to engender cultural productions in the public domain. The methodology eschewed the researchers merely observing or reporting artistic work. Nor was our role simply one of mediators in the production of art. Rather, as curatorial 'interlocutors' we were involved in connecting research to aesthetic practices (cf. Denzin, 1993): an interplay between developing a practice-based research and a research-based practice. We sought to put into play a series of connections across different domains of academic and creative practices.

The fluidity of the methodology enabled innovations to take place during the project. In particular, after the generation of the poetry, its sonorous call intimated that more than one kind of sonic response was possible. Subsequently, the composer Francis Silkstone, was also invited the opportunity to respond to poetry, which resulted in the production of the provocative *Post-Colonial War Requiem* composition and live performance (see Silkstone, 2011). This was a double response; first to the poetry we presented to him and secondly to Benjamin Britten's *War Requiem*, which had inaugurated the newly built Coventry Cathedral in 1962 after the Blitz.

It was crucial that *Noise of the Past* avoided setting up a project with the academicians possessing the critical knowledge and authority, and the creative practitioners merely servicing the project by offering the means of public engagement and dissemination. There were a range of expertise and knowledge practices – academic, archival, poetic, filmic, visual, sonic and musical – at play in the project, and it was important that autonomy of practices was maintained, while re-imaginations were exchanged. Sharing authority for a researcher is easier claimed than achieved in reality. University funding procedures and extant academic hierarchies do not encourage researchers to divest their authority as directors of a funded project. One is required to maintain the direction of a project so that it fulfils its stated funding aims and objectives. We avoided adopting a 'controlling curatorial position' (Bennett, 2006), and offered direction without explicitly directing. The call-and-response methodology enabled *autonomy and exchange* between collaborators from different fields, inhabiting different forms of social, cultural and economic capital. Collaboration invariably can lead to tensions that are manifested 'as a struggle between a centripetal tendency towards the unity of a research project "we" and a centrifugal tendency towards difference and the opening up for a plurality of voices' (Phillips, 2009: 2). Louise Phillips maintains that a project should not seek to dissolve differences among the collaborators and, in our case, between the researchers and creative practitioners and between the creative practitioners themselves. Rather, it should involve being open to otherness (Pearce and Pearce, 2004), and the call-and-response approach created the conditions for these kinds of 'ethical' encounters by dialogically 'tuning-in' to each other's autonomy of practice. However, we would be covering over our research tracks if we claimed the project was without tension, presented by differing scales of economy and authorial control.

It would not have been possible to realize the *Noise of the Past* project without a curatorial methodology. Cross-disciplinarity, creativity and exhibition were at the heart of a project driven by a roaming sociological imagination that was willing to mutate sociology. As researchers, embarking on sociological curation meant forgoing the security of our academic authority and institutionalized control of a funded project. Collaboratively working with a range of practitioners required an approach that was sensitive to different knowledge practices by activating a dialogic exchange. In particular, using artistic practices, via film, sound and exhibition in the form of a curated event at the Coventry Cathedral instigated a 'live' sociological event. This was a key stage of the methodological process of the project; here the event called out to the public and thereby put in place iteration to the call-and-response method. *Noise of the Past* uniquely gathered together a multicultural audience at the Cathedral; the screening of *Unravelling* and live performance of *Postcolonial War Requiem* deepened the call-and-response methodology of the project. The architectural site was very much a part of the visceral audience responses we hoped to generate. Curating sociology involves exposing researchers to the 'real' world, and making academics 'accountable' to publics without following *a priori* notions of either taste or constituency. *Noise of the Past* risked academic 'failure', though taking such risks enabled a public intervention to be made possible *and* meaningful.

We would like to end our discussion of this project by noting some of the responses provided by audience members on the night of the event in the Cathedral:[16]

I think it's wonderful . . . so much of the cathedral was used and the surrounding area. Also the theme of reconciliation is very important to Coventry . . . It's been an education. (Interviewee #3)

The last speaker, praised this as a new communication . . . opening doors. I thought it was a fantastic setting. Especially for opening old encrusted ideas of what religion is, what our human rights are . . . And the cathedral is a poignant start to all of this. (Interviewee #4)

It's really brilliant. I really liked the film. I liked the politics. I liked the way, the music was extended to the war in Iraq. But in the main film narrative, I felt that women were completely missing. It's very much a male narrative – grandfather to grandson, no mention of women. It's a great work, but probably that something could have been addressed. But overall, brilliant. It's high time the contribution of other people to the War was recognised and accepted, and the community came to terms with it, from both sides. I'm from India, we wage wars. (Interviewee #6)

Conclusions

We are witnessing a growing interest among scholars to discover creative methodological practices in sociology. What constitutes sociology continues to expand in the forging of collaborative relationships and inter-interdisciplinary forms of knowledge-production. We are likely to develop a richer resource for developing these directions, if time is granted and attention is paid to the earlier moments of creative practices in sociology which experimented with multimodal forms of telling about society. There continue to be implications for aggrandizing the boundaries of sociology when pursuing collaborative and interdisciplinary labour. Nonetheless, it is important to bear in mind the scope and analytical depth of the sociological imagination: the ways in which this imagination 'roams' and invites us to consider how we collaborate, create the exhibition space and public events. The nature of collaborative exchange is, however, not a straightforward matter. If knowledge production is to be truly dialogic, rather than a simple case of transferring knowledge from the academy to practitioners, our practices must resist the latter group merely acting as 'service providers' for academicians who maintain their intellectual and institutional authority.

Many of the curatorial strategies developed during the *Noise of the Past* were discovered as the project evolved. This led to the research project requiring intense effort, an effort that blurred the boundaries between intellectual and creative labour. The curatorial research approach incited connections across academic concerns with dynamic artistic practices. As academics we became apprentices in the craft of curatorship through practice. In this respect, curating sociology is an intervening methodology that reflexively works with practitioners to produce cultural co-productions engaged in the transformation of research problems. Explicit research questions can be critically transformed into aesthetic practices intervening in the public arena. This may involve learning to reconfigure and occupy public space, as evident in the *Noise of the Past* project.

The Sociological Review, 60:S1, pp. 40–63 (2012), DOI: 10.1111/j.1467-954X.2012.02116.x

Curating sociology innovates a methodological approach that can be adopted to address a multiplicity of contemporary social and political concerns vis-à-vis dialogic and creative collaborations. Curation enables sociological ideas to be made public, whether through dramaturgy, exhibition or live events. Research ideas, issues and concerns can be vitalized, and invested with an affective force beyond a sociology bounded to its disciplinary conventions. Curating sociology is not a specialist practice for those researchers only interested in collaboration or artistic practice. Rather, it offers us compelling new ways of re-imagining and *doing* sociology. We are thus presented with the possibility of energizing conventional methods, of borrowing and sharing from other disciplines, to make sociological mutations that facilitate forms which keep conceptual problems live. Curation makes sociological ideas as an event in new ways – as it did with *Noise of the Past*.

Acknowledgements

We would like to thank Les Back for his thoughtful feedback on earlier drafts. We are grateful to Jennifer Mason, Chris Shilling, Motamedi Fraser, Emma Uprichard, Noortje Marres, Clare Williams and the other referees for helping us to shape the final form of the article through their productive suggestions.

The funders who made the *Noise of the Past* project possible were the AHRC, Coventry Peace Festival, Arts Council England, LCACE, Goldsmiths (University of London) and Brunel University.

Without Kuldip Powar, Sawarn Singh, Francis Silkstone, Nitin Sawhney and the incredible film crew this project would not have happened in the way it did.

Noise of the Past was invited back to Coventry Cathedral on 14 November 2011 to mark the 70th anniversary of the Coventry Blitz. This time we did not curate a stand-alone large-scale event but the film *Unravelling* and the performance *Post-colonial War Requiem* were granted slots amid a range of events selected by Canon David Porter, the Director of Peace at Reconciliation at the cathedral and Lee House from Coventry Peace Festival. We seek to return again in 2012 for the cathedral's golden jubilee.

Notes

1 In the etymology of the term there are christian ecclesiastical references to, for instance, a curate-in-charge of a parish; bearing spiritual oversight.
2 Though this may be the case, of which we can find instances in sociology. For instance, Howard Becker went back to study photography. Geddes had a keen interest in medieval masque plays and in fact wrote a dramatic pageant himself, which will be discussed later.
3 Splits in early British sociology (Halliday, 1968), specifically between Brandford and Geddes, (whose influences included Comte, William James, Bergson, George Elliott, William Morris and the arts and craft movement) and the contrasting perspectives of L. T. Hobhouse at the LSE were integral to the direction in which they sought to define sociology (Scott and Bromley, 2012).

4 Rouch who was heavily influenced by surrealism, blurred the boundaries of fact and fiction, myth and reason, drama and fantasy as well as imagination and fieldwork in his ethnography, as evidenced in his films, such as the controversial 'Mad Masters' (*Les Maîtres Fous*, 1955). For his part, having already written about film, stardom and popular visual culture in *The Cinema, or The Imaginary Man* (1956) and *The Cinema* and *The Stars* before these fields were considered respectable (English translations, Morin, 1960, 2005), Morin saw both myth and magic as a part of modernity.

5 Morin carried participatory methods into his written work too (*The Red and the White*, 1970). He has also written a six-volume collection on Method. Inter-disciplinary collaboration has been key to how his work has been presented beyond the page. Interestingly his first book *L'an zéro de l'Allemagne* (1946) was the inspiration for Roberto Rossellini's neo-realist movie *Germany Year Zero* (*Germania Anno Zero*). He also collaborated with the visual artist Karel Appel on a study of New York (1984).

6 *A Seventh Man* involved one of many collaborations between Berger and the photographer Jean Mohr. Mohr collaborated with Edward Said on what was initially controversial but then became a world famous touring exhibit of images on *After the Last Sky: Palestinian Lives* (Said and Mohr, 1986).

7 Many of these initiatives involved collaborations with film too, located in what became understood as cultural studies rather than strict sociology (see for example, Minh-ha, *Surname Viet Given Name Nam*, 1989).

8 To view the film online visit: http://www.darkmatter101.org/site/2012/04/03/aaj-kaal-yesterday-today-tomorrow-video/

9 See 'Sociologists Talking' by Elisabeth Simbuerger at the ReInvention Centre, Warwick University, http://www2.warwick.ac.uk/fac/soc/sociology/rsw/undergrad/cetl/filmspublications/sociologiststalking/

10 For example, Latour's team had ample funding, he did not need to worry about numbers of audiences, he did not have to be a 'success', according to some pre-existing criteria, funding or otherwise, and the 1,000-page catalogue (Latour, 2005) could be vast and academic in style.

11 Cluster analysis has itself borrowed from biology (see Byrne and Uprichard, 2012), as has sequence analysis (Abbott, 1995).

12 We are likely to see further collaborations between information technologies, sociologists and artists, such as the EPSRC-funded project, 'Supporting Shy Users in Pervasive Computing', co-led by Susie Scott, which has developed an interactive art exhibition.

13 Today art has arrived at a point where reflexivity of the exchanges between economic and symbolic capital in the art world, which has been a focus of Haacke's work, have become incorporated into conversations in the sector.

14 We have now put into play the call-and-response method in further projects involving collaborations across sectors and specialists. For instance, the film project *Cinema III* (dir. Puwar and Sharma, 2010) funded by the British Academy.

15 For the curation of the site, among other artistic influences were the artistic directions of Alan Kaprow on 'happenings', as well as the acoustic dramaturgy of sound instituted by the composer Luigi Nono. John Cage's 'Lecture on the Weather' fittingly provides space for further reflection on the thunder storm that took the electricity out for some minutes on the night. As well as generating light flashes and shocks of fear in the production team, the film had to re-start from the beginning.

16 These interviews were generated from immediate 'vox-pop' responses by audience members after the film screening and musical performance.

References

Abbott, A., (1995), 'Sequence analysis: new methods for old ideas', *Annual Review of Sociology*, 21: 93–113.

The Sociological Review, 60:S1, pp. 40–63 (2012), DOI: 10.1111/j.1467-954X.2012.02116.x

Andreasen, S. and Larsen, L. B., (2010), 'The middleman: beginning to think about mediation', in P. O'Neill (ed.), *Curating Subjects*, London: Open Editions.

Back, L., Cohen, P. and Keith, M., (1996), *Finding the Way Home*. Working Paper 1, Issues of Theory and Method, Centre for New Ethnicities Research, University of East London.

Back, L., Haddour, A. and Puwar, N. (eds), (2009), 'Special issue: Post-colonial Bourdieu', *The Sociological Review*, 57 (3): 371–546.

Barry, A., Born, G. and Weszkalnya, G., (2008), 'Logics of interdisciplinarity', *Economy and Society*, 37 (1): 20–49.

Bauman, Z., (1998), 'On art, death and postmodernity – and what they do to each other', in M. Hannula (ed.), *Stopping the Process: Contemporary Views on Art and Exhibitions*, Helsinki: NIFCA.

Becker, H., (1984), *Art Worlds*, London: University of California Press.

Becker, H., (2007), *Telling about Society*, London and Chicago: University of Chicago Press.

Bennett, T., (2006), 'Exhibition, difference and the logic of culture', in I. Karp, C. A. Kratz, L. Szwaja and T. Ybarra-Frausto (eds), *Museum Frictions: Public Cultures/Global Transformations*, 46–69, Durham and London: Duke University Press.

Berger, J. and Mohr, J., (2010 [1975]), *A Seventh Man*, London: Verso.

Boardman, P., (1978), *The Worlds of Patrick Geddes*, London: Routledge & Kegan Paul.

Boone, P., (2003), 'When the "Amen Corner" comes to class: an examination of the pedagogical and cultural impact of call-response communication in the black college classroom', *Communication Education Journal*, 52 (3/4): 212–229.

Bourdieu, P., (1993 [1987]), 'The historical genesis of a pure aesthetic', (trans. C. Newman), *The Journal of Aesthetics and Art Criticism*, 46: 201–210.

Bourdieu, P., (2003), 'Interview with Franz Schultheis', in *Algeria: Testimonies of Uprooting*, United Kingdom edn, Camera Austria, Graz.

Bourdieu, P., (2007), *The Bachelors' Ball*, Chicago: University of Chicago Press.

Bourdieu, P. and Haacke, H., (1995), *Free Exchange*, Stanford, CA: Stanford University Press.

Bradley, J., (2003), 'International exhibitions: a distribution system for a new art world order', in M. Townsend (ed.), *Beyond the Box: Diverging Curatorial Practices*, Canada: Banff Centre Press.

Bryan-Wilson, J., (2003), 'A curriculum for institutional critique, or the professionalisation of conceptual art', in J. Ekeberg (ed.), *New Institutionalism*, Verksted No. 1, Oslo: Office for Contemporary Art.

Burawoy, M., (2005), 'For public sociology', *American Sociological Review*, 70 (4): 4–28.

Byrne, D. and Uprichard, E., (2012), *Cluster Analysis* (4 vols: *Logic and Classics*; *Useful Key Texts*; *Cluster Analysis in Practice*; *Data Mining with Classification*), London: Sage.

Clifford, J. and Marcus, G. E. (eds), (1986), *Writing Culture: The Poetics and Politics of Ethnography*, Berkeley, CA: University of California Press.

Cohen, P., (2009), *Questioning Ethnographies: Essays in Cultural Politics*, Basingstoke: Palgrave Macmillan.

de Nooy, W., Mrvar, A. and Batagelj, V. (eds), (2005), *Exploratory Social Network Analysis with Pajek*, Cambridge: Cambridge University Press.

Denzin, N., (1993), *Performance Ethnography: Critical Pedagogy and the Politics of Culture*, London: Sage.

Evans, D., (1986), *Le Play House and the Regional Survey Movement in British Sociology 1920–1955*, unpublished M.Phil thesis, City of Birmingham Polytechnic/CNAA. Available at: http://www.dfte.co.uk/ios (accessed 6 May 2006).

Farquharson, A., (2003), 'I curate, you curate, we curate', *Art Monthly*: 7–10.

Ferguson, M. C., (2011), 'Patrick Geddes and the Celtic Renascence of the 1890s', thesis for Doctorate of Philosophy in History, University of Dundee.

Fortier, A. M., (2007), *Multicultural Horizons: Diversity and the Limits of the Civil Nation*, London: Routledge.

Gielen, P., (2010), *The Murmuring of the Artistic Multitude: Global Art, Memory and Post-Fordism*, Denmark: Valiz.

Greenberg, R., Ferguson, B. W., and Nairne, S., (1996), *Thinking about Exhibitions*, New York: Routledge.

Guggenheim, M., (2011), 'Notes on an acoustic sociology of science', in R. Hannes (ed.), *Videogramme: die Bildwelten biologischer Experimental systeme als Kunst und Theorieobjekt*, Zürich: Scheidegger & Spiess.

Hall, S., (2001), 'Constituting an archive', *Third Text*, 15 (54): 89–92.

Halliday, R. J., (1968), 'The sociological movement, the sociological society and the genesis of academic sociology in Britain', *The Sociological Review*, 16 (3): 377–398.

Halsey, A., (2004), *A History of Sociology in Britain*, Oxford: Oxford University Press.

Hitchcock, P., (1993), *Dialogics of the Oppressed*, London: University of Minnesota Press.

Hubble, N., (2006), *Mass Observation and Everyday Life: Culture, History and Theory*, Basingstoke: Palgrave Macmillan.

Kochman, T., (1990), 'Force fields in black and white communication', in D. Carbaugh (ed.), *Cultural Communication and Intercultural Contact*, 193–217, Hillsdale, NJ: Lawrence Erlbaum.

Latour, B., (2005), 'From realpolitik to dingpolitik or how to make things public', in B. Latour and P. Weibel (eds), *Making Things Public: Atmospheres of Democracy*, Cambridge, MA: MIT Press.

Latour, B., (2007), 'Interview with Bruno Latour: making the "Res Public" by Tomás Sánchez Criado', *Ephemera. Theory and Politics in Organization*, 7 (2): 364–371.

Logan, P., (2011), *Humphrey Jennings and British Documentary Film: A Re-assessment*, Farnham: Ashgate.

Millard, R., (2001), *The Tastemakers: UK Art Now*, London: Thames Hudson.

Miller, J., (1996), 'The show you love to hate: a psychology of the mega-exhibition', in R. Greenberg, B. W. Ferguson and S. Nairne (eds), *Thinking about Exhibitions*, London: Routledge.

Mills, C. Wright, (1959), *The Sociological Imagination*, New York: Oxford University Press.

Minh-Ha, T. T., (1991), *When the Moon Waxes Red: Representation, Gender and Cultural Politics*, London: Routledge.

Morin, E., (1946), L'an zéro de l'Allemagne, Éditions de la Cité universelle, Paris.

Morin, E., (1960), *The Stars*, trans. Richard Howard, New York: Grove Press.

Morin, E., (1970), *The Red and the White*, New York: Pantheon Books.

Morin, E., (2003), 'Chronicle of a film', in Jean Rouch, *Cine-Ethnography*, ed. and trans. S. Feld, London: University of Minnesota Press.

Morin, E., (2005), *The Cinema, or The Imaginary Man: An Essay in Sociological Anthropology*, trans. Lorraine Mortimer, Minneapolis: University of Minnesota Press.

Morin, E. and Appel, K., (1984), *New York: La Ville de Villes*, Paris: Galilaee Editions.

O'Neill, P., (2007), 'The curatorial turn: from practice to discourse', in J. Rugg and M. Sedgwick (eds), *Issues in Curating Contemporary Art and Performance*, Bristol: Intellect Books.

O'Neill, P., (2010), 'The Politics of the Small Act: Interview with Peter O'Neill', *ONCurating.org*, The Political Potential of Curatorial Practise, Issue 04/10: 6–10.

Osborne, T., Rose, N. and Savage, M., (2008), 'Editors' Introduction Reinscribing British Sociology: Some critical reflections', *The Sociological Review*, 56 (1): 519–534.

Pearce, W. B. and Pearce, K., (2004), 'Taking a communication perspective on dialogue', in R. Anderson, L. Baxter and K. Cissna (eds), *Dialogue: Theorizing Difference in Communication Studies*, 39–56, London: Sage.

Peterson, D. E., (1993), 'Response and call: the African American dialogue with Bakhtin', *American Literature*, 65 (4): 761–775.

Phillips, L., (2009), 'Analysing the dialogic turn in the communication of research-based knowledge: an exploration of the tensions in collaborative research', *Public Understanding of Science*, 1: 1–21.

Portelli, A., (1991), 'On methodology', in *The Death of Luigi Trastulli, and Other Stories: Form and Meaning in Oral History*, 27–42, Albany: State University of New York Press.

Portelli, A., (1997), 'There's always goin' be a line: history-telling as a multivocal art', in *The Battle of Valle Giulia: Oral History and the Art of Dialogue*, 24–39, Madison, WI: Wisconsin University Press.

The Sociological Review, 60:S1, pp. 40–63 (2012), DOI: 10.1111/j.1467-954X.2012.02116.x

Portelli, A., (n.d.), 'A dialogical relationship: an approach to oral history'. Available at: http://www. swaraj.org/shikshantar/expressions_portelli.pdf (accessed 1 June 2011).

Puwar, N., (2011), 'Noise of the past: spatial interruptions of war, nation, and memory', *Senses and Society*, 6 (3): 325–345.

Puwar, N., (2012), 'Mediations on the making of Aaj Kaal', *Feminist Review*, 100: 124–141.

Puwar, N. and Sharma, S., (2011), 'Introduction: war cries', *Senses and Society*, 6 (3): 261–266.

Rathzel, N. and Cohen, P., (2008), *Finding the Way Home: Young People's Stories of Gender, Ethnicity, Class, and Places in Hamburg and London* (*Transkulturelle Perspektiven*, 7), Göttingen: V&R Unipress.

Rogers, R., (2009), *The End of the Virtual: Digital Methods*, Amsterdam: Vossiuspers UvA.

Rugoff, R., (1999), 'Rules of the game', *Frieze* magazine, 44, January/February.

Said, E. and Mohr, J., (1986), *After the Last Sky: Palestinian Lives*, London: Faber & Faber.

Savage, M., (2010), *Identities and Social Change in Britain since 1940: The Politics of Method*, Oxford: Oxford University Press.

Scott, J., (2000), *Social Network Analysis: A Handbook*, 2nd edn, Newberry Park, CA: Sage.

Scott, J. and Husbands, C. T., (2007), 'Victor Branford and the building of British sociology', *Sociological Review*, 55 (3): 460–485.

Scott, J. and Bromley, R., (2012), *Visions of Reconstruction*, Albany, NY: SUNY Press.

Sennett, R., (2009), *The Craftsman*, London: Penguin Books.

Shanas, E., (1945), 'The *American Journal of Sociology* through fifty years', *American Journal of Sociology*, 50 (6): 522–533.

Sharma, S., (2011), 'Unravelling difference: towards a sensory multiculture', *Senses and Society*, 6 (3): 284–305.

Silkstone, F., (2011), 'Composing post-colonial war requiem: issues and processes', *Senses and Society*, 6 (3): 267–283.

Stanley, L., (2001), 'Mass observations fieldwork methods', in P. Atkinson, A. Coffey, S. Delamont, J. Lofland and L. Lofland (eds), *Handbook of Ethnography*, London: Sage.

Strathern, M., (2004), *Commons and Borderlands*, Wantage: Sean Kingston.

Tanner, J., (2003), *Sociology of Art: A Reader*, Oxford and New York: Routledge.

Tannert, C. and Tischler, U. (eds), (2004), *MIB – Men in Black: Handbook of Curatorial Practice*, Berlin: Revolver Books.

Ungar, S., (2003), 'In the thick of things: Rouch and Morin's *Chronique d'un été Reconsidered*', *French Cultural Studies*, 14: 5–22.

Velthuis, O., (2007), *Talking Prices: Symbolic Meanings of Prices on the Market for Contemporary Art*, Princeton, NJ: Princeton University Press.

Vishmidt, M., (2006), 'Twilight of the widgets', in J. Krysa (ed.), *Databrowser 0.3: Curating Immateriality*, London and New York: Autonomedia.

Wells, L., (2007), 'Curatorial strategy as critical intervention: the genesis of facing cast', in J. Rugg and M. Sedgwick (eds), *Issues in Curating Contemporary Art and Performance*. Bristol: Intellect Books.

Music Performance

Silksone, F., (2008), *Post-Colonial War Requiem*, Coventry Cathedral.

Seeing it whole: staging totality in social theory and art

Alberto Toscano

Abstract: Can, or should, social theory try to 'see it whole'? This article explores some of the aesthetic, political and conceptual issues that arise when we pose the problem of representing social totality today. It revisits two influential assertions of theory's calling to generate orienting and totalizing representations of capitalist society: C. Wright Mills' plea for the 'sociological imagination' and Fredric Jameson's appeal for an 'aesthetic of cognitive mapping'. Mills and Jameson converge on the need to mediate personal experience with systemic constraints, knowledge with action, while underscoring the political urgency and epistemic difficulty of such a demand. The article contrasts these perspectives with the repudiation of a sociology of totality in the actor-network theory of Bruno Latour. It explores this contrast through the 'panorama' as a visual practice and a metaphor for theory itself. Against Latour's proposal to reduce and relativize totality, it argues that sociology can learn from contemporary artistic efforts to map social and economic power as a whole. 'Pano-ramic' projects in the arts, such as Allan Sekula's and Mark Lombardi's, can allow us to reflect on sociology's own deficit of imagination, and on the persistence of the desire to 'see it whole' – especially when that whole is opaque, fragmented, contradic-tory. A live sociology can only gain from greater attention to the critical experiments with forms and methods of representation that are being carried out by artists preoc-cupied with the staging of social totality.

Keywords: capitalism, cartography, Fredric Jameson, Bruno Latour, Mark Lom-bardi, C. Wright Mills, panorama, Allan Sekula, totality

> The movements of the stars have become clearer; but to the mass of the people the movements of their masters are still incalculable.
>
> Bertolt Brecht, *The Life of Galileo*

Across the contemporary arts and social theory – in domains of production and practice difficult to pigeonhole and categorize – the past years have witnessed, alongside a resurgent concern with politics (Day *et al.*, 2010), a veritable efflo-rescence in efforts to provide models, diagrams or narratives that might allow us to orient ourselves around the world-system. In a manner that both mirrors and inflects a broader cultural and visual predicament, critical representations

The Sociological Review, 60:S1, pp. 64–83 (2012), DOI: 10.1111/j.1467-954X.2012.02117.x

of society increasingly appear as mediated by cartography, be it literally or metaphorically.[1] The most interesting artists and groups producing work in this register demonstrate a capacity to address the question of cartography in a practically reflexive and formally challenging manner, thwarting fantasies of locational transparency while strategically deploying the visual repertoire of mapping – acutely aware that overview is often another name for oversight.[2] To the extent that social theory counts various modes of mapping and diagramming within its methodological repertoire, and frequently uses these notions as broader watchwords for the tasks of the discipline as a whole, there is much to be gained from bringing the social research of contemporary artists into dialogue and contrast with what we could call the 'aesthetics of social theory', or the regimes of visibility and sensibility that pervade different ways of doing sociology.

For all of the limitations, easily classified under the headings of ocularcentrism or reification, of contemporary invocations of 'mapping' – a practice that has been intimately entangled with the epistemic and political histories of colonialism (Wood, 2010; Harley, 2001) and capitalist domination (Farinelli, 2009) – their frequency indicates a widespread demand for critical or oppositional forms of orientation around contemporary capitalist society. Today this need and these forms proliferate mostly *outside* the academic social sciences. There is undoubtedly something problematic in claims that the TV series *The Wire* provides the best ethnography of contemporary US society (cited in Penfold-Mounce *et al.*, 2011: 157; Kinkle and Toscano, 2009), or that films like *The Flaw* or *Debtocracy* foster a critical intelligence about the financial crisis that university-based research either cannot or is not interested in attaining (Chakrabortty, 2011; Kinkle and Toscano, 2011). But it is difficult to gainsay that an urgent public need to 'see it whole' is rarely met by the contemporary social sciences, whose 'impact' is most often channelled into governmental or corporate channels which have little interest in the disquieting, antagonistic or counter-intuitive consequences of trying to think totality. After all, among the first products of a genuine striving for orientation is disorientation, as proximal coordinates come to be troubled by wider, and at times overwhelming vistas.

There are numerous plausible narratives for this predicament, and a glance at the history of social-scientific disciplines will reveal that lamentations about irrelevance, specialization, instrumentalism, and so on, have a long pedigree (which is of course no reason to dismiss them). What attention to the figurations of the social in current aesthetic research alerts us to, however, is an important inflection of the immemorial conundrum about the interrelation of knowledge and action – which has taken names as varied as 'scientific socialism', 'critical theory' and 'public sociology'. To the limits of second-hand theorizing[3] or of the isolated case-study, the 'cartographic' turn in the arts responds with a genuine and at times militant curiosity for the mutations being wrought by global capitalism and the oppositional counter-moves that sometimes meet it 'on the ground'. To the stereotyped formatting of research by private and governmental bodies it responds with experiments in different institutional bases for investigation and production.[4] Most significantly for my purposes here, it runs against the grain of those new, and increasingly fashionable iterations of the refusal of totalization which has accompanied social theory throughout its development.[5]

The moment of 'theory', like that of postmodernism, with which it was so closely entangled, may have passed, but if this is so it is more by way of a diffusion and complication of the energies that brought it to the fore, than by a new consolidation of the disciplines, or a return of philosophy (though the latter has had some effect on recent discussions of art and politics). If, following Jameson (2009), we can regard theory as a desire for a system without the ideological fantasy of autonomy and completion – that is, for the establishment of a sovereign and encyclopaedic philosophy as world-view – then this is a desire which may wax and wane but not vanish. Yet this desire for systematicity, for totalization, is in turn deeply ambiguous. For, or at least so the Jamesonian proposal goes, we are always already totalized, albeit in ways which largely lie beyond our control and outside our knowledge. So that theory, in its meta-political or para-political impetus, is in some respects an effort at counter-totalization, at totalizing the totalizer (society, state, capital) – not necessarily to impel change, but at least to locate the functioning levers and sensitive nerve-centres. And, as the proposal of live methods for a live sociology suggests (Back, 2012), discerning and describing such pressure points within social relations is rendered particularly challenging when the technologies of representation have themselves become – in uneven, contested and frequently manipulative ways – massively 'socialized'; what's more, when a desire for cartographic representations, both immediately practical and more metaphorical, is pervasively embodied in social media and digital devices.

To the extent that we can consider a resurgence of the political in art and theory along the axes of principled affirmation and cognitive inquiry, decision and totalization, will and knowledge, it is helpful to return to some of those intellectual moments – moments of relative ebb, stasis and anxiety – at which the problem of orientation, and the tension between knowledge and action were most acutely posed. The more proximate theoretical template for our cartographic conjuncture, Jameson's 'cognitive mapping', was itself first formulated in the mid-1980s, in the midst of Reaganite neo-liberalism and at a low-point of Left energies in the North (and not only) (Jameson, 1988). It is a thesis that resonates strongly with another programmatic text written amid political doldrums, C. Wright Mills' *The Sociological Imagination*, published in 1959, as an attempt to define something like a politics of inquiry and research that could dislocate technocratic one-dimensionality. It is not by chance, I think, that broadly aesthetic and projective terms – mapping, imagination – drive investigations aimed at thinking politically in anti-political times, nor that such texts continue to speak to present efforts to link political intervention and the comprehension of power's fulcrums, structures and devices.

Mills' bitter salvo has dated far less than many of the prophetic declarations of his contemporaries ('the end of ideology', for one): 'Ours is a time of uneasiness and indifference – not yet formulated in such ways as to permit the work of reason and the play of sensibility. Instead of troubles – defined in terms of values and threats – there is often the misery of vague uneasiness; instead of explicit issues there is often merely the beat feeling that all is somehow not right' (1959: 11). Among the unrelenting themes of *The Sociological Imagination*, drawing together its ethos of intellectual craftsmanship and its political ideal of 'collective self-control over the structural mechanics of history' (1959: 116), is an image of the social sciences as concerned with biography, history and the intersections of these in the social structure. In a metaphor that links craft to clear-sightedness Mills reminded his readers of the need, at once political and theoretical, 'to grind a lens through which we can perhaps see a little more clearly the world in which we live' (1959: 151). At first glance, this might seem anodyne enough: linking individual trajectories to systemic trends via their collective and institutional mediations – to employ a bit of what Mills derided as 'socspeak' – is general enough to describe, rather than motivate, much social research. But, as the no-holds-barred attacks on Parsonian 'grand theory' and the 'abstracted empiricism' of research bureaus suggest, Mills thought that this 'classical' imperative of social thought was imperilled, with grave political consequences. Against this, he called for a 'fresh perception' that 'involves the capacity to unmask and to smash the stereotypes of vision and intellect with which modern communications swamp us' (1959: 69), and for a form of intellectual work that could combine playfulness with 'a truly fierce drive to make sense of the world' (1959: 211) – a vision which links a ludic aesthetics, running from Schiller to Marcuse, with a public and political vocation to know and explain. 'Serious play' could indeed be an evocative formulation for the updating of the sociological imagination proposed under the banner of live sociology (Back, 2012).

Exemplifying the very capacity to shift between levels of abstraction that he identifies with the 'imaginative and systematic thinker' (1959: 34), he pointed to the neglected ties between disciplinary questions corralled off as 'methodological' or 'theoretical', on the one hand, and the deep anxieties of his age, on the other. Not only was 'the sociological imagination' something that exceeded the boundaries of sociology, it could also (like Gramsci's recasting of philosophy) be regarded as the object of an often muted but collective capacity or desire. Mills' estimation of the enormous administrative and ideological obstacles to the continuation of what he called 'classical' social analysis was accompanied by a sense that the 'qualities of mind' that constitute the tradition 'are becoming a common denominator of our general cultural life' (1959: 21) – an observation that could certainly be transferred to the proliferation of attempts to 'see it whole' outside of an academy which is, for different reasons, generally unaffected by (or scornful of) the desire for totalization.

In fact, this disparity, between public need and academic practice, was what led Mills to sound harsh notes of reprobation against 'the social scientists of the rich societies', whose unwillingness to confront social problems was 'surely the greatest human default being committed by privileged men in our times'

(1959: 176). Instead, the vocation of the imaginative social thinker, with the privilege to bring craftsmanship to bear on this 'common denominator', was to be able to span the hiatus between individual anxieties and collective transformations, in so doing acquitting a task that was simultaneously intellectual and political – one which the shift from intellectual insurgency to administrative practicality threatened, and threatens, to render impossible. As Mills writes:

> The 'basic problem' . . . and its answer, usually require attention both to the uneasiness arising from the 'depth' of biography, and to indifference arising from the very structure of an historical society. By our choice and statement of problems, we must first translate indifference into issues, uneasiness into trouble, and second, we must admit both troubles and issues in the statement of our problem. In both stages, we must try to state in as simple and precise a manner as we can, the several values and threats involved, and try to relate them. Any adequate 'answer' to a problem, in turn, will contain a view of the strategic points of intervention – of the 'levers' by which the structure may be maintained or changed; and an assessment of those who are in a position to intervene but are not doing so. (1959: 131)

Of particular note in this statement, redolent of what some have termed Mills' 'disillusioned radicalism' (Geary, 2009: 191), is the idea that the civic task of the sociological imagination is not to create a pacifying knowledge, but to sharpen and concretize what would otherwise be a vague and powerless anxiety, while at the same time providing a realistic estimate of the powers necessary to alter, however minimally, the course of history. As we read in a fine biography of Mills, *Radical Ambition*: 'Rather than situating the individual in a particular institutional setting, Mills traced the influences of larger and more impersonal forces on the individual' (Geary, 2009: 209). Foremost among the intellectual imperatives advocated by *The Sociological Imagination* is that of 'seeing it whole', of endeavouring to grasp one's epoch in its totality, while not treating this effort at totalization as an excuse to justify any kind of determinism, or apologia for social and historical fate. Likewise, Mills inherited from what he called 'plain Marxism' the idea, as he put it in *The Sociological Imagination*, that we 'live in a historically unique epoch; capitalism is an epochal, cultural formation affecting all human activity', though recognition of this should not entail neglect of what he termed 'the human variety' (1959: 55).

What are we to make of such theoretical demands today, in a moment when the Cold War conformism that Mills was struggling against seems distant? It is worth recalling that Mills perceived his own epoch as a threshold and was in fact one of the first to make theoretical use of the idea of the 'post-modern' to qualify what he called 'The Fourth Epoch', a period 'in which for the first time the varieties of social worlds it contains are in serious, rapid, and obvious interplay' (1959: 150). Mills' idea of the sociological imagination can be read into the later debate around postmodernism, and specifically in Fredric Jameson's suggestion that one of the needs arising with the socio-economic shifts of the 1970s was a kind of 'cognitive mapping' – a term he borrowed from Kevin Lynch's classic primer in urban design, *The Image of the City*, incidentally published the same year as *The Sociological Imagination*. In the context of a notorious discussion of the Los Angeles Bonaventure Hotel as a material allegory of the postmodern, Jameson spoke of 'the incapacity of our minds, at least at present, to map the great global multinational and decentred communicational network in which we find ourselves caught as individual subjects' (Jameson, 1998: 16) – in other words, of the impossibility of creating that very articulation of biography, history and social structure demanded by Mills, and which for Jameson was at the heart, among others, of Jean Paul Sartre's 'biographies' of Flaubert and Genet, as well as his *Critique of Dialectical Reason*, which rendered this idea with the concept of totalization (Jameson, 2009). Ultimately, an inability to cognitively map the contours of the world system is as debilitating politically as being unable to mentally map a city would be for a city dweller.

Whereas Mills, though recognizing its latency as the 'common denominator' of the age, linked the sociological imagination to the public practice of social science, for Jameson, cognitive mapping, though not limited to art, is an 'aesthetic' question – a question of the figurability or representability of the present. Such mapping is a precondition for seeking out any political 'levers', and goes hand in hand with any sketch of an archaeology of the future that might elucidate the ontology of the present. Mills' requirement that social thought manifest 'the capacity to range from the most impersonal and remote transformations to the most intimate features of the human self – and to see the relations between the two' (1959: 7), persists for Jameson, though it could be argued that he is at times even glummer than Mills about the viability of shifting convincingly between these levels – not least because he is less persuaded of the contemporary stability of the self, as his foregrounding of schizophrenia in *Postmodernism* suggests. But 'seeing it whole' remains crucial for Jameson, who, in an explicitly Hegelian formulation, calls the objective of cognitive mapping, a 'cartography of the absolute' (Jameson, 1992: 3). The works that would emerge under the banner of this aesthetic would allow individual subjects and collectivities to understand their local situation in a globalized world: 'to enable a situational representation on part of the individual subject to that vaster and properly unrepresentable totality which is the ensemble of society's structures as a whole' (1991: 51). This recalls very closely a line from Mills' *White Collar*, where he writes 'that the individual cannot understand his own experience or gauge his own fate without locating himself within the trends of his epoch and the life-chances of all the individuals of his social layer' (2002: xx). It is for this very reason that theory can appear as both an individual and a social need, at least if we understand theory in the sense proposed by Mills in a letter to a friend in 1941: 'All new things are "up in the air". If you stay too close to the "earth", you can never fly over new regions. Theory is an airplane, not a pair of heavy boots; it is of the division of reconnaissance and spying' (cited in Geary, 2009: 37).

Reconnaissance, spying, cartography, 'situational representation' – Mills and Jameson can be seen to share in an aesthetics which, in its para-military and urbanist references, speaks to us of the entanglement between a totalizing vision (its absence, or present impossibility) and a strategic imperative: finding and eventually controlling the 'levers'; diminishing powerlessness. That one of the most resonant present challenges to the regulative and ethico-political ideal of totality in social theory should come with its own 'aesthetics', its own arsenal of metaphors, should be of no surprise. Bruno Latour, whose recent aesthetic and curatorial ventures (Latour, 2002b; Latour and Weibel, 2005) would warrant separate treatment, has recently proposed that we put the totalizing theories generated by 'sociologies of the social' in their circumscribed and specific place, as fragile and monadic *panoramas*. I want to explore Latour's mobilization of this term, how it encapsulates his dismissal of critical sociology, and the manner in which its presence in the practices and writings of some recent artists engaged in social and political research might return us instead to the troubles and anxieties pinpointed by Mills and Jameson, showing in the end that, *pace* Latour, the theoretical desire for totality is not incompatible with a painstaking attention to traces, objects and devices.

The fact that Actor-Network Theory should lend itself to metaphors drawn from cartography ('mapping' controversies, sketching a 'topography of the social'), as well as logistics, forensics, accounting, and so on, is no surprise, and exquisitely self-aware. It is also part of a broader trend (Bosteels, 1996). Latour's choice of metaphor for its supposedly hegemonic rival, the sociology of the social, or the social theory of totality, is more intriguing and indicative. The cover of his *Reassembling the Social* (2002a) sports a lithograph depicting the construction of a rather late panorama, a 'Taking of Antananarivo' from the *Exposition de Madagascar* in the 1900 Paris Universal Exhibition. Visually, we are presented with an impeccably 'critical' move. Despite the currency of the term, panorama is a modern neologism, dating from the early 1790s, to describe massive 360 degree oil paintings, exhibited in cylindrical buildings and viewed from platforms that hid the devices of light and architecture which made the immersion into the image possible (Sternberger, 1977; Hyde, 1988; Miller, 1996; Oetterman, 1997; Comment, 2002; Verhoeff, 2007). More broadly, it covers a whole set of perceptual constructions, from Daguerre's diorama to the Kaiser-panorama, from the diaphanorama to the stereorama, which constitute 'nineteenth-century examples of the image as an autonomous luminous screen of attraction, whose apparitional appeal is an effect of both its uncertain spatial location and its detachment from a broader visual field' (Crary, 2002: 19; also Benjamin, 2002 and 2006). Thus, where Latour's lithograph shows all of the 'work-net' (2002a: 143) that goes into the production of the panorama-effect – the painters, the scaffolding, the workers, the heaters, the coat-racks, and so on – the projected viewer of the panorama would have wandered, with the help of studiously designed features, in a 'continuous boundaryless field' (Crary, 2002: 20).

The panorama also makes an appearance in Latour's nuanced and intriguing collaboration with the photographer Emile Hermant in *Paris: Invisible City* (1998), a book and Internet project which fleshes out the aesthetics of actor-network theory in a constant and compelling conflict with the problem of illustrating theory. Weaving together representations, textual and visual, of sites and modes of representation, to follow the pathways of the representation of the social – even as it does so to suspend the totalizing confidence with which we supposedly approach such concepts in our disciplinary common sense – *Paris: Invisible City* can be fruitfully compared to some recent photographic attempts at social mapping, though one wonders to what extent the methodological repudiation of totality imposes a skewed frame onto Hermant's photowork. Tellingly, and programmatically – though as ever with a heavy dose of Latourian irony – the book begins with a partially obsolescent 'panorama' of *Tout-Paris* in the *grand magasin la Samaritaine*, a 360 degree porcelain relief on the perimeter of the building's roof, which no longer quite matches up with the capital's skyline (Latour and Hermant, 1998, 2006).

By exploring and photographing some of the sites and conduits for the production and circulation of the representations of 'Paris' (deposits for street signs, meteorological stations, metro command and control centres), Latour and Hermant present us with partial totalizations, channelling the conviction that the city is 'moulded by an accumulation of series of views, one after the other, juxtaposed but never summed up' (1998: 125; 2006: 88), both accounting for and undermining the spherical projections and scalar hierarchies that supposedly structure our (aesthetic) common sense about the social and the city. In identifying totalization with circumscribed and 'blind' sites (dioramas, panoramas), Latour enlists the photographic investigation in a political polemic, or rather a polemic against the politicization of 'sociologies of the social', which does not refrain from using an explicitly political rhetoric. *Paris: Invisible City* doubles as a photographic education of those 'Romantics', who

> always dream of an assembly that, with neither schedules nor lists, signs nor intermediaries, transparently reveals Society in its immediate solar presence. By dreaming of a full, entire reality, common sense simply dreams of a diorama enclosed in a narrow room. For four thousand years we haven't had the good fortune of living in a Swiss canton, gathered in the town square to decide on current affairs, hands raised. It's been a long time that Society hasn't seen itself entirely in a single glance. (1998:19–20; 2006: 7–8)[6]

But these same 'Romantics', friends of political transparency and social totalization (Latour's critical arsenal here replicates the traditional one of anti-utopian and anti-socialist discourse), are also ones who allegedly 'scorn the poor actors overwhelmed by the environment', who, we are confidently told, *pace* Mills and his 'trouble', 'are never particularly overwhelmed, let's rather say they know they are numerous, populous, mixed, and that they ceaselessly sum up in a single word whatever it is that binds them in action' (1998: 134; 2006: 91).

As a metaphorical device, that is a real, if mostly obsolescent device enlisted as a metaphor, Latour's panorama fills a precise function: it permits him to 'regionalize' (or perhaps more literally, belittle) the pretensions of social theory to 'see it whole', in the name of the right of actors to frame their own worlds and the duty of researchers to pay all the 'transaction costs' involved in moving from one frame to another, one actor to the next. Latour is perfectly cognizant of the Millsian desire to see it whole, as evidenced by his enumeration of the kind of questions that would lead to the conjunction of the sociological imagination and a desire for politics: 'There is something invisible that weighs on all of us that is more solid than steel and yet so incredible labile' (2002a: 21); 'Why are we all held by forces that are not of our own making?' (2002a: 43). But, in a strange re-edition of a Weberian injunction, he wants to cut the very knot pointed to by Mills and Jameson, the one that ties together (individual and collective) disorientation, theoretical elaboration and political action. One of his (curiously disembodied) examples is worth citing here:

> A worker, who labors all day on the floor of a sweatshop, discovers quite quickly that his fate has been settled by invisible agents who are hidden behind the office walls at the other end of the shop. . . . So, it is perfectly true to say that any given interaction seems to overflow, with elements which are already in the situation coming from some other time, some other place, and generated by some other agency. . . . Although there is indeed, in every interaction, a dotted line that leads to some virtual, total, and always pre-existing entity, this is just the track that should not be followed, at least for now: virtual and shadowy it is, virtual and shadowy it should remain. Where political action has to proceed forward, sociologists should fear to tread. Yes, interactions are made to exist by other actors, but, no, those sites do not form a context around them. (2002a: 166)

It is particularly significant here that, despite the supposed primacy of the actor, and the ways in which Latour appropriates for his own ends the long line of critiques of the silencing of marginal and minoritarian (and proletarian) actors, he is suggesting that the workers' drive to see it whole be thwarted – apparently under the pretext that, *contra* Mills, this 'theoretical' drive is not that of the actors, and, moreover, that sociology and politics should be compartmentalized, not allowed to slip into hybridity. When Latour writes that 'It is little use to respect the actors' achievement if in the end we deny them one of their most important privileges, namely that they are the ones defining relative scale' (2002a: 184),[7] we could easily retort, and the examples are legion, that most (human, exploited) actors have rather some difficulties in defining the relative scales within which they work and live. Instead of simply ignoring the often debilitating constraints under which agents produce representations of their action, the kind of co-research advocated under the rubric of live sociology (Back, 2012) could open up critical avenues for inquiring into representational struggles, at the level of everyday life and collective action, to define the scale and scope of actors' agency.

While merely referring concrete experiences of dispossession to capitalism or the state or power and leaving it at that is no doubt sterile, I would argue, contrary to Latour, that the struggle to investigate, represent and undo the pressure of 'virtual and shadowy' agencies is precisely the point at which the 'spontaneous sociology' of actors and the everyday life of sociologists meet on a common terrain (after all, most sociologists also sell their labour, or at least try). Precisely

The Sociological Review, 60:S1, pp. 64–83 (2012), DOI: 10.1111/j.1467-954X.2012.02117.x
© 2012 The Author. Editorial organisation © 2012 The Editorial Board of the Sociological Review

to the extent that both the methods of social research and the demand for social explanation far exceed their compartmentalization within sociology as an academic discipline (Back, 2012), any attempt to enforce the demarcation between political action and sociology would require an artificial segregation of the will to knowledge and the desire for justice which, in claiming to respect actors' achievements, pays all too little heed to their difficulties and frustrations.

Considering the centrality of capitalism to the development of the 'sociology of the social', it is little mystery that this should be one of Latour's bugbears. As he notes: 'From the floor of the sweatshop is there any canal that goes to a "capitalist mode of production" or to an "empire"? . . . Capitalism is certainly the dominant mode of production but no one imagines that there is some *homunculus* CEO in command, despite the fact that many events look like they obey some implacable strategy' (2002a: 167). Precisely, no one – and certainly not theorists like Mills or Jameson – imagines that capitalism as a totality possesses an easily grasped command-and-control-centre.[8] That is precisely why it poses an *aesthetic* problem, in the sense of demanding ways of representing the complex and dynamic relations intervening between the domains of production, consumption and distribution, of making the invisible visible.

The empiricist demand that unless one is able to draw a *continuous* thread from the sweatshop to Capitalism, one should stop speaking about the latter altogether, is obscurantist on a number of levels. To begin with, for legal and economic reasons that ANT practitioners could surely illuminate, many of those 'canals' are deeply opaque, and the forms and informations that circulate through them are very asymmetrically controlled by different actors and their groupings (some prehistoric thinkers used to call them classes). But not only is the imperative to follow traces forgetful of who is allowed to follow and who isn't, it also privileges certain types of accounts of how the social circulates. Thus, if an overarching conception of capitalism – not as a homunculus or a monolith, but as a totality full of contradictions, unevennesses and tendencies – is perceived as panoptical, conspiratorial and unaccountable, the privileging of 'centers of calculation' or 'oligopticons'[9] will provide accounts whose descriptive power does not seem up to the task of responding, sociologically, to those questions which Latour feigned to respect, such as 'Why are we all held by forces that are not of our own making?' In *Reassembling the Social*, Latour writes that

> capitalism has no plausible enemy since it is 'everywhere', but a given *trading room* in Wall Street has many competitors in Shanghai, Frankfurt, and London . . . that may shift the balance from an obscene profit to a dramatic loss. Yes, Wall Street is connected to many places and in this sense, but in this sense only, it is 'bigger', more powerful, overarching. However, it is not wider, larger, less local, less interactive, less an inter-subjective place than the shopping center in Moulins, France or the noisy and smelly market stands in Bouaké, Ivory Coast. Don't focus on capitalism, but don't stay stuck on the screen of the trading room either: follow the connections, 'follow the actors themselves' (2002a: 179).

Though it is possible to gain immensely useful insights into the metric and mathematical machinations of contemporary finance armed with such injunctions (see MacKenzie, 2009), they should, to my mind, be disjoined from the high-handed and sterile dismissal of social-theoretic accounts of capitalism. If we don't 'focus' on capitalism 'itself', phenomena like the crisis that surfaced in 2008 will be artificially banished from the purview of our inquiry. That a theory of crisis, for instance, could be dismissed due to its inevitable incapacity to trace *all* the 'canals', seems to move beyond an important methodological polemic to a lobotomy of the relation between social research and political action, as well as to a *de facto* muzzling of those 'actors', rising in number, who seek such explanations. And, though they constitute an important part of the story, treatments of the performative effects of economic theories on crisis, or descriptions of the precise connections between centres of calculation,[10] do not obviate the need to provide totalizing *explanatory* accounts that do not cleave to ANT's simultaneously ascetic and plethoric demands.

It is beyond doubt that it often costs little to make generic gestures towards capitalism, or other totalizing horizons; to treat individual agents and objects as mere husks for some Spirit or other. The methodological requirement that one locate and localize the sites for the production of globality, or of scale, is surely both an important investigative injunction and an antidote to a metaphysical treatment of totalities. The 'question of staging the totality' (Latour, 2002a: 188), as Mills and Jameson stressed, is a crucial question of the imagination, of aesthetics, of method and of politics. But Latour's way of localizing the global, in the name of a methodological ethics of flattening (2002a: 165–172), proves to misunderstand both staging and totality. Speaking of modernist masters of the panorama like Hegel and Marx, Latour writes:

> They design a picture which has no gap in it, giving the spectator the powerful impression of being fully immersed in the real world without any artificial mediations or costly flows of information leading from or to the outside. Whereas oligoptica are constantly revealing the fragility of their connections and their lack of control on what is left in between their networks, panoramas give the impression of complete control over what is being surveyed, even though they are partially blind and nothing enters or leaves their walls except interested or baffled spectators. . . . Most of the time, it's this excess of coherence that gives the illusion away. (2002a: 188)

But the modern panorama (there is no other kind) is precisely not the static, mastered totality that Latour wants to stage. As the cases of Mills and Jameson suggest, it is only those who believe that theories of the totality conform to a Stalinist caricature of 'dialectical materialism' that would tax them with an 'excess of coherence'. A social theory of capitalism as a totality, and the imaginations and aesthetics that strive toward it, could only be marked by an 'excess of coherence' to the extent that it papered over the incoherence (or contradictoriness, difference, unevenness) in its object, and refused to acknowledge its own theoretical activity – with all of its highly artificial stylistic, political and methodological devices. If anything, great dialectical writing would constitute precisely the kind of panorama that could, like the lithograph on the cover of Latour's book, present both the totality and its constituent devices.[11]

It was indeed one of the more heterodox of the 20th-century's dialectical thinkers who noted that, somewhat in the way of a Leibnizian monad, the panorama's truth could be drawn precisely from its closure. In trying to understand the physical and fantasy spaces of an emergent 19th-century commodity culture, Walter Benjamin pointed to the panorama as a space in which the blindness of the interior was a precondition of perspective, but also where fiction was a condition of truth: 'The interest of the panorama is in seeing the true city – the city indoors. What stands within the windowless house is the true. Moreover, the arcade, too, is a windowless house. . . . What is true has no windows; nowhere does the true look out to the universe' (Benjamin, 2002: 532). In *The Arcades Project*, he quotes Baudelaire, 'These things, because they are false, are infinitely closer to the truth' (2002: 536). In a sense, it is for Benjamin in plunging into the closed, 'false' perceptual worlds generated by capitalism that we can draw sustenance for thinking against it.

But we could also note, following Jonathan Crary, that the panoramas of the 19th century did not in the end elicit a totalizing perception that would provide the kind of seamless illusion of mastery, of vision wedded to knowledge, that Latour repudiates. Though the panorama on one level 'provided an imaginary unity and coherence to an external world that, in the context of urbanization, was increasingly incoherent', it 'was in another sense a derealization and devaluation of the individual's viewpoint'. In fact, 'the panorama image is consumable only as fragments, as parts that must be cognitively reassembled into an imagined whole. A structure that seems magically to overcome the fragmentation of experience in fact introduces partiality and incompleteness as constitutive elements of visual experience' (Crary, 2002: 21).[12]

It is precisely in the relationship between the will to a totalizing vision, cognitive and perceptual fragmentation, and the opacities and blind-spots generated by political and economic transformations, that the most interesting invocations or practices of the panorama in the contemporary arts reside. In particular, I am thinking of various attempts to 'see it whole' which have confronted the complexity of that 'it' – be it contemporary capitalism and/or the political machinations of an imperial security state – by turning to various forms of social and political research. Two of these artists, Mark Lombardi and Allan Sekula, are of particular note for their turn to the very concept of 'panorama' as a resource to grasp the aesthetic and cognitive challenges of tracing or representing totalizing processes.

Lombardi is best known for a series of captivating, large-scale drawings of networks of finance, collusion and covert activity, which he tellingly named 'narrative structures'. After his death by suicide in 2000, one of them, a diagram of the relations between the Bush family and Harken energy, notoriously drew the attentions of the FBI in the wake of the attacks on 11 September 2001, tracing as it did an elaborate, if minimalist and under-determined pattern of relations that linked, among others, G.W. Bush and Bin Laden. On one level, Lombardi's art would seem to verify Latour's oft-stated suspicions about critical theory and critical art descending into forms of conspiratorial thought, in which the network is not a careful method for the tracing of associations, but a paranoid representation of a total and unverifiable Power. Indeed, Lombardi has been criticized by other practitioners of art as political research (or political research as art) for producing beautiful images whose cognitive consistency is as tenuous as the pencil-drawn lines between the named 'nodes' of collusion (Paglen, in Bhagat and Mogel, 2007). But if we attend to the genesis of these images, perspicuously interpreted by Hobbs (2003),[13] this impression is complicated considerably.

Among Lombardi's papers are in fact two unpublished manuscripts, one on the 'parapolitical' links between the US government and the drug trade, *On Higher Grounds*; the other a history of the panorama as art form. Lombardi, who had developed artistically within the domains of minimalism and conceptual art, had in fact begun to produce his drawings – which interestingly shifted from a timeline approach to spherical figurations – as aids in his own research into neglected and covert dimensions of US state power. The diagrams eventually attained an autonomy, to become, one could argue, the contemporary equivalent of the kind of enclosed and encompassing history paintings that graced many of the panoramas studied in his other manuscript. In doing so, they arguably replicated the same fruitful tension between totalization and fragmentation, clarity and opacity, overview and oversight, which, following Crary, we can note in actual panoramas. Rather than fantasies of an all-knowing eye, or indeed conspiracy *theories*, they become records of research at the same time as aesthetic goads to inquiry. Though that inquiry – to the extent that this is possible in covert or proprietary domains, which is not in the least obvious – may indeed gain much in carefulness and inventiveness from the negative protocols set out by Latour, it also points to a drive for 'cognitive mapping' which is increasingly present in a world where coercion and secrecy, on the one side, and the seemingly unrepresentable super-power of 'the economy', on the other, pose significant problems for social research, political action and aesthetic representation.

That the term panorama, as colloquially used, derives from those obsolescent but formative devices of modernity that so fascinated Benjamin, is indicative of the force that artificial constructions of perception have both on our everyday life and on our experience (or lack thereof) of our place in a broader order or dynamic. But modernity, as the photographer and critic Allan Sekula has detailed in *Fish Story* (1995) – his critical montage of photographs, long essays, and observations on the mutations of maritime capitalism – is also a passage from panorama to detail, from a mercantile ideology of the sea as an object of strategic overview to an increasingly Taylorized and militarized 'forgotten space', in which the difficulty in producing an aesthetic 'realism' concerning capitalism's more abstract dimensions is redoubled by the rendering invisible, and powerless, of living maritime labour. While Sekula's photographs resist, with their attention to the slowness and materiality of labour at sea, the immaterialization of global capitalism into a smooth space of flows, his essays track the passage from the panorama to the detail.

The LNG carrier Hyundai Utopia, designed to transport liquified natural gas from Indonesia to South Korea, nearing completion. Hyundai Heavy Industries shipyard, Ulsan. These images are taken from Allan Sekula, Fish Story (Sekula, 1995). The author would like to express his gratitude to Allan Sekula for permission to reproduce them here.

Model of ironclad "turtle ship" used by Admiral Yi Sun-Sin to defeat invading Japanese fleet in 1592. Hyundai shipyard headquarters.

The Sociological Review, 60:S1, pp. 64–83 (2012), DOI: 10.1111/j.1467-954X.2012.02117.x
© 2012 The Author. Editorial organisation © 2012 The Editorial Board of the Sociological Review

Finishing propeller shaft in the engine shop. Hyundai shipyard.

Company golf course reserved for visiting shipowners. Hyundai shipyard.

The Sociological Review, 60:S1, pp. 64–83 (2012), DOI: 10.1111/j.1467-954X.2012.02117.x

This can also be thought of as a passage from one panorama, the kind that played a key role in the unfolding of maritime power in the 17th-century, to another 'panorama', best exemplified perhaps in those control towers in container ports in which the immensely profitable modularization of maritime logistics is monitored through organizational and calculative activities on screens – veritable oligopticons of the sea. It is also a shift between different worlds of capital, namely, towards a financialized world that 'submits the totality to the same pecuniary accounting procedures with which it had grasped the fragments' (Sekula, 1995: 44).[14] If considered in terms of the aesthetic and economic transformations of the sea, modernity, that well-known Latourian bugbear, 'dissolved the edifying unity of the classical maritime panorama' (1995: 106). But this process is not one of seamless integration: 'under conditions of social crisis . . . the bottle of representation can burst, and the sea again exceeds the limits imposed upon it by a de-radicalized and stereotypical romanticism' (1995: 107).

It could also be argued that the end of the 17th-century panorama, of that kind of visual-mercantile dominion, gives way to a proliferation of panoramas, first as an attempt to encompass the world in a closed space, then directly to control, shape and measure it. But, contra Latour, rather than this being a liberation from totalization, it is a molecular or capillary form of totalization-by-assemblage or totalization-by-control (witness the explicitly totalizing aims of Geographical Information Systems, and their political and economic use). Against Latour's asseverations against 'seeing it whole', Sekula's practice, in its 'impure', reflexive and multiple approach, its systematic montage of media and formats, shows that it is indeed possible to do considerable justice to the sociological imagination in both social theory and artistic practice. Sekula too criticizes a view of frictionless transactions, seeing it in fact as a contemporary fetishization of finance and the immaterial, and he undoes through his photographic practice the idea of a commanding overview of the totality[15] – but he does so from the standpoint of a critique of the particular ways in which de-totalization and de-nationalization has taken place, not as an ontology but as a strategy.

As I hope to have intimated with relation to the ideas and images of mapping and panorama, many of the ethical and political contests in contemporary social thought are accompanied by disputes regarding the interrelations between knowledge, action and perception. By moving between the aesthetics of social theory and those ventures in the visual arts that challenge the sociological reluctance or refusal to 'see it whole' – especially when that 'whole' is far from seamless, contradictory, or even, as Adorno would have it, untrue – I want to defend the notion that a critical urge towards totalization is indispensable for social theory and research. That is, if the latter are not content with leaving the imaginative representations of the social, and of the mediations (or lack thereof) between everyday life and systems of compulsion and constraint, to a domain circumscribed, and belittled, as aesthetic or artistic. The incorporation of methods of social research into practices with their origins in art should at the very least compel sociologists and social theorists to interrogate the limits of the institutions, methods and self-understandings that currently define their own practice. Not in order to seek some instrumentalist inter- or trans-disciplinarity, but to renew the cognitive, ethical and political vocation to 'see it whole'.

Ours too is a time of uneasiness, though a catastrophist anxiety has taken the relay from the indifference of one-dimensional society. If we understand the 'aesthetic' dimension of social research not as a supplement or an ornament, but as a matter of our modes of representing, figuring or imaging the social, then there is much to learn from those critical artistic practices which at one and the same time seek to 'see it whole' and to explore the numerous ways in which such sight is imposed or occluded, modulated and mutable.

Critics and artists like Mark Lombardi, Trevor Paglen and Allan Sekula, among several others, have incorporated many of the most vital developments in critical social theory into expansive and experimental practices of research capable of truly responding to the 'desire called cognitive mapping'. Their fidelity to the totalizing aims of critical theory and materialist geography has also involved, as a necessary corollary, the exploration of the truncated, instrumental or illusory representations of the whole. This has also entailed a rigorous exploration of modes of representation (from art-historical tropes to technological devices), institutions of representation (from museum archives to state surveillance agencies), but also representational publics and counter-publics. Their projects have thus embodied the 'promise' of the sociological imagination in a way that the vast majority of contemporary social research, out of what we may term false modesty, has not. The bleak and turbulent horizon of the present demands a panoramic vision. But this is not that of a simple and secluded model – which, contra Latour, is an impoverishing interpretation of the classics of social thought – but rather the construction of a 'complex seeing' (Williams, 1979: 193), one that will be far closer to the dialectical montages of the 1920s or the experimental geographies of the past few decades than to the panoramas of the 19th century.

Notes

1 Indicative surveys and advocacies of a cartographic political aesthetics include Bhagat and Mogel (2007), Thompson and Independent Curators International (2009; see also Paglen, 2009b), Abrams and Hall (2006) and Harmon (2009). In recent journals, *Printed Project* 12, and *Afterall* 27 are dedicated to mapping. The exhibition *Uneven Geographies: Art and Globalisation*, curated by T. J. Demos and Alex Farquharson at Nottingham Contemporary, brought together much of this recent work.
2 Paglen's critical reflections on Mark Lombardi's network drawings, and the limitations of 'mapping' as a catch-all horizon for aesthetic research into contemporary spatial configurations of power (Bhagat and Mogel, 2007: 43–44) are significant in this respect, echoing as they do Neil Smith's comments on the limitations of the mapping metaphor in his very important *Uneven Development* (Smith, 2008: 223–229). See also Paglen (2009a) and Kinkle (2010); and Paglen (2010) for the experimental geographer's artwork, and for his account of his 'Sources and Methods' (2010: 144–151).
3 Of which I am well aware this essay is an instance.

The Sociological Review, 60:S1, pp. 64–83 (2012), DOI: 10.1111/j.1467-954X.2012.02117.x

4 Paglen's reliance on communities of plane- and satellite-spotters for his research on extraordinary renditions and the 'deep state' is a vivid instance of how to involve communities of research in an attempt to map the complex and covert operations of the new security state (Paglen, 2009a; Paglen and Thompson, 2007). The activist architect work of An Architektur on the *Geography of the Fürth Departure Centre* is an important and compelling case of militant and experimental geography (see the map in Bhagat and Mogel, 2007, and the interview on pp. 51–67). Of special note for its nuanced and systematic attempt to establish a *sui generis* institution for spatial research is the work of the Center for Land Use Interpretation (Coolidge and Simons, 2006). Wood (2010) provides a rich critical survey of 'counter-mapping'.

5 So much so that Bruno Latour has sought to locate its dramatic nucleus in the confrontation between Gabriel Tarde and Émile Durkheim over the direction of French sociology, and to re-enact it for the present (Viana Vargas *et al.*, 2008).

6 'Nature at a glance' was the name under which Robert Barker first patented what later came to be known as the panorama in 1787 (Oetterman, 1997: 6).

7 Tellingly, Latour treats the notion that there 'is a pecking order from top to bottom', as a political and epistemological 'prejudice' (2002a: 183).

8 The same could be said for the claim that 'People will go on believing that the big animal [ie Society] doesn't need any fodder to sustain itself; that society is something that can stand without being produced, assembled, collected, or kept up; that it resides behind us, so to speak, instead of being ahead of us as a task to be fulfilled' (2002a: 184). One supposes that Latour would argue that the myriad theories of reproduction put forward by Marxists, Bourdieusians, feminists, etc, are just not theories of reproduction.

9 'We . . . are not looking for utopia, but for places on earth that are fully assignable. Oligoptica are just those sites since they do exactly the opposite of panoptica: they see much *too little* to feed the megalomania of the inspector or the paranoia of the inspected, but what they see, they *see it well*' (Latour, 2002a: 181).

10 An ANT-inspired inquiry into the legal, technological, metric and political devices allowing rating agencies such as Standard & Poor's to function as they do would surely be a fine contribution to critical sociology.

11 For a brilliant reading of Marx in this direction, see Pepperell (2010).

12 A similar observation can be found in Allan Sekula's *Fish Story*: 'The panorama is paradoxical. topographically "complete" while still signalling an acknowledgment of and desire for a greater extension beyond the frame. The panoramic tableau, however bounded by the limits of a city profile or the enclosure of a harbor, is always potentially unstable: "If this much, why not more?" The psychology of the panorama is overtly sated and covertly greedy, and thus caught up in the fragile complacency of disavowal. The tension is especially apparent in maritime panoramas, for the sea always exceeds the limits of the frame' (1995: 43).

13 There is a major proviso to my appreciation of Hobbs's introductory essay to the catalogue of Lombardi's narrative structures: his reliance on Deleuze's notion of the rhizome to comprehend Lombardi's work is at odds with the totalizing drive of the drawings, also suggested by Lombardi's concern with the panorama.

14 Sekula is also extremely attentive to the material and strategic conditions of possibility of this shift: 'Coal-fired boilers, torpedoes and long-range naval guns introduced a new abstractness to the maritime space of combat. Abstract measured distance – from coaling stations, from one gun to another – came to matter more than the immediate and local vagaries of the wind. . . . The ultimate and likewise contradictory result of the "distancing" of determining factors [coaling stations, link to the land, targeting, etc.] was that the detail, rather than the panorama, became crucial. At the level of naval "intelligence" details became the analytic fragments that had to be entered into a vast statistico-taxonomic grid, a grid that compared and weighed the fleets of the world' (1995: 107). His totalities are results of concrete processes of abstraction, full of actors and devices, not seamless overviews of a homogeneous capitalism.

15 It is fruitful in this regard to compare his work with that of Edward Burtynsky, which in its visual style and its attempt to represent both society and ecology shows the limitations in a certain approach to 'seeing it whole'.

References

Abrams, J. and Hall, P. (eds), (2006), *Else/Where: Mapping – New Cartographies of Networks and Territories*, Minneapolis: University of Minnesota Design Institute.

Back, L., (2012), 'Live sociology: social research and its futures', *The Sociological Review*, 60 (S1), 18–29.

Benjamin, W., (2002), *The Arcades Project*, ed. R. Tiedemann, Cambridge, MA: The Belknap Press of Harvard University Press.

Benjamin, W., (2006), *Berlin Childhood around 1900*, Cambridge, MA: The Belknap Press of Harvard University Press.

Bhagat, A. and Mogel, L. (eds), (2007), *An Atlas of Radical Cartography*, Los Angeles: Journal of Aesthetics and Protest Press.

Bosteels, B. A., (1996), 'Misreading of maps: the politics of cartography in Marxism and poststructuralism', in S. Barker (ed.), *Signs of Change: Premodern, Modern, Postmodern*, Albany: State University of New York Press.

Chakrabortty, A., (2011), 'Debtocracy: the samizdat of Greek debt', *The Guardian*, Thursday 9 June.

Comment, B., (2002), *The Panorama*, London: Reaktion.

Coolidge, M. and Simons, S. (eds), (2006), *Overlook: Exploring the Internal Fringes of America with the Center for Land Use Interpretation*, Los Angeles: Metropolis Books.

Crary, J., (2002), Géricault, the panorama, and sites of reality in the early nineteenth century', *Grey Room*, 9: 5–25.

Day, G., Edwards, S. and Mabb, D., (2010), 'What keeps mankind alive? The Eleventh International Istanbul Biennial: Once more on aesthetics and politics', *Historical Materialism*, 18: 135–171.

Farinelli, F., (2009), *La crisi della ragione cartografica*, Torino: Einaudi.

Geary, D., (2009), *Radical Ambition: C. Wright Mills, the Left, and American Social Thought*, Berkeley, CA: University of California Press.

Harley, J. B., (2001), *The New Nature of Maps: Essays in the History of Cartography*, ed. P. Laxton, Baltimore, MD: The Johns Hopkins University Press.

Harmon, K., (2009), *The Map as Art: Contemporary Artists Explore Cartography*, Princeton, NJ: Princeton Architectural Press.

Hobbs, R. (ed.), (2003), *Mark Lombardi: Global Networks*, New York: Independent Curators International.

Hyde, R., (1988), *Panoramania! The Art and Entertainment of the 'All-Embracing' View*, London: Trefoil.

Jameson, F., (1988), 'Cognitive mapping', in C. Nelson and L. Grossberg (eds), *Marxism and the Interpretation of Culture*, Champaign, IL: University of Illinois Press.

Jameson, F., (1991), *Postmodernism, or, The Cultural Logic of Late Capitalism*, London: Verso.

Jameson, F., (1992), *The Geopolitical Aesthetic: Cinema and the World-System*, London: British Film Institute.

Jameson, F., (1998), *The Cultural Turn: Selected Writings on the Postmodern, 1983–1998*, London: Verso.

Jameson, F., (2009), *Valence of the Dialectic*, London: Verso.

Kinkle, J., (2010), 'Filling in the blanks: Trevor Paglen's parapolitical geography', *Site*, 29/30: 3–4.

Kinkle, J. and Toscano, A., (2009), 'Baltimore as world and representation: cognitive mapping and capitalism in *The Wire*', *Dossier* (online) available at: http://dossierjournal.com/read/theory/baltimore-as-world-and-representation-cognitive-mapping-and-capitalism-in-the-wire/ (accessed 9 September 2011).

Kinkle, J. and Toscano, A., (2011), 'Filming the crisis: a critical survey', *Film Quarterly*, 65 (1), 39–51.

The Sociological Review, 60:S1, pp. 64–83 (2012), DOI: 10.1111/j.1467-954X.2012.02117.x

Latour, B., (2002a), *Reassembling the Social: An Introduction to Actor-Network Theory*, Oxford: Oxford University Press.

Latour, B. (ed.), (2002b), *Iconoclash: Beyond the Image Wars in Science, Religion and Art*, Cambridge, MA: The MIT Press.

Latour, B. and Hermant, E., (1998), *Paris ville invisible*, Paris: La Découverte/Les Empêcheurs de danser en rond.

Latour, B. and Hermant, E., (2006), *Paris: Invisible City* (online). Available at: http://www.bruno-latour.fr/virtual/PARIS-INVISIBLE-GB.pdf (accessed 15 August 2011).

Latour, B. and Weibel, P., (2005), *Making Things Public: Atmospheres of Democracy*, Cambridge, MA: MIT Press.

Mackenzie, D., (2009), *Material Markets: How Economic Agents are Constructed*, Oxford: Oxford University Press.

Miller, A., (1996), 'The panorama, the cinema, and the emergence of the spectacular', *Wide Angle*, 18 (2): 34–69.

Mills, C. W., (1959), *The Sociological Imagination*, New York: Oxford University Press.

Mills, C. W., (2002), *White Collar: The American Middle Classes*, New York: Oxford University Press.

Oetterman, S., (1997), *The Panorama: History of a Mass Medium*, Cambridge, MA: MIT Press.

Paglen, T., (2009a), *Blank Spots on the Map: The Dark Geography of the Pentagon's Secret World*, New York: Dutton.

Paglen, T., (2009b), 'Experimental geography: from cultural production to the production of space', *The Brooklyn Rail*, March (online). Available at: http://www.brooklynrail.org/2009/03/express/experimental-geography-from-cultural-production-to-the-production-of-space (accessed 16 August 2011).

Paglen, T., (2010), *Invisible: Covert Operations and Classified Landscapes*, New York: Aperture.

Paglen, T. and Thompson, A. C., (2007), *Torture Taxi: On the Trail of the CIA's Rendition Flights*, Cambridge: Icon Books.

Penfold-Mounce, R., Beer, D., and Burrows, R., (2011), 'The wire as social science-fiction?', *Sociology*, 45 (1): 152–167.

Pepperell, N., (2010), *Disassembling Capital*, PhD thesis, RMIT University, Melbourne, Australia (online). Available at: http://www.roughtheory.org/wp-content/images/Disassembling-Capital-N-Pepperell.pdf (accessed 16 August 2011).

Sekula, A., (1995), *Fish Story*, Rotterdam: Witte de With and Dusseldorf: Richter Verlag.

Smith, N., (2008), *Uneven Development: Nature, Capital and the Production of Space*, Athens, GA: University of Georgia Press.

Sternberger, D., (1977), *Panorama of the 19th Century*, Oxford: Basil Blackwell.

Thompson, N. and Independent Curators International (eds), (2009), *Experimental Geography: Radical Approaches to Landscape, Cartography, and Urbanism*, New York: Melville House.

Verhoeff, N., (2007), 'Panorama behind glass: framing the spatial and visual design of highways', (online) MIT 5: Creativity, Ownership and the Digital Age, International Conference, 27–29 April 2007, Massachusetts Institute of Technology. Available at: http://web.mit.edu/comm-forum/mit5/papers/Verhoeff_PanoramaBehindGlass_MiT5.pdf (accessed 15 August 2011).

Viana Vargas, E., Latour, B., Karsenti, B., Aït-Touati, F. and Salmon, L., (2008), 'The debate between Tarde and Durkheim', *Environment and Planning D: Society and Space*, 26: 761–777.

Williams, R., (1979), *Modern Tragedy*, London: Verso.

Wood, D., (2010), *Rethinking the Power of Maps*, New York: Guilford Press.

Once upon a problem

Mariam Motamedi Fraser

Abstract: This article investigates the specificity of sociological materials and methods in relation to other disciplines and practices (art, literature, science and journalism) and questions the opportunities for sociological attentiveness, experimentation and failure in the context of contemporary UK professional, institutional and academic/intellectual constraints. It asks whether materials and methods are 'sociological' to the extent that they tell about the problems of *society*, or whether it is the unique relation *of* sociology *to* its materials and methods that defines sociological practice. Exploring these questions in relation to a project that was researched and written during an extended period of unpaid leave (ie outside the profession and the institution), the article also examines some of the consequences of a changed relation between sociology and experience. What would be the implications if the aim of sociology was not only to theorize and explain experience but also, sometimes, to be an 'informed provocation' of experience? The second part of the article considers what the concept of 'make-believe' might offer sociology – not in terms of what sociology *is*, but rather in terms of what it does with its materials and methods. Finally, the article returns to the most common material that sociologists work with – words – and asks how it is possible to stay receptive to the vitality of words as forces in the research process.

Keywords: sociology, failure, experience, make-believe, words, imagination

Mamlekat-e emkānant
The country of possibilities

In his book *Telling about Society*, Howard Becker discusses a vast range of materials and methods. As he describes it:

> from the social sciences, mathematical models, statistical tables and graphs, maps, ethnographic prose and historical narrative; from the arts, novels, films, still photographs and drama; from the large shadowy area in between, life histories and other biographical and autobiographical materials, reportage (including the mixed genres of docudrama, documentary film, and fictionalized fact), and the storytelling, map-making, and other representational activities of laypeople. (Becker, 2007: 4)

The Sociological Review, 60:S1, pp. 84–107 (2012), DOI: 10.1111/j.1467-954X.2012.02118.x
© 2012 The Author. Editorial organisation © 2012 The Editorial Board of the Sociological Review. Published by Wiley-Blackwell Publishing Ltd, 9600 Garsington Road, Oxford OX4 2DQ, UK and 350 Main Street, Malden, MA 02148, USA

Becker does not bother to ask *whether* these materials and methods tell about society; rather, assuming that they do, he seeks to examine 'what the problems of different media have in common and how solutions [to representing society] that work for one kind of telling look when you try them on some other kind' (Becker, 2007: 3).

Although the diversity of materials and methods that Becker considers is not conventional – indeed he claims at the outset that '[t]his was never a conventional research project' (Becker, 2007: xi) – insofar as he expects the representations he examines to tell about *society,* the book sits comfortably, as it is intended to do, within sociology. This is not to suggest that Becker adopts an unproblematized conception of society, or indeed of telling. Modes of telling, as he illustrates, are cross-cut by different distributions of labour, competing conceptions of intelligibility, and unequal social relations. Becker dedicates several chapters to an examination of how different users read and understand representations of society, and considers some of the conflicts – often cast in moral terms (Becker, 2007: 88) – that arise between users and makers of such representations. It is nevertheless striking, particularly as Becker explores materials and methods from a wide variety of domains ('from the social sciences . . . from the arts . . . from the large shadowy area inbetween'), that he should find that they *all tell* and, in telling about *society,* they all do sociological work (Becker, 2007: 5–10).[1]

Becker's aim is generous. It is to illustrate that sociologists do not have privileged access to social analysis. Nevertheless, while this generosity is appealing, it is also the aspect of *Telling about Society* that prompts me to ask whether Becker might not, inadvertently, be giving away the potential specificity of sociology and sociological practice too quickly. I do not ask about this (I hope) in order to make 'a standard professional power grab', as Becker puts it (Becker, 2007: 6).[2] My intentions are rather to explore, perhaps more cautiously, what the nature of the 'gift' of sociology might be (allowing that it might be more than one thing). For example: are the materials and methods that Becker identifies sociological because *they* tell about the problems of society? Or is it that the relation of sociology *to* its materials and methods is what enables *it* – that is, sociology – to lure those materials and methods into posing *their own* problems? If it is the latter, and if it transpires that a set of materials and methods did not tell, and/or if they did not tell about society, would they also not be sociological?

I have explored some of these issues elsewhere, by asking what would happen if the sociological problem (as it is defined by C. Wright Mills) was refracted through the virtual problem (Fraser, 2009).[3] My intention in this paper is to address them again, in a more practical vein, with reference to a project that has preoccupied me for the last three years. As I will be discussing below, this project came out of a series of unlikely coincidences and strange encounters which led me to take three years out of the institution and out of the profession in order to write what other people have called, on my behalf, a documentary novel or documentary fiction. A book, anyway, which may or may not be sociological. I will be exploiting the undecided status of the book (as sociology, or not) to ask, towards the end of the first part of this paper, how far a method, or a set of materials, can push at the boundaries of sociology before tipping it over into something else (art, perhaps, or literature). This is, again, a way of exploring the specificity of a 'sociological' problem, and how it might be defined. Using my project as the focus, I will suggest that the extraction of a problem from a research project requires a quality of attentiveness[4] to materials and methods, to their particularity, and a willingness to be transformed by them. Transformation is more likely to be possible if the 'participants' in a research project are understood to be relational (that is, constituted in part through their relations with each other).[5] Relationality is a helpful concept in this context, I think, because it implies that the problem is distributed across the research assemblage as a 'whole' rather than being located in the researcher, in the subject of research, in 'society', or even in their (methodological, epistemological, affective, etc) relations. Relationality also, inevitably, implies conflict (Fraser, 2009).

I have organized the first part of the paper around the question, 'Where, or when, does a project begin?' which I will ask three times. I have done this because the discussion that follows focuses mainly on my own experiences, and this question is a way of drawing attention to the particularity of the analysis. It is also, perhaps, another way of asking 'where, or when, does a story start?' and storying[6] is very much at the heart of my project and of this paper which, as I have already indicated, is partly about telling. In the spirit of storying, I end the first section with a few brief comments on what make-believe, as contrasted with making (Sennett, 2008) or making up (Clifford, 1986), might offer in terms of understanding sociological practice. The second part of the paper is something of a line of flight. Here, I consider the most common material that sociologists work with – words – and asking what are the implications of, and how it is possible to stay receptive to, the vitality of words as forces in the research process?

Material relations

So where, or when, does a project begin? It is always difficult to know. I could say that I was browsing through periodicals in the School of Oriental and African Studies library when, entirely by chance, I came across a reference to a story called *Irradiant*, written by a tribesman from Lorestan in World War II occupied Iran. That story, and the correspondence relating to it, is in an archive in the Bodleian Library in Oxford. One reason why it is there, in the Bodleian Libraries' Oriental Section and Indian Institute, is because *Irradiant* is believed, by some, to be an epic account of an ancient Mithraic or possibly pre-Zoroastrian religion in Iran (Zaehner, 1965, 1992).

The first time I came across a reference to *Irradiant* I only made a mental note of the story. But when I came across a second reference, also by accident

The Sociological Review, 60:S1, pp. 84–107 (2012), DOI: 10.1111/j.1467-954X.2012.02118.x
© 2012 The Author. Editorial organisation © 2012 The Editorial Board of the Sociological Review

(and let it be said that references to *Irradiant* in the English-speaking world are rare), I was prompted to trace the story to the Bodleian Library in Oxford. It took a while for the library, by their own high standards, to locate *Irradiant* for me but eventually the archivist e-mailed on 20 March 2009. That date happened, that year, to be the day of the vernal equinox. The day of the vernal equinox is New Year's day in Iran, the first day of the Iranian calendar, No Ruz, the most holy and joyful festival of the Zoroastrian year.

The Bodleian Library took some time to find the *Irradiant* archive because it did not, until I asked to read it, have a permanent shelf-mark. Indeed it did not have a permanent shelf-mark until I *kept* reading it. I am the first systematic reader of the archive (as a whole) and its most recent champion. I began by creating a rough catalogue of the contents for my own use (see also Bivar, 1998), which was sometimes a disorienting experience, early on, because the materials were often transferred overnight, over a series of nights, into renumbered acid-free boxes and, in the process, slightly reorganized. That feeling of delirium, in the morning, on finding new boxes, and finding things, or not being able to find things in them. The *Irradiant* archive is still officially uncatalogued, and will probably remain so until the paper in it has been conserved. This is something I am working on with the Bodleian. The materials in the *Irradiant* archive have transformed me from reader into sometime-archivist.

Previously, I had taught sessions to postgraduates on the philosophy and methodology of working with archives. Now, I attended courses on the principles and practices of researching and documenting information about archives. This involved learning how to arrange and describe information according to national and international archival standards and how to use archival software, such as EAD (Encoded Archival Description). I did this in order to be able to catalogue the archive professionally, or to be in a position to properly understand the cataloguing process were it undertaken by someone else, and/or to be well-informed about the process when it came to writing grant applications. With the support of Dr Gillian Evison, Head of the Bodleian Libraries' Oriental Section and Indian Institute, I met with Virginia Lladó-Buisán, Head of Book and Paper Conservation at the Bodleian, to make a 'pitch' for the conservation of *Irradiant*. That meeting quickly taught me (with much amusement, at the time, and with some shame, later) how reduced my own understanding of the archive was. For me, conservation meant conserving the *words* in the archive – minimally, by transcribing them and/or better, and ideally, by having them digitized. For Virginia, it referred to all aspects of the archive, beginning, in the case of *Irradiant*, with the paper on which the words were written.

It was not as if I had not felt the thrill of the archive as a physical object, especially on that very first day when, in place of the single book I had been expecting, Colin Harris, Superintendent of the Special Collections Reading Room, wheeled out a trolley stacked high with odd-shaped boxes. It was not as if I had not stifled my laughter in the sombre reading room when I realized it was not *dust*, as Carolyn Steedman (2001) put it, but *rust* which better characterized the *Irradiant* archive. (The rusting binders on the files and the paperclips.) Nor was I unaware of the important role played by paper – mostly as a hindrance – throughout the life of *Irradiant*. And certainly, as I will be discussing below, I already carried with me a sense of the viscerality of words. But it was only during the meeting with the Head of Paper that the archive finally, literally, *materialized* before my eyes as Virginia talked me through the different papers and inks in it, and later invited me, generously, to the studios to see what kinds of papers the Bodleian Libraries have there, and what they do with them. Our application to the National Manuscripts Conservation Trust was not successful. But Virginia Lladó-Buisán, Gillian Evison and Joan Lee decided nevertheless to go ahead with the conservation of parts of the *Irradiant* archive. When this is completed, it will be possible to apply for further grants for transcription and digitization. And, ultimately, for cataloguing.

Clearly, the *Irradiant* archive is being transformed. I do not mean by this that by the activities of humans the documents are being differently organized, or differently shelved, or that they are supported on a page by a hinge of Japanese RK17 tissue, using wheat starch paste, rather than pierced by a fat metal file binder. Although there is this. What I mean is that, insofar as the 'participants' in the archive are constituted by their relationality, the archive is always, necessarily, in the process of becoming itself differently. *All* the 'participants' in the research process – the archival documents and objects, the forces which act on them (such as the law), and on which they act, the researchers/readers/archivists who work with them – are *constituted by* and *transformed through* their relations with each other. The letter that Cousin John opens in 1943, which tells of a Lor tribesman, is not the same letter that I open in the arched light of the Special Collections Reading Room. It is not the same letter in part because the 'participants' have changed, as have the patterns of our relations, but also, as importantly, because the many and diverse *modes* of relationality are different. This latter point is especially significant because it suggests that being attentive means not just being in *a* relation to materials; it is also about learning, in part from the materials, what *kind* of relation we are in. How do I open this letter? How does this letter open me? I will return to the significance of kinds of relations below and in the conclusion.

Where, or when, does a project begin? I started to answer this question by recounting the story of my discovery of *Irradiant*. But my discovery is only the most recent event in *Irradiant's* own story, which is long and twisty. A second response, then, could be to begin with *Irradiant* itself, which for many years, and in keeping with the notion that Britain rules Iran with a hidden hand,[7] was thought to be a literary hoax. This belief was fuelled by the temporary 'disappearance' of the manuscript and by the kinds of people who claimed to have seen it, some of whom were instrumental in the 1953 coup against Dr Mohammad Musaddiq, the hugely popular – if not, now, iconic – democratically elected Prime Minister of Iran, who sought to nationalize Iranian oil. When I learnt who had been involved in the story of *Irradiant*, I expanded the field of my research and began to read documents relating to these figures, and the role they played in the coup, in the British National Archives at Kew. This is partly

The Sociological Review, 60:S1, pp. 84–107 (2012), DOI: 10.1111/j.1467-954X.2012.02118.x

what my book is about. My book tells of how and why *Irradiant* came to be written; how it was lost, and then found; how it brought people together, how it separated them. I further amplify the *Irradiant* story in my book by making stories out of the many forces and relations that shaped *Irradiant* at the micro-level (paper, as I have already mentioned, is a crucial part of the life of *Irradiant*), as well as at the macro-level (I explore, for example, the role of British academics in devising and executing British foreign policy). In addition to this, I fold into the book a wide range of texts, including Iranian and British published memoirs; academic and popular histories; government and newspaper reports; reviews; classical and modern literature (poetry and novels); children's stories and nursery rhymes; and my own fictional inventions (characters and events). I also 'met with many . . . people', as Becker describes the research practices of literary writers (Becker, 2007: 215).

All of which sounds like a lot of telling. Yet the very proliferation of materials in this project, the excess of them even, suggests to me that these materials *do not want to tell*; or at least, that they are not for telling *about*; and certainly, that they will not be *told*. At the time, I did not know what to do with them or how to enter relations with them. Thus,[8] although I found the *Irradiant* archive while I was on funded sabbatical leave, I arranged to have the rest of the year unfunded and later took a further two unfunded years.[9] This put me in a position to cultivate, as Chris Salter describes it, 'another type of attentiveness' to the materials, the kind of attentiveness that often does not produce immediate (or even any) results, and that takes time (Salter, 2011: 13).

It seems appropriate – before returning for a third time to the question 'Where, or when, does a project begin?' – to take the time to consider some of the relations between the practical conditions under which UK academics work and the more 'abstract' problem of the distinctiveness or not of British sociological methods, projects and their limits. To make the point again (and again and again), the conditions under which most academics work in the United Kingdom do not usually allow, and increasingly disallow, for anything but the most over-determined and familiar 'attention' to materials and methods. Time is short. Research must be decided in advance. It must be decided in order for sabbaticals (that most material of professional academic resources) to be justified, and for funding to be secured. It seems especially significant to me, or symptomatic rather, that outputs – the form and number of them, as well as their places of dissemination – are often required to be identified *before* the research has been carried out. This is no less true of speculative research funding, which requires in advance some evidence that a piece of research will be 'adventurous and innovative' (http://www.ahrc.ac.uk/FundingOpportunities/Pages/RG-SpeculativeResearch.aspx).[10] Although knowing what is going to happen in a research project is not always problematic,[11] it often is. With regards to archival research, for example, the possibility of stumbling into an unread or unresearched archive, and of living there for a while without knowing what it will yield, if it yields anything at all, is important because, in the UK, sources such as official correspondence and memoranda, in particular where recognized public figures are concerned, are very often *over-catalogued.* Or as Peter Jackson puts it, 'weeded heavily before being released for public consumption' (Jackson, 2010). Such stumbling-into usually occurs by way of lucky accident. But even accidents need the conditions to support them.

As do failures. It is interesting to note in this context that while scientific experiments and literary works frequently fail (differently, and with different implications), sociological failures are quite well hidden within the profession. And yet one of the ways that the materials with which sociologists work might be enabled to 'express' their own view on the purposes to which they are suited – whether, for example, they are suited to the mode of telling or not, and if so, how so, etc – is if sociologists were more able to admit to those occasions when particular questions, concepts, methods, were *not* fit for purpose. In the current political climate in Britain, no academic (research project) can afford to fail, institutionally, unless it is for a reason that is acceptable to the institution.[12] Before my unpaid leave was agreed, Human Resources sought my assurance that, during the period I was away, the work I would be doing would continue to contribute to my academic career. One of the reasons I was unwilling to answer this question in the affirmative was, I now think, not because I feared failure per se – I have certainly experienced and continue to experience the fear of failure of my book – but because I feared *not* being able to fail *as a sociologist.*[13] Universities have become remarkably adept at absorbing, under the rubric of creativity, innovation, resourcefulness, experimentation, etc, all kinds of outcomes. In practice, this is often something to be thankful for. But it has a cost.

How, then, to fail? One way, as I have already implied, would be to produce something that is not fit for purpose. In *Telling about Society,* Becker suggests that a representation *is* whatever its makers and users agree to believe it is. He calls this 'the social agreement to believe' (Becker, 2007: 115). It means that an object is judged by whether it is 'plenty good enough' for the purpose to which it is agreed to be put. For example: 'If it's a "realistic" novel, it doesn't include factual stuff that, if you look into it, isn't factual' (2007: 117). 'We would feel differently', Becker argues, about Dickens' *Bleak House* if it was not 'a realistic account of events that might well have happened' (2007: 124–125).[14] We would 'probably judge it a smaller achievement' (2007: 125). More broadly, and more fundamentally, Becker makes claims for the aesthetic and affective importance of *truth* as 'an essential element in our appreciation of the work as art' (2007: 128).

Should the facts be factual then, and the fiction fictional, in order for a 'representation', as Becker puts it, to be fit for purpose? There is much at stake for sociology, raised as it was 'between literature and science' (Lepenies, 1992), in the organization of the relations between facts, truths and fictions. Isabelle Stengers suggests the 'new mode of togetherness' invented by modern science turns on precisely this contrast: '[t]he whole of human invention, imagination, intentionality, and freely engaged passion is . . . mobilized in order to establish that there is one interpretation only, the "objective one," owing nothing to

The Sociological Review, 60:S1, pp. 84–107 (2012), DOI: 10.1111/j.1467-954X.2012.02118.x

invention, imagination, and passion' (Stengers, 2002: 251).[15] It is not surprising, in view of this modern, Western, scientific conception of the world, that these relations should have so troubled C. Wright Mills when he stalked the fields of science and literature, of abstracted empiricism and grand theory, in search of sociological imagination. None of these would ultimately do for Mills, not '[s]tudies of contemporary fact' (Mills, 2000: 23) nor contemporary literature (Mills, 2000: 17): 'What fiction, what journalism, what artistic endeavor', Mills wrote, 'can compete with the historical reality and political facts of our time? What dramatic vision of hell can compete with the events of twentieth-century war? What moral denunciations can measure up to the moral insensibility of men in the agonies of primary accumulation?' (Mills, 2000: 17).

Mills' book was published on the eve of the 1960s, which was the decade in which the writers associated with the new journalism[16] might well have raised their hands in positive answer to these questions. Truman Capote's (1981 [1965]) *In Cold Blood*, Tom Wolfe's (1981 [1965]) *Kandy-Kolored Tangerine-Flake Streamline Baby*, Joan Didion's (1974 [1968]) *Slouching towards Bethlehem,* Norman Mailer's (1968) *Armies of the Night,* and Hunter S. Thompson's (1972 [1971]) *Fear and Loathing in Las Vegas*[17] were among the works that developed, John Hartstock argues, 'in response to significant social and cultural transformation and crisis. These were reflected in the civil rights movement, assassinations, disruptions in prevailing middle-class culture, the drug culture, growing environmental awareness, and of course the Vietnam War' (Hartstock, 2000: 192). These novels and other shorter pieces of journalistic writing impress by their fieldwork, real-life observation, accumulation of empirical detail and by their atmosphere of authenticity and realism (Underwood, 2008: 136) – captured, for example, in Wolfe's 'linguistic pyrotechnics that seemed to pose a taunt to advocates of standard English usage' (Hartstock, 2000: 195). It is for these very same reasons, however, that these works are disquieting for they are, also, fictitious. Gay Talese, described by Tom Wolfe as the founder of the new journalism, summarizes the different aspects and ambitions of the genre, claiming that while it reads like fiction, 'it is not fiction. It is, or should be, as reliable as the most reliable reportage although it seeks a larger truth than is possible through the mere compilation of verifiable facts' (Talese in Hartstock, 2000: 193). But this, for John Hersey, is exactly the problem. The reader of journalism, unlike the reader of fiction, should feel secure that 'NONE OF THIS WAS MADE UP' (Hersey in Becker, 2007: 130). For Hersey, the ethics of journalism demands that every journalist recognize the 'distortion that comes from adding invented data' (Hersey in Becker, 2007: 130).

Hersey's point is indicative of 'an interesting asymmetry', as Sundar Sarukkai puts it, between the fictional and the real wherein '[a] drop of fiction is enough to spread through a narrative and make the whole narrative fictional. Whereas, on the other hand, a fistful of reality does not make a narrative a real one' (Sarukkai, 2006–2007: 53–54). Literature no less than science, Sarukkai argues, is invested in the difference, and perhaps for good reason: the 'self-conscious' and 'carefully cultivated' appropriation of the fictional by literary practitioners and critics serves to protect literature from 'attempts to regulate artistic expression though constraints such as the real' (Sarukkai, 2006–2007: 54). It also denies literature, however, the 'pragmatic nonchalance' with regards to fictions and 'unrealities' that, despite the ideal conception of science described by Stengers, characterizes some branches of science, and especially mathematics (Sarukkai, 2006–2007: 59). The very term 'distortion' for example, as Hersey means it (as an undesirable departure from 'reality'), is displaced in the use that physicists make of mathematical models. As Nancy Cartwright explains:

> it is not essential that the models accurately describe everything that actually happens . . . The requirements of the theory constrain what can be literally represented. This does not mean that the right lessons cannot be drawn. Adjustments are made where literal correctness does not matter very much in order to get the correct effects where we want them; and very often, as in the staging example [the staging of a historical episode], one distortion is put right by another. That is why it often seems misleading to say that a particular aspect of a model is false to reality. (Cartwright, 1983: 140)

How then, in the light of these different patterns of relations between facts, fictions, truths and realities, have I tried to understand my own book project? To what purpose is it fit?

Although the realism/realist genre in my book is discontinuous, it is partially organized around real historical people and events and in this respect it would be legitimate to ask whether, were one 'to look into it', as Becker puts it, the facts are factual. Somewhat problematically, my answer would have to be that although the book includes 'factual stuff', it is *neither* fact *nor* fiction. There are two reasons for this. First, many of the materials out of which the book is fabricated are not themselves strictly factual. Archival documents, for instance, are 'artful' in a banal sense insofar as an archive is, necessarily, a collection of artificially gathered-together entities.[18] In the *Irradiant* archive, a number of the memoirs and diaries, and some of the letters, are also more literally artful: they have the distinct feel of fiction about them, or at the very least might be said to be highly edited with a view to privacy, posterity or possible publication. If anything were to be described as 'fictionalized reportage' in this context, it would be these documents.

Of course the original meaning of a document as 'a piece of paper with words that attested evidence' (Coles in Plummer, 2001: 67) has long been contested. Document, the noun, derived from the Latin *docere,* to teach (to tell?), might still attest, but *of what* it teaches, or attests, is no longer considered to be self-evident. This point can be extended, without too much difficulty, from the archival materials on which my book partly drew to the published historical accounts of the period that I also used. These texts often have a literary quality in themselves, but also, more interestingly, frequently seem to be dramatizations of *each other.* Consider, for example, the following descriptions of a single event, the occasion on which two (maybe, or maybe more) secret service agents (or US Army colonels, or British diplomats) visited Ashraf Pahlavi, the twin sister of the Shah of Iran, to enrol her support in the coup against Musaddiq. The first set of extracts are accounts of what Pahlavi was offered in return for her help:

'a blank check' (Pahlavi, 1980: 136).

'an unauthorized promise that he [her brother, the Shah of Iran] would be supported in the style to which he had become accustomed by the United States if the coup failed' (Gasiorowski, 1987: 273, based on a confidential interview with the Colonel who was present on the occasion).

'if the coup failed, the United States would give her [Ashraf Pahlavi] sufficient financial support to go on living abroad in the style to which she was accustomed' (Elm, 1992: 301, (mis)quoting Gasiorowski).

'a great wad of notes' (Dorril, 2001: 588).

'a mink coat and a packet of cash' (Kinzer, 2003: 7).

'a mink coat and a substantial though unspecified amount of cash (Louis, 2006: 783).

And these are accounts of her response:

'her eyes lit up' (Louis, 2006: 783, quoting Dorril).

'her eyes lit up' (Kinzer, 2003: 7, quoting Dorril).

'her eyes lit up' (Dorril, 2001: 588, citing Special Operations Executive Norman Darbyshire).

'I was so stunned I didn't even hear the rest of what he was saying. Although I had very limited funds at this time, the suggestion that I would take money for an operation that would help my country made me lose my temper' (Pahlavi, 1980: 136).

It is possible to describe my book as neither fact nor fiction because the materials on which it draws mostly refuse to identify themselves as clearly one or the other (regardless of the author's intentions or of the disciplinary, professional, institutional, legal, and commercial processes by which a text comes to be constituted as, say, a work of history).[19]

More significantly, however, the book is fit for purpose neither as the new journalism nor as sociology because it does not have a referent – 'truth' or 'society' – against which the distance required to conceive of fact and fiction could be measured. Should such a referent be taken for granted or is it an achievement, won or stolen and secured at a price? The reason that my book does not have a referent is not because of my theoretical and/or political commitments to, for instance, a particular conception of 'the real' or because of my aesthetic sensibilities and preferences, etc. It is, rather, because the book is concerned with a period in Iranian history when the relations between facts, truths and fictions were used and abused by some Iranians and especially by the British and the Americans. Or, more accurately, a period when many of the scales and perspectives by which realities are commonly constituted were purposely or inadvertently rendered inoperative. When there was no longer a 'horizon', as Veena Das puts it, 'within which [to] place the constituent objects of a description in their relation to each other and in relation to the eye with which they are seen' (Das, 2007: 4). If the materials on which I draw in my book, when they are gathered together, that is, put into a relation with each other, do not tell, or do not tell about, and if they will not be told, perhaps one reason is because telling, as a method, as a 'how', as Alfred North Whitehead might put it (Whitehead, 1978: 23) (telling as a mode of becoming), produces too stable a 'what' for the context, a too-unproblematized tale told, under the circumstances.[20] For Becker, all materials and methods tell *of* something (society). But *of* is a place, a position, or a relation. What if there were no 'of' through which to lure a tale? No 'of' through which to be lured? 'What is it to lose one's world?', Das asks (Das, 2007: 2). My book is about stories and storying. It is about words, language, literacy, educating, editing, translating and publishing. It is about the material and emotional experiences of reading and writing, and of learning to read and write. It is about propaganda, rumour, plots, plotting, coup-making and conspiracy-mongering. It is about authorship, signatures and signatories. Wilful obfuscation, lies and secrets are principal themes in the book.

This brings me, finally, to a third way of responding to the question 'Where, or when, does a project begin?' and to the words that are stitched into the emotional heart of the book: *yekee bud, yekee nabud*. In direct translation, this Iranian equivalent of 'once upon a time' means 'one there was, one there wasn't'. The words, with which so many Iranian stories begin, alert the reader to the instability of stories and their contents. They are an invitation to ask: To what does a story refer? Of what and when does it tell? In what different kinds of ways is it possible to believe in a story, or not believe, and with what consequences?

My book is an alloy of fact and fiction because, in order to problematize the tale and its telling, I not only tell tales, but I also story the activity of storying itself. I want the book not just to *represent* the feel of Iranian politics and the part played by the British in creating that feeling, but to actually walk the tightrope between the paranoid style, as Ervand Abrahamian (1993) puts it, that characterized politics in Iran (and which finally 'legitimated' the execution of thousands of so-called spies and traitors) and the justifiable suspicion of foreign powers, and especially the British establishment, based on well-documented accounts of their cloak-and-dagger activities. I want the book to be about the problem of storying, to story, and also to pose the problem of storying to the reader. In short, if these materials do not exactly *tell*, they are intended to provoke. In the book, this provocation unfolds in a number of different ways, by foregrounding the process of storying (or historying) for example or by exploiting historical facts, fictions, and the fact of historical fictions (such as *Irradiant*) to create a paranoid reader who cannot be sure – as one could not be sure, in Iran – of the tale told, the telling, or the teller.[21]

Could a book that seeks to provoke a feeling, the emotion of frustration (at least), or paranoia (at best), be fit for purpose as sociology? Or would it be a

94

failure? For Becker, sociology tells about society. Why should it be obliged to do anything else? Other fields, especially art and literature, seek more explicitly to produce affect and to create novelty. In sociology, experience is usually something to be theorized and explained (how are experiences shaped? How they are produced? What is the relation between experience and the subject?) before it is something to be generated or manipulated (see Fraser, 2009: 68). But what if the aim of sociology was, also, sometimes, an 'informed provocation' of experience? Is this a 'legitimate' activity for sociology? What would be the criteria for judging 'good' sociology if it were?

* * *

At the end of his book, Becker compares himself to a preacher. In his final lines he writes (somewhat dismally): 'Like every preacher, I hope the congregation listens, but I'm not too hopeful' (Becker, 2007: 287). Perhaps he is right not to be too hopeful. It is difficult to be in a relation with a preacher who not only tells, but who also often ardently believes in what he is telling. I want to finish this first part of the paper by commenting very briefly on make-believe as another way of thinking not about what sociology *is* but about what it *does* with its materials and methods. The concept of make-believe is helpful, I think, because it does not exactly sacrifice the element of belief that is implicit in Becker's description of the sociologist as preacher, but nevertheless brings some reflexivity and humour to it. Make-believe is also, importantly, a way of acknowledging sociology's debt to, and its possible departure from, some of the more familiar ways of organizing the relations between facts, truths and fictions.

There has, recently, been some considerable comment on *making* in sociology (for example, Richard Sennett's (2008) *The Craftsman*) and there has always been much to say about *making things up* in the social sciences. In his controversial introduction to *Writing Culture* (1986), James Clifford substituted the word 'fiction' for 'partial' and argued that anthropological ethnographies can be 'properly called fictions' not just in the sense of 'something fashioned', but in the sense of 'inventing things not actually real' (Clifford, 1986: 6). Since *Writing Culture* was published, a vast and diverse body of literature has focused on what might be described as 'the telling of telling', which illustrates how the sciences and social sciences are a kind of story-telling, packed with hidden moralities, power relations, exclusions, rhetorical tricks, styles, and so on.

Making and making up: but not, interestingly, make-believe. This is curious, given how often make-believe features in anthropology. Perhaps it is something for the other, and not for the self.[22] Make-believe does not, at least at first glance, appear to be an especially sophisticated concept but it has a useful elasticity about it and seems to me to have more integrity than making up. Make-believe does not mock or ridicule its element of belief in the way fiction potentially can and often does. As in Iran: 'you don't actually believe that do you? The British made it up!'. At the same time the 'make' in make-believe foregrounds the artificiality of belief. It is a reminder that sociological beliefs are something that have to be crafted, and also that belief is dangerous when it is manufactured. Make-believe can be methodologically pragmatic. It is often helpful for sociologists, no less than for physicists, to proceed, at different points in a research project, *as if* something were true, or to experiment with the location of the boundaries of 'existential commitment' (Cartwright, 1983: 128–131). To suspend, at least for a while, their sense of *disbelief* in order to continue to think through (and with, and against) a problem. In this respect, make-believe is an aid to sociological imagination. However, if proceeding *as if* implies distance from and control over a piece of research, it is also the case that, sometimes, sociological make-believe is closer to faith: intimate, committed, complete. C. Wright Mills sought to exercise what he called 'the political task of the social scientist' in work, in educating, and in life (Mills, 2000: 187). In *Life and Words*, Veena Das writes of her 'anthropological kind of devotion to the world' (Das, 2007: 221).[23] But make-believe is also resonant of magic, that most material of arts, which, like sociology – to gloriously corrupt the title of Wolf Lepenies' (1992) history of sociology – lies somewhere 'between literature and science'.

My focus is on make-believe rather than making-believe (cf. de Certeau, 1984). This is in keeping with my introductory claim that, if a problem is to be extracted from research, it will be extracted from the 'whole' of the assemblage rather than any single aspect of it or any subject who participates in it (whether as researcher or researched). Make-believe is less about an author, is less *author*itative, than either making up or making. One of the difficulties with Mills' and Sennett's work on craft is that, in both their books, novelty is for the most part located in the figure of the craftsman rather than in the problem. (And this is the case even when, or perhaps especially when, it is the craftsman who actively seeks out problems). To find novelty in the problem itself is not to exclude the craftsperson (or the researcher) but it is to hold open the significance of that figure in problem-making. Finally, I think that make-believe is a fragile activity. It tends to be short-lived, and is contingent upon the materials at hand. Also, it is often tender.

Words as things

Although the story I have told so far is not wholly retrospective, in fact my main feeling, while I was working on my project, was *words*. Initially, as indicated by my earliest conception of the archive as mainly or even solely composed of sound-images (see the account above, of my meeting with Virginia Lladoó-Buisán, Head of Book and Paper Conservation at the Bodleian), I understood words to be basically discursive, primarily related to other words, and (therefore) essentially detachable from any material or other support. This conception changed over the course of the project, which is perhaps not surprising: I was 'handling' a lot of words, written in many kinds of texts; I was thinking about how words are, and could be, generated and generative, manipulated and manipulative; I was reading and writing about a writer, and how he came

The Sociological Review, 60:S1, pp. 84–107 (2012), DOI: 10.1111/j.1467-954X.2012.02118.x

to write a novel in a third language; I was experimenting with writing myself, and with two different languages; I was not doing much else. Ultimately, my experience of the book began to feel closer to sculpting (something material) than writing (something discursive). In a most real sense, in relation to words, this distinction between the material and the discursive did not hold for me. Words are arguably the most common material that sociologists work with and yet it is often difficult to see them as 'participants' in research, with a force and productivity of their own. One possible reason for this is that, unlike other research materials, the use of words seems for the most part to be chosen and, conversely, unable to be unchosen. I want to end this paper with a suggestion as to how to remember the liveliness or vitality of words, which is to think of them, sometimes, as not necessarily or inherently bound to language or literacy.

Tim Ingold would surely recognize the kind of 'reduced attentiveness' that describes my initial relation to words as a symptom of the separation, in the Western world, between speech and song. For Ingold, it is not looking or vision per se, the word as sound-image, that has led the affective capacity of words to be diminished (as Walter Ong argues), rather, it is because words have lost their physical trace. 'Though we say of an author that he writes, referring archaically to the result of his work as a manuscript, this is evidently the one thing he does not do' (Ingold, 2007: 26). Ingold is thinking here of writing as a handicraft, literally *hand writing*, as physically incisive trace-making. As he puts it: 'I compare [handwriting] to practicing my cello. When I practice – which I do as often as I can – the sound pours out from the contact between bow and strings. In just the same way, handwriting flows from the moving point of contact between pen and paper' (Ingold, 2011).[24] Unlike music, Ingold illustrates that words are no longer important in themselves, for the sound they make or 'for the effects that they have on us' (Ingold, 2007: 6).[25] Instead, words are delivery-vehicles for intentions and meanings that lie elsewhere.

Ingold's 'archaeology of lines' – and writing is for Ingold but one species of line-making – is suggestive when it comes to thinking generously about words. Ingold cares about the silence of words and the absence of the trace of the gesture on the page. In doing so, he moves away from the problem of words *and* things – *Les Mots et Les Choses* (1966) as Foucault summarized it – and towards words *as* things.[26] Words as things-in-themselves rather than words as things-that-represent-other-things. Not words *in* language or even *for* literacy but words as entities with properties, qualities, intensities and extensities which emerge from the relations into which they enter or are entered. Bruno Latour admires Isabelle Stengers for creating worlds not words (Latour, 1997: viii). But might not words be worlds too? 'Recall', Ingold writes, 'that for readers of medieval times, the text was like a world one inhabits, and the surface of the page like a country in which one finds one's way about, following the letters and words as a traveller follows footsteps or waymarkers in the terrain' (Ingold, 2007: 24).

Mostly, it is literary writers, who are attentive to the work and play of words, and artists, who are attentive to materials, who best capture the physical, emotional and affective dimensions of words. The writer Eudora Welty's 'love for the alphabet' *precedes* her being able to read the letters (Welty, 1984: 9). And: '[i]n my sensory education I include my physical awareness of the *word*. . . . The word "moon" came into my mouth as though fed to me out of a silver spoon. Held in my mouth the moon became a word' (Welty, 1984: 10). One might ask: to what extent is thinking led not only by conscious, reasoning thinkers who *choose* their words, but by the affective or aesthetic resonance, the sound, feel, touch, place, position, direction, sense and sensation of words that, for one reason or another, they have entered into relations with? These are the kinds of relations with words I am thinking of, when I think of words as material participants in the research process. I am thinking, for example, of something akin to the relations with words forged in ancient and contemporary Middle Eastern calligraphic art.

I choose this example specifically because it is difficult to define calligraphic letters as either written or drawn,[27] or as belonging to art, literature or sculpture. Or are these letters part of the animal world? *Nasta'liq*, the 'hanging script', was perfected in the 15th century after Mir Ali al-Tabrizi dreamt of flying geese. A special term, *hurufiyya*, has been coined for this calligraphic trend in the Middle East, after the Arabic word *harf,* meaning letter, but also because *hurufiyya* alludes to the occult properties of letters (Porter, 2006). Words can be magic and often – this is calligraphy's inheritance – they are divine. They may be for beauty, and not for reading. Words cover walls and decorate buildings in every city and town and in nearly every village in Iran. Sonorous speech is woven into everyday life, from the poetry that can be heard daily on the radio, in restaurants and between television programmes, to the more familiar call of the *azān*. How are these words similar to, or how do they differ from, the font and print that also map these spaces, and that direct the flow of human and other traffic? Brands may not leave physical traces on the surface of billboards, but as Celia Lury shows, they are no less able to enter into and organize the movement and rhythm of a body for that (Lury, 2008).[28] How distant are these patterns of words from Ingold's description of writing as landscaping, as the creation of a landscape *through which* the reader moves, rather than *at which* the reader looks? Words can be strange attractors, with pulls that are often difficult, if not impossible, to resist. They have the power to lead or to lead on, to stop or to block. Words can be prompts for action or prompted into action. Single words, assemblages of words, word-ecologies. Words with histories, trajectories and associations that are not necessarily intelligible on account of their relations within language. Words-as-things do not always *follow from* experience, or *come after* experience, or *describe* experience, but can be understood as experience-participants, parts of experience assemblages, or themselves assemblages.

This is how, for now, I would define writing: as relations-with-words. This definition nods towards language, which can be understood as a system of relations between words, but is more fundamentally different from it, insofar as it does not assume in advance that relations-with-words are necessarily systematic. It follows, therefore, that I am not thinking of a grammatological concep-

The Sociological Review, 60:S1, pp. 84–107 (2012), DOI: 10.1111/j.1467-954X.2012.02118.x
© 2012 The Author. Editorial organisation © 2012 The Editorial Board of the Sociological Review

tion of substance, such as biology as systematicity or the writing skills of DNA. Nor am I assuming that words are necessarily related to other words, or that relations-with-words always refer to the relations of humans with words. Words-as-things are forces to be reckoned with. They are powerful because they are attached to people. But sometimes they are powerful because they are not. Veena Das (2007) brilliantly illustrates how words, untethered from subjects, groups of subjects or from the state, can lead to destruction and death.

Das's analysis of the chains of connection (rather than the chains of causation) that were ignited in the light of Indira Gandhi's assassination on 31 October 1984 is especially compelling in the context of this article because it illuminates a conception of the social 'in terms of unfinished stories' (Das, 2007: 108). Das describes how rumours about Indira Gandhi's death and the identity of her killers spread *before* official announcements were made. 'People somehow "knew"', she writes, 'that she [Indira Gandhi] had been killed by her Sikh body-guards' (Das, 2007: 109). They 'knew' because this 'calamitous national event' (Das, 2007: 110) was experienced, by most people, as part of a seriality of unfolding events which included, most recently, Operation Blue Star. Operation Blue Star had been launched four months earlier, in July 1984. The Indian Army forcibly entered the Golden Temple in Amritsar – literally, forced their way in the *gurudwara,* the doorway to the Guru – to, allegedly, 'flush out the militants' (Das, 2007: 109). During the exercise the Sikh militant leader, Bhindranwale, was, again allegedly, killed. Allegations and counter-allegations followed, and these served, in their turn, to shape perceptions of, and rumours about, Indira Gandhi's assassination (Das, 2007: 130–131). Most Sikhs for example, even if they were not sympathetic to the militant cause, considered Operation Blue Star to be a deliberate desecration of the temple and an insult to the religious community. After the assassination, some claimed that Bhindranwale had not in fact died and that, like a 'sleeping bull', he would 'rise to lead the Sikhs against the Indian State' (Das, 2007: 130). Many Hindus on the other hand believed that the Indian Army had, as the army itself claimed, entered the temple in order to rescue 'innocent pilgrims' who the 'terrorists' were using as human shields. This provided Hindus with evidence of the 'fanaticism' of Sikhs, willing to sacrifice themselves and their children in the cause of their religion. The assassination of Indira Gandhi, it was said, was only the first step in what would be a violent avenging of Operation Blue Star. Sikhs 'had gathered in *gurudwaras* to attack Hindus in large numbers' (Das, 2007: 133). Trains full of dead bodies were arriving from Punjab.

The force and credibility of the 'uncanny knowledge' about Indira Gandhi's assassination turned not just on the presence, in the present, of the immediate past (the recent event of Operation Blue Star) but also on experiences of the Partition riots, 'as if "having seen" such things [such violent things] in 1947 showed the veracity of what has heard [sic] in 1984' (Das, 2007: 122). Das shows how, as the rumours thickened, the categories of aggressor and victim were reversed: a sense of vulnerability was created among Hindus, in parallel with a conception of Sikhs as aggressive, mad, and possessed by demons.

> The characteristics of this crisis were a mounting panic that signalled the breakdown of social communication, the animation of a societal memory seen as constitutive of incomplete or interrupted social stories, and the appearance of the panic rumor as a voice that was unattributed, unassigned, and yet anchored to images of self and other that had been circulating in the discourses of militancy. The withdrawal of trust from normally functioning words constituted a special vulnerability to the signifier, leading one to ways of acting over which all control seemed to have been lost. (Das, 2007: 117)

Three thousand Sikhs died in the violence that began on the evening of the assassination of Indira Gandhi.

Das's analysis, here and in her book more generally, is a profound illustration that the liveliness of words is neither necessarily desirable nor is it always benign. Vitality does not have an inherently ethical disposition (Blencowe, 2011).

Countries of possibilities

Mamlekat-e emkānant, 'the country of possibilities', is an Iranian expression, which usually refers to Iran. I have extended it here to include sociology as well. A country of possibilities is a country of imagination, and it is imagination, especially sociological imagination, that has subtended much of the discussion in this paper. 'What', Sundar Sarukkai asks, 'is the role of imagination after the real has been brought forth?' For him, the answer depends on whether imagination is for science or for art:

> Scientific imagination is essential for the discovery of new truths, but once this task is over, imagination is replaced by the real. Imagination, for science, is a means to an end – the end that is the articulation of the truths of the world. For art, imagination is all there is; there is no reality in which it can hide. Really, there can be no end to art, to the work of imagination. (Sarukkai, 2010: 217)

And sociology? Sociology seeks neither to 'discover' (or invent) realities, nor to dispense with them. It nevertheless struggles on occasion, as journalism does, with the boundaries between facts and fictions. Should it be journalism, then, rather than science, art or literature, through which sociology comes to a better understanding of itself?

Paul Rabinow and George Marcus, speaking of anthropology, insist that there can be no comparison with journalism. The reason for this, they argue, is because, unlike journalism, scholarly activity is (ideally) untimely. They take this term from Nietzsche's *Untimely Meditations* which, as Rabinow describes it, 'seeks to establish a relationship to the present different from reigning opinion' (Rabinow and Marcus, 2008: 59). Journalists, Rabinow continues, cannot do untimely work – it is 'the one thing journalists absolutely cannot do' (Rabinow and Marcus, 2008: 59) – because they operate under severe genre and time constraints and, perhaps more importantly, because the temporality of relevance is, for them, contracted to the immediate present. For anthropologists by contrast 'sustained practice' secures a different kind of relevance to the present, albeit one that may not be instantly recognizable. It is this kind of sustained practice, this untimely activity, which is currently endangered by the changes that are being imposed on higher education.

Although the implications of these changes are important, as I have suggested, and contesting them is urgent, they are not the only factors that shape the temporality of academic work or forms of academic attentiveness and experimentation. George Marcus asks '[w]here does this untimely work occur?' (Rabinow and Marcus, 2008: 60) and answers, interestingly, with a critical analysis of the burdens that are now placed – 'now' being since his own co-edited *Writing Culture*, which I discussed briefly earlier, was published – 'on the mythic scene of fieldwork and writing ethnography' (Rabinow and Marcus, 2008: 60). He writes: 'With its additional load of developing theory, assessing the present, sustaining a kind of moral discourse, being inventive and original, and so forth, anthropological ethnography, as text, has become very little accountable to the data that comes from fieldwork' (Rabinow and Marcus, 2008: 60). Marcus's point explicates, I think, the difficulties that come from working within a professional discipline which may require juggling between the things a researcher believes her research cannot, for whatever reason, do without and which might indeed be enabling of it but which also, potentially, serve to disable the task of establishing rich and adequately complex relations with the subject of scholarly attention.

Concepts can do this, be disabling, as can forms of explanation. '[S]o much of what is of interest' (Collini, 2011: 11) withers under the glare of pre-given analytical categories. I am returned to the issue of sociological reductionism (Fraser, 2009), or 'sociological fundamentalism' as Stefan Collini puts it. Collini uses these words to describe Ernest Gellner and, in particular, Gellner's work on nationalism. Notably, in his critique of Gellner, Collini (quoting Benedict Anderson) twice uses words associated with magic. 'Or as Anderson puts it', Collini writes, ' "[w]hereas Weber was so bewitched by the spell of nationalism than he was never able to theorise it, Gellner has theorised nationalism without detecting the spell" ' (Anderson in Collini, 2011: 12). This is a challenging balancing act: to be able to recognize the magic of social life, without also being spellbound by it. And to bring sociological knowledge to a problem, without presuming to know what the problem with the problem is in advance. With regards to this latter point, and to return to a key theme in this paper, how is it possible, how possible is it, is it possible, for sociology to allow a problem to pose *itself*? Is it possible, given not only the constraints of contemporary professional academic life but, also, sociology's 'own' investments (as all disciplines are invested) in particular sets of concepts, categories, words, ambitions, desires, commitments and so forth?

My intentions in making this point are not to advocate or endorse especially the 'shift to dialogic or participatory forms of social investigation' (Back, 2007: 18) in sociological research. While it is important that research participants have a 'voice' in the research process, in practice, as Les Back illustrates, the 'gesture towards more democratic forms of research practice may also contain ethical sleights of hand' (Back, 2007: 18). Moreover, as I have noted several times, if the problem lies in the research assemblage as a 'whole', then it cannot by definition be extracted from or located within any single (group of) 'participants'. I do, however, refer to Back's critique of sociological research methods for a reason. It is illustrative, I think, of the sophistication that sociologists bring to bear on the issue of methods in general, and especially their own use of methods. Back goes on to say (and show), for example, how '[e]ven the most righteous research keeps a firm grasp on analytical control and sociological authority' (Back, 2007: 18).

It is the very making of this point that exemplifies, for me, the potential strength – perhaps it is indeed the gift – of 'sociology', and it is here, I think, in the relation of sociology *to* its materials and methods that the answer to the question as to what imagination is 'for' in sociology lies. It is less interesting, ultimately, to ask whether sociology *is* science, or art, or literature than it is to consider what it is that sociology *does*, and perhaps even what it is uniquely able to do. Sociology, as Becker illustrates, has shown itself to be singularly open to the vast diversity of methods that it has (chosen to have) at its disposal. But it is also, more importantly I think, singularly cognizant of, and alive to, the ontological, epistemological, political and ethical implications of different uses of different methodologies and methods and the role they play in enabling alternative, imaginative, patterns of relationality – patterns, that is, of experience. Herein lies the usefulness, as I suggested earlier, of the concept of relationality in research: it necessarily invites questions about the *kinds* of relations we are in or, indeed, the kinds of relations we *could* be in, and what specific arrangements of relations do or do not allow. In one respect at least therefore, to draw attention to relationality is to privilege methods and methodology, for what are methods, after all, but different modes of relating? This is why I think it is a mistake to assume to know in advance what methods are best suited to a set of materials, or what they will or will not produce. It may be a representation of society. Or it may not be. 'Where does untimely work occur?' Marcus asks. In sociology, I think it could occur not in a place, but in an activity. Specifically, in the activity of holding open the question of, and experimenting with, what kinds of relations (experiences) different modes of relating (methods) give rise to or allow. When this is possible (*emkān*), sociology can make-believe realities imaginatively, without also abandoning its disciplinary distinctiveness.

Acknowledgements

As my first publication on *Irradiant*, I would like to thank, above all, Gillian Evison, Virginia Lladó-Buisán, Colin Harris, Vicky Saywell, and Joan Lee at the Bodleian Library, Oxford, for making my experience of working with the archive so joyful. Thanks also to Masserat Amir-Ebrahimi for providing the initial inspiration for this article, and to Gholam Khiabany and Celia Lury for their constructive comments on it. Special thanks to the editors, Nirmal Puwar and Les Back, for their generous and careful readings, and especially for their patience. All errors etc are my own.

Notes

1 Which is not to say that Becker is claiming that this is all they do: 'But even the most formalist critic should realize that some part of the effect of many works of art depend on their "sociological" content' (Becker, 2007: 8).

2 Although professional, disciplinary and other systematized practices are relevant to these issues, as I will be discussing at various points below. For example: while it may well be that a novel tells about society, institutionalized constraints – which are often invoked, it should be noted, by sociologists themselves – mean that a novel is unlikely to be considered a wise/legitimate output for submission by a sociology department to a research evaluation exercise in the UK.

3 I also discuss, in this paper, the problems of writing about sociology as if it were a coherent, homogenous entity. I would like to reference and reiterate those points once again (Fraser, 2009: 65) and to further underscore that the 'sociology' which I am imagining is British/Anglo-American.

4 Although I do not, for the most part, draw directly on Les Back's (2007) work in this article, I am indebted to its spirit. It would be interesting to reflect on the difference between a sociology that *tells* and one that *listens*.

5 The word 'participants' will appear in inverted commas throughout this article because it implies too much that a research project is composed of autonomous entities that have temporarily gathered together.

6 One of the reasons I use the word 'storying' in this article, rather than story-telling, is to displace the privilege that telling has acquired in relation to stories. Although stories are indeed often told, they also emerge from discursive and non-discursive, human and non-human patterns of relations. The notion of storying is in keeping with my comments on problems and their distribution across (or within) a research assemblage and on the difference, as I will be discussing below, between making-believe and make-believe. It is, in short, consistent with a conception of the relationality of the 'participants' that constitute the boundaries of research.

7 A belief known, in Iran, as 'Uncle Napoleanism'. The phrase derives from Iraj Pezeshkzad's (2006) satirical account of the relation between Iran and Britain in *My Uncle Napoleon (Da'i jan Napoleon)* which was first published in Tehran in 1973. As will be clear below, my own view is that while this belief – that foreigners (and especially the British) are behind much of what happens in Iran – has often been justified, it has also been exploited, especially since 1979, with politically damaging and violent consequences.

8 'Thus': my use of this word, which both institutes and confirms a chain of causation, is disingenuous. Of course there were many reasons for taking unpaid leave, some of which are not for telling in a public article. Others are unfathomable, and seem likely to remain so, at least to me.

9 For this I am exceptionally grateful to the generosity of my colleagues in the department, and especially Celia Lury, who made this period of leave possible often against the wishes of the institution. The efforts of all the Heads of Sociology at Goldsmiths during this time meant that my department was always able to employ someone in my place.

10 Interestingly, the AHRC's speculative research route for funding folded in January 2011 in part on account of 'the small numbers of applications received'. Applications for 'adventurous and innovative' research are now being processed through the standard route.

11 For at least two reasons that I can think of here. First, it can sometimes be important (politically important, for example) to be able to use, quickly, efficiently, and with confidence, well-

established and robust sociological methods to contribute to debates about issues of social and political significance. Secondly – a rather different point – it is often the case that, in practice, a research interest unfolds over a long period, sometimes over the length of a career, sometimes over a lifetime, and therefore while it may be that a single project is somewhat over-determined by the demands of the institution or the profession the research *overall* is not. The question is: to what extent is even that 'overall' being squeezed out of existence by changing working conditions?

12 It should be clear that I am not thinking of failure in terms of the description of the limitations of a research project that is inevitably included in a section at the end of a report and which is, now, part of the institutionalized process of succeeding.

13 This is one, intellectual, reason. There were others. For example, I find the use of the notion of 'vocation' – which is how academic work is often described – to justify unrewarded productivity for the institution, whether in or out of paid employment, deeply problematic.

14 Is this really the case? The point would certainly seem to be supported by the historian Carolyn Steedman's account of her relation to the Little Watercress Girl, a child street-trader from the mid-19th century, with whom she 'had a stickily sentimental and 20-year obsession' which ended 'the moment I discovered that she was not "real"' (Steedman, 2008: 21, references omitted). But, are novels such as *Bleak House* obliged to be 'realistic' in the same way that history is?

15 Scientific – and indeed literary – practice is far more complex than this 'ideal' conception allows. I will be returning to this point below.

16 The use of empirical research in literary novels has a long history. Doug Underwood (2008) dates it back to the rise of the novel itself. What makes the new journalism of the 1960s and 1970s 'new', according to John Hartstock (2000), is the critical recognition that it achieved. My discussion of the new journalism here will be confined to the content and form of the text. Other approaches are possible. Hartstock (2000), for instance, explores the implications of the genre in relation to author subjectivity/objectivity.

17 Which is more frequently described as gonzo journalism. Thompson challenged 'the very notion of what qualifies as the correct state of consciousness (sobriety) in reporting on the world' (Hartstock, 2000: 201).

18 The unity conferred on a collection of objects ·and/or documents by its provenance is easily shattered. For example: regardless of the Bodleian Library's *ownership* of the *Irradiant* archive, unless copyright has also been donated to the library, it remains with the different authors of the individual documents in the archive.

19 This is not to judge these books negatively. Rather, in line with Alessandro Portelli, I would prefer to displace the conventional significance attributed to wrongness, error, invention and lies in history-making (Portelli, 1997) and to draw attention instead, as Michel de Certeau does, to the different ways in which belief is established. It is notable, given my own focus here on citations and their various repetitions, that de Certeau should highlight the significance of citation – 'the ultimate weapon for making people believe' (de Certeau, 1984: 188) – in a context where 'the real' is instituted not with reference to what *oneself* believes, but what one believes that *others* believe (de Certeau, 1984: 188–189).

20 But note, importantly, that 'to say that a historical telling cannot be about what happened is not at all to say that nothing happened, or that the past did not happen (whatever saying that might mean)' (Steedman, 2008: 21).

21 Perhaps there is something about conspiracy stories that inspires this splicing together of fact and fiction. One might consider in this context Oliver Stone's controversial film *JFK* (1992). Unlike *JFK,* my 'documentary fiction', if that is what it is, is fully referenced and is therefore probably more in keeping with the style and spirit of Clio Barnard's *The Arbor* (2010), in which 'real' words (that is, words transcribed from interviews) are mouthed by actors in sometimes self-consciously contrived, and sometimes realistic, settings.

22 Although there are of course exceptions. See for example Stoller (2005).

23 I am grateful to Sundar Sarukkai for drawing my attention to the pragmatic dimension of make-believe and for thinking through, with me, the difference between this and make-believe as a form of faith.

24 'In Old English the term *writan* carried the specific meaning "to incise runic letters in stone"' (Ingold, 2007: 43, references omitted). Writing was literally a *drawing* of a sharp point over a surface (much as Ingold describes the drawing of a bow across the strings of a cello).

25 Some of the most affective words are those that lie on the border between speech and song. In this context, Ingold considers plays, which he describes as 'halfway to . . . a score' (Ingold, 2007: 12), and poetry. I am also reminded of theological debates on the recitation of the Qur'an which, according to the rules governing its recitation (tajweed), must be spoken and not sung.

26 Again, I am thinking of 'a thing', minimally, as a pattern of temporarily enduring relations. Words are both *parts of patterns* and *patterned*.

27 See also Cy Twombly's calligraphy-style graffiti paintings and the work of Henri Micheaux.

28 Lury shows that Nike bodies do not *wear* words, nor is the word Nike *secondary* to these bodies. These *are* word-bodies or body-words. This is a problematic example, of course, because Lury is analysing the Nike 'tick' rather than the word Nike. I have included it here, however, because, at this point in my thinking about words, it is not clear to me what precisely a word is. Is a word always made up of letters? With regards to this particular example, one could argue that the Nike tick composes, as letters usually do, the word Nike. Clearly, anyway, there is more to bodies and words than the hand and the gesture. Studies of reading are often quite well attuned to the relation between bodies and words perhaps because, in Antiquity and the Middle Ages, written marks directed readers to audible sounds (see Manguel, 1996; Ingold, 2007: ch. 1 and esp. pp. 13–24).

References

Abrahamian, Ervand, (1993), *Khomeinism: Essays on the Islamic Republic*, Berkeley, CA: University of California Press.

Back, Les, (2007), *The Art of Listening*, Oxford: Berg.

Becker, Howard S., (2007), *Telling about Society*, Chicago: University of Chicago Press.

Bivar, A. D. H., (1998), 'Reassessing Mirdrakvandi: mithraic echoes in the 20th century', in Nicholas Sims-Williams (ed.), *Proceedings of the Third European Conference of Iranian Studies*, 55–70, Wiesbaden: Reichert.

Blencowe, Claire, (2011), *Biopolitical Experience: Foucault, Power and Positive Critique*, London: Palgrave Macmillan.

Capote, Truman, (1981 [1965]), *In Cold Blood: A True Account of a Multiple Murder and its Consequences*, London: Sphere.

Cartwright, Nancy, (1983), *How the Laws of Physics Lie*, Oxford: Oxford University Press.

Clifford, James, (1986), 'Introduction: impartial truths', in James Clifford and George E. Marcus (eds), *Writing Culture: The Poetics and Politics of Ethnography*, Berkeley, CA: University of California Press.

Collini, Stefan, (2011), '"What's not to like?", review of *Ernest Gellner: An Intellectual Biography*, by John Hall', *London Review of Books*, 33 (11): 10–12.

Das, Veena, (2007), *Life and Words: Violence and the Descent into the Ordinary*, Berkeley, CA: University of California Press.

De Certeau, Michel, (1984), 'Believing and making people believe', in *The Practice of Everyday Life*, Berkeley, CA: University of California Press.

Didion, Joan, (1974 [1968]), *Slouching towards Bethlehem*, Harmondsworth: Penguin.

Dorril, Stephen, (2001), *MI6: Fifty Years of Special Operations*, London: Fourth Estate.

Elm, Mostafa, (1992), *Oil, Power, and Principle: Iran's Oil Nationalization and its Aftermath*, New York: Syracuse University Press.

Foucault, Michel, (1966), *Les Mots et Les Choses*, Paris: Gallimard.

Fraser, Mariam, (2009), 'Experiencing Sociology', *European Journal of Social Theory*, 12 (1): 63–81.

Gasiorowski, Mark, J., (1987), 'The 1953 coup d'etat in Iran', *International Journal of Middle Eastern Studies*, 19: 261–286.

Hartstock, John C., (2000), A *History of American Literary Journalism: The Emergence of a Modern Narrative Form*, Amherst: University of Massachusetts Press.

Ingold, Tim, (2007), *Lines: A Brief History*, London: Routledge.

Ingold, Tim, (2011), 'In defence of handwriting', available at: http://www.dur.ac.uk/writingacrossboundaries/writingonwriting/timingold/ (accessed 28 April 2012).

Jackson, Peter, (2010), '*Working with the archival material of intelligence and security agencies of Britain, France and the US: comparative perspectives'*, paper delivered at The Political Life of Documents: Archives, Memory and Contested Knowledge, *CRASSH*, Cambridge, 15–16 January.

Kinzer, Stephen, (2003), *All the Shah's Men: An American Coup and the Roots of Middle East Terror*, New York: John Wiley and Sons.

Latour, Bruno, (1997), 'Introduction', in Isabelle Stengers, *Power and Invention: Situating Science*, trans. Paul Bains, Minneapolis: University of Minnesota Press.

Lepenies, Wolf, (1992), *Between Literature and Science: The Rise of Sociology*, Cambridge: Cambridge University Press.

Louis, Wm. Roger, (2006), *Ends of British Imperialism: The Scramble for Empire, Suez and Decolonization*, London: I. B. Tauris.

Lury, Celia, (2008), 'Marking time with Nike: the illusion of the durable', *Public Culture*, 11 (3): 499–526.

Mailer, Norman, (1968), *Armies of the Night: History as a Novel, the Novel as History.* New York: New American Library.

Manguel, Alberto, (1996), *A History of Reading,* London: HarperCollins.

Mills, C. Wright, (2000 [1959]), *The Sociological Imagination*, Oxford: Oxford University Press.

Pahlavi, Princess Ashraf, (1980), *Faces in a Mirror: Memoirs from Exile*, Englewood Cliffs, NJ: Prentice-Hall.

Pezeshkzad, Iraj, (2006 [1973]), *My Uncle Napoleon*, trans. Dick Davis, New York: The Modern Library.

Plummer, Ken, (2001), *Documents of Life 2: An Invitation to Critical Humanism*, London: Sage.

Portelli, Alessandro, (1997), *The Battle of Valle Giulia: Oral History and the Art of Dialogue*, Madison: University of Wisconsin Press.

Porter, Venetia, (2006), *Word into Art: Artists of the Modern Middle East*, London: The British Museum Press.

Rabinow, P. and Marcus, G. E. with Faubion, J. D. and Rees, T., (2008), *Designs for an Anthropology of the Contemporary*, Durham and London: Duke University Press.

Salter, Chris, (2011), 'JND: An artistic experiment in bodily experience as research', in Deniz Peters, Gerhard Eckel and Andreas Dorschel (eds), *Bodily Expression in Electronic Music: Perspectives on a Reclaimed Performativity*, New York: Routledge.

Sarukkai, Sundar, (2006–2007), 'Literary reality and scientific fiction', *Jadavpur Journal of Comparative Literature*, 44: 48–66.

Sarukkai, Sundar, (2010), 'Many faces: reimagining the moon', *Leonardo*, 43 (3): 216–217.

Sennett, Richard, (2008), *The Craftsman*, London: Penguin.

Steedman, Carolyn, (2001), *Dust*, Manchester: Manchester University Press.

Steedman, Carolyn, (2008), 'Intimacy in research: accounting for it', *History of Human Sciences,* 21 (4): 17–33.

Stengers, Isabelle, (2002), 'Beyond conversation: the risks of peace', in C. Keller and A. Daniell (eds), *Process and Difference: Between Cosmological and Poststructuralist Postmodernisms*, New York: State University of New York Press.

Stoller, Paul, (2005), *Stranger in the Village of the Sick: A Memoir of Cancer, Sorcery and Healing*, Boston: Beacon Press.

Thompson, Hunter S., (1972 [1971]), *Fear and Loathing in Las Vegas: A Savage Journey to the Heart of the American Dream*, London: Paladin.

The Sociological Review, 60:S1, pp. 84–107 (2012), DOI: 10.1111/j.1467-954X.2012.02118.x
© 2012 The Author. Editorial organisation © 2012 The Editorial Board of the Sociological Review

Underwood, Doug, (2008), *Journalism and the Novel: Truth and Fiction, 1700–2000*, Cambridge: Cambridge University Press.

Welty, Eudora, (1984), *One Writer's Beginnings*, Cambridge, MA: Harvard University Press.

Whitehead, Alfred N., (1978), *Process and Reality*, corrected edition, ed. D. R. Griffin and D. W. Sherburne, New York: The Free Press.

Wolfe, Tom, (1981 [1965]), *Kandy-Kolored Tangerine-Flake Streamline Baby,* London: Picador.

Zaehner, R. C., (1965), 'Zoroastrian survivals in Iranian folklore', *Iran: Journal of the British Institute of Persian Studies*, III: 87–96.

Zaehner, R. C., (1992), 'Zoroastrian survivals in Iranian folklore II', *Iran: Journal of the British Institute of Persian Studies*, XXX: 65–76.

Learning to be affected: social suffering and total pain at life's borders

Yasmin Gunaratnam

Abstract: The practice of live sociology in situations of pain and suffering is the focus of this article. An outline of the challenges of understanding pain is followed by a discussion of Bourdieu's 'social suffering' (1999) and the palliative care philosophy of 'total pain'. Using examples from qualitative research on disadvantaged dying migrants in the UK, attention is given to the methods that are improvised by dying people and care practitioners in attempts to bridge intersubjective divides, where the causes and routes of pain can be ontologically and temporally indeterminate and/or withdrawn. The paper contends that these latter phenomena are the incitement for the inventive bridging and performative work of care and live sociological methods, both of which are concerned with opposing suffering. Drawing from the philosophy of total pain, I highlight the importance of (1) an engagement with a range of materials out of which attempts at intersubjective bridging can be produced, and which exceed the social, the material, and the temporally linear; and (2) an empirical sensibility that is hospitable to the inaccessible and non-relational.

Keywords: death, interdisciplinarity, migrants, ontology, palliative care

My 'live sociology' takes its vital inspiration from death.

For the past 15 years or so, pushed and pulled by biographical events, I have been researching migrants, illness, death and dying.[1] There is an existential and carnal density to this world of life at its limits that makes tangible a central sociological problematic – that of intersubjective communication and understanding. In Les Back's preliminary sketching of 'live sociology', understanding the experiences of others is an abiding methodological concern and one which carries an ethical charge: sociologists have a responsibility to seek out and bring to publicity 'the fragments, the voices and stories that are otherwise passed over or ignored' (2007: 1). Here, through a discussion of pain and disadvantaged dying migrants, I show how following idiosyncratic fragments and the fleeting can bring us not only to the larger and longer lasting, but also to the recessive, indeterminate and discontinuous qualities of life.

What is sociologically interesting and distinctive about transnational dying is that it is a situation constituted by two radical and simultaneous registers and

The Sociological Review, 60:S1, pp. 108–123 (2012), DOI: 10.1111/j.1467-954X.2012.02119.x

thresholds of estrangement: the spatio-temporal and the phenomenological. There is a dramatic ethico-political significance to such borders Derrida tells us, making explicit the edges of belonging, language and territorialization and where 'borders of property' are not only grounded but also carry a metaphysical resonance connoting 'the right of property to our own life' (1993: 5). The idea of life as 'property' is a complicated one, evoking life as a province – a territory that is as much temporal as it is spatial – marked by borders to the unknown,[2] rendering it discontinuous and choppy, never at one with itself. And because all human life is characterized by thresholds and 'a common ontological condition as vulnerable' (Turner, 2006: 9) there are wider inferences to be made from the worlds of dislocated dying. Despite the ever-increasing contests over territorial boundaries, as Dikeç *et al.* remind us 'what is also always with us are the borders, thresholds, and turning points of ordinary, embodied existence. And these are no less significant than the more concrete figures of mobility and transition' (2009: 11).

Here, through a focus on pain, I will explicate something of what I have learned about methodology and ontology from the improvisations of dying migrants and care professionals at life's thresholds. There are two main things that I want to do. First, I suggest the value of multiple and interconnected analytic registers by bringing into conversation sociological accounts of 'social suffering' (Bourdieu, 1999) with what in palliative care is called 'total pain'. Total pain interpolates, and at times creolizes, physical, social, psychological and spiritual pain (Saunders, 1964). It also gives recognition to pain that is accrued over a lifetime.

Total pain is a multimodal method of auscultation and care as much as it is a philosophy. It seeks to invent and legitimize ways of reading and becoming receptive to multifarious situations *as* pain. In this regard, it is a performative method and care practice that both describes and helps to bring to symbolization the phenomena it tries to apprehend and get close to. A distinctive value of the inventiveness of total pain is how it provides for the assembling of heterogeneous phenomena within the domains of pain. However, unlike a flat ontology (DeLanda, 2002), it avoids a 'smear of equivalence' between entities (Lorimer, 2005: 88) by not presupposing that phenomena have an analogous status and by allowing for that which is ontologically and temporally insecure and/or withdrawn. The latter entities are not fully accessible in the here and now. They can lack a referent and/or inherent, stable qualities (see also Barad, 2007). I will argue that it is the excessive haunting of the withdrawn that incites the experimental bridging work of care, where improvised attempts to alleviate suffering cannot always rely upon an evidence base in sensual knowledge. In this regard, responsibility for – and accountability to – what is withdrawn constitutes a space of ethics (Levinas, 1994). And sometimes of politics.

Second, and relatedly, I examine the effects of these complex interfaces between entities and the work that they inspire, in relation to my knowledge exchange practices and the movements between circuits of 'learning to be affected' (Latour, 2004) by a diversity of realities and perspectives, and being affected and provoked to learn. This is an interdisciplinarity where the limitations of existing knowledge can produce transformations in a given 'logic of ontology' of pain (Barry *et al.*, 2008). But more of this later. Let me first contextualize some more by describing the challenges of accounting for painful experiences.

Pain

> Physical pain does not simply resist language but destroys it, bringing about an immediate reversion to a state anterior to language, to the sounds and cries a human being makes before language is learned. (Scarry, 1987: 4)

At the heart of attempts to apprehend human pain and suffering is an implicit falling short of methodology and analysis (Bourdieu, 1999; Harrison, 2007). These experiential states, however loud and flailing, are deemed to mark a certain aporetic; a detachment and retreat from word and world. As Harrison puts it 'experiences of suffering are quasicontradictory experiences in that they tend towards the limits of experience, towards the unexperienceable and irrecuperable' (2007: 595). This falling back of the self into a depth of experiencing disturbs long-standing philosophical injunctions from Descartes' *cogito* to Nietzschian vitalism. It is also problematic for Anglophone interpretative social science and the pervading legacy of Verstehende approaches where a defining claim is that 'subjective understanding is the specific characteristic of sociological knowledge' (Weber, 1947: 104).

Yet even in the most radical accounts of pain as a destroyer of language, recognition is given to the role of pain translation and advocacy and to those such as physicians, where the success of the medical practitioner is dependent upon 'the acuity with which he or she can hear the fragmentary language of pain, coax it into clarity, and interpret it' (Scarry, 1987: 6). The role of pain translation and advocacy also exists in the social sciences where the demands that pain, trauma, vulnerability and suffering make upon social analysis have been given sustained attention (Bar-On, 1999; Harrison, 2007; Frost and Hoggett, 2008; Waddell, 1989; Warin and Dennis, 2008).

What characterizes these social science discussions is the recognition that pain and distress can be produced by the social: by inequality, marginalization, injustice, powerlessness and persecution. It is perhaps not surprising that such forms of suffering can manifest at the end of life for socially disadvantaged migrants, where lives are looked back on, regret and losses can (re)surface, and selves and bodies can become both more salient and more vulnerable as illness progresses and also at different stages of the care pathway that involve varying degrees and rhythms of exposure (Gunaratnam, 2008b). In a Swedish study, nurses reported that caring for refugees and for survivors of the Nazi concentration camps often demanded greater attention to the routines and technical procedures of bodily care. One nurse described how 'we had a patient who had been in a concentration camp . . . it was awful of course . . . talking about

The Sociological Review, 60:S1, pp. 108–123 (2012), DOI: 10.1111/j.1467-954X.2012.02119.x
© 2012 The Author. Editorial organisation © 2012 The Editorial Board of the Sociological Review

gas . . . she had great difficulty in breathing and it was extremely hard and there were so many memories involved in it all . . .' (Ekblad *et al.*, 2000: 628).

I have also found that at diagnosis, particularly if it is perceived to be problematic, commonly expressed questions of 'why?' (Saunders, 2006) and 'why me?' (Stanworth, 2004) can, for dying migrants, take on a twist of 'is it me?' A story recounted in a focus group interview by Mita, a Cancer Nurse Specialist, speaks of how the felt injustices of diagnostic care can resonate with the injuries of racism, producing a layered distress. Mita's story concerned an Indian Hindu patient with terminal cancer. The man's cancer had been repeatedly misdiagnosed leaving him feeling angry and distressed. The patient had been a teacher in India and on settlement in the UK could not get a teaching job, so had worked in factories and as a bus driver. In Mita's words:

> I think it (his feelings of being excluded from professional employment) had an impact on how he dealt with his condition, because unfortunately his diagnosis had been quite delayed. For a year he'd been going backwards and forwards to the GP, telling him all the classic symptoms of what he'd got . . . he still had this idea and he said 'I know I'm educated and I know I'm completely in the wrong box. I think they haven't treated me properly because I am who I am, because saying I was only good enough for bus driving, not for teaching and for the same reason they didn't think I was important enough to be diagnosed early enough to be treated in the right way.' And I found that very hard. That was really difficult, that was hard for me to take. I mean what can you say? . . . What can I actually say to him that's actually going to make a difference to him? And I found that really difficult. (Gunaratnam, 2008a: 35)

For Mita, the intractable problem is how to respond to and alleviate the patient's anguish at the multiple injustices he feels. In the study *The Weight of the World* (1999), first published in French in 1993, Pierre Bourdieu uses the term 'social suffering' to recognize such experiences and to examine the relationships between *la grande* misère (material inequality) and *la petite* misère or the 'ordinary suffering' of living with inequality and injustice. The *Weight of the World* combines ethnographic and interview methods to produce a series of pen portraits of ordinary suffering across and within different social strata. In the study there is a continuous overlapping between the social, the somatic and the 'spiritual' as Bourdieu calls it.

The weight of the world

Because of the difficulties in expressing social suffering, sociological attentiveness to it has to be cultivated Bourdieu argues, through 'active and methodological listening' (1999: 609). In the project, interviewers often had a long-standing connection to, and embodied familiarity with the research sites and the participants, a practice developed by the research team to reduce social asymmetries and the risks of symbolic violence. In some respects and despite claims to the contrary, the methodological disposition that Bourdieu and his collaborators sought to develop – 'to situate oneself in the place the interviewees occupy in

the social space in order to understand them as necessarily *what they are . . .*'
(1999: 613, author's emphasis) – appears close to an affective empathetic version
of Weber's Verstehen. However, for Bourdieu, the aim was to confect an
extraordinary attentiveness and proximity in the interviews in order to cut
through the 'we've already seen and heard it all' (1999: 614) cynicism of the
researcher, and to reach a practical understanding of how social structures and
histories can be *felt* in each research participant's 'idiosyncrasy'.

Angela McRobbie (2002) has criticized Bourdieu's study for its sentimental-
ity, lack of thick description and methodological rigour. The careful documenting and exposition of the negotiation between subjectivity and objectivity and
theoretical and practical knowledge that usually characterize Bourdieu's empirical research, although present, are certainly more muted in this project. Instead,
the pain translation and advocacy role of the sociologist is emphasized and situated in her ability to give time, space and self to the interviewee and 'like a
mid-wife' (1999: 621) to bring deep buried suffering and discontent into the
world of expression and understanding. This is not the 'communication as com-
munion' (Shields, 1996: 276) model of Verstehen that Rob Shields has critiqued
so vigorously. 'Against the old distinction made by Wilhem Dilthey', Bourdieu
contends 'we must posit that *understanding and explaining are one*' (1999: 613,
author's emphasis). In such qualifications and differentiations, Bourdieu appears
acutely aware of the normative and controversial nature of his empirical
approach to suffering:

> at the risk of shocking both the rigorous methodologist and the inspired hermeneutic
> scholar, I would say that the interview can be considered a sort of *spiritual exercise*
> that . . . aims at a *true conversion of the way we* look at other people in the ordinary
> circumstances of life. The welcoming disposition, which leads one to make the respon-
> dent's problems one's own, the capacity to take that person and understand them just
> as they are in their distinctive necessity, is a sort of *intellectual love* . . . (1999: 614,
> emphasis in original)

The words 'spiritual'[3] and 'love' emphasized so provocatively by Bourdieu point
to the limits of the 'scientific intent' (1999: 621) of social research. In its place
Bourdieu institutes sociology as a 'craft', entailing improvisation and intersubjective and intercorporeal bridging work between the interviewer and research
participant 'so as to help respondents deliver up their truth, or, rather, to be
delivered of it' (1999: 621).

Social suffering and the more-than-social

Mindful of McRobbie's critique of *The Weight of the World*, I am interested in
what Bourdieu and his colleagues were trying to get at with their flagrant, if
ambivalent, detours outside of methodological orthodoxy and into the more-
than-social. In many respects their stubborn allegiance to the specific social
constitution of suffering is very much in evidence throughout the project, ensuring that 'ordinary suffering' remains within sociological reach: it can be com-

prehended, thematized and explained empirically. But there is also a more intermittent acknowledgement of how attention to the 'idiosyncrasy' of suffering can necessitate a move outside of disciplinary traditions, so that analysis and methodology overflow into such matters as spirit and love that breach and offend scientific enterprise, categories and language. In this respect, and taking into account the long history of forensic attention to methodological practice that marks Bourdieu's research, there seems to be something more profound and artful going on than the 'sociological opportunism' that Angela McRobbie has read into the researchers' empirical rule-breaking (2002: 134). In the context of my research experiences, I want to suggest that Bourdieu's forays into the more-than-social can be read as a contact with the vitality and anti-thematizing qualities of suffering and the impossibility of limiting the affects and effects of the painful to one sphere of life and being.

The unruliness of pain, and the coincidence of the thresholds of the geo-social and the phenomenological, can be found in the situation of Ibrahim, a 46-year-old Ghanaian refugee with kidney cancer. Ibrahim had migrated to the UK in the 1980s as a part of a cohort of Ghanaians escaping political persecution. I interviewed him in his hospice bed, ten days before he died. Ibrahim's physical pain percolated into the form and content of our interview. He alternated between sitting up and lying down to relieve his pain. Spasms of pain were perceptible in his intonation and in the recuperative pauses and breaths that he took when speaking, leaving the transcript punctured by ellipses. My concerns about Ibrahim meant that I ended the interview prematurely and we made plans to resume our conversation a couple of days later. By that time Ibrahim was slipping into unconsciousness and I did not talk to him again.

The one interview that I had with Ibrahim was taken up by stories of his illness, diagnosis, and migration to the UK: '*I knew if I didn't move out of the country I would either lose my, my peace or my life altogether*'. He talked at length about his economic concerns: the financial future of his partner and 16-month-old baby in the UK, and how his extended family and two children in Ghana would survive without his regular remittances. Ibrahim worried aloud about the cultural identity of his baby son. At the time when we met, hospice doctors were overhauling Ibrahim's drugs to better control his pain and hospice social workers had secured a small grant to ease the family's financial burdens. Ibrahim had come up with his own solution to the problem he saw facing his baby. He wanted to be buried in Ghana:

> I want my son to (. . .) one day not just melt away into this society, but think of a place where he comes from and one day, or once in a while go back there, and when he goes there and then there's this grave stone standing there and say 'Oh that's your Dad lying down there' just gives him some kind of attachment to a place which I will cherish (. . .) yeah, but if he stays here, just melts away into society and that's the end (. . .).

The constituency of Ibrahim's situation and the materials that he talked of using to bridge the thresholds of life and death, and here and there, bring into view the affective, physical and metaphysical dimensions of the geo-social. We can understand something of Ibrahim's improvisations socially with regard to his citizenship status, cultural and masculinist concerns of inheritance, wider transnational networks and repatriation death rituals amongst Ghanaian migrants (see Krause, 2008). All of these phenomena provide insight into the movements of material and semiotic resources in Ibrahim's life. Nevertheless, to reduce these diverse matters to the social would be to abolish the many novel coordinates of Ibrahim's predicament. In a Northern European context, Ibrahim's desire for a post-death connection with his son is an anti-rational temporization, which, following Lisa Adkins (2009a), we might call 'event time'. For Adkins, event time marks a departure from the normative dominance of mechanical clock time that characterized industrial capitalism. In contrast, event time signifies a temporality that 'no longer stands outside phenomena . . . but unfolds *with* phenomena' (Adkins, 2009b: 336, original emphasis). Event time is thought to be a product of contemporary transformations in the social field from a territory to a contingent circulation.

The problem of how to ensure a child known in the present connects with a country he may have no experience of in the future, and where in the past his father was endangered, is a new affective and spatio-temporal drama and source of distress for Ibrahim. It is a predicament where questions of territory and circulation are coincident in the production of time. In these complicated circumstances, the attempt to forge an attachment, or to perhaps make a claim upon his son's future identity, is made by casting a lifeline[4] from a speech act requiring social (understanding of intention) and material (repatriation, burial, Ghanaian soil) uptake.

In this ethnographic study, I was able to follow what happened to Ibrahim after his death: his family in the UK could not afford to bury him in Ghana. The social *a priori* in such circumstance is imposing and seemingly determining, inhibiting the actualization of Ibrahim's desire for a post-mortem agency, and pointing to the force of broader socio-economic patterns. Valuable as ethnographic methods are in following the movement of practices and affects (Mol, 2006), they have their limits in tracking the contingencies, non-linearities and metaphysics of uptake and actualization; the ways in which Ibrahim's desire for a lifeline to his son might end with his burial in the UK, or might yet unfurl through unpredictable, and for me unknowable and untraceable, future events.

If Ibrahim's story brings into view the multiple layers of the geo-social, it also pushes attentiveness to improvisation outside of the social – to such matters as flesh, soil and spirit, and to the weird temporalities and idiosyncrasies of event time. However, Ibrahim's bridging work is more of a once-in-a-life-time method (a technique) than a developing methodology (a systematic theoretical and philosophical framework). It is in the work of care practitioners, who are involved in the daily work of attempting to bridge intersubjective divides that I have been able to better understand the value of the ontology of total pain and how it is relevant to the practising of live sociology.

Total pain: 'all of me is wrong'

> I remember one patient who said, when asked to describe her pain: 'Well, doctor, it began in my back but now it seems that all of me is wrong,' and she then described her other symptoms. She went on . . . 'I could have cried for the pills and injections but knew that I must not. My husband and son were wonderful but they were having to stay off work and lose their money.' She was suffering a 'total pain'. . . . It is, in a way, somewhat artificial thus to divide a whole experience but it may give an internal checklist on meeting a new patient. (Saunders, 1988: 171–172)

The biopsychosocial challenges of alleviating the chronic pain that characterizes terminal disease preoccupied Cicely Saunders, a philosophy student, turned nurse, social worker and then physician.[5] Saunders collected over 1,000 patient narratives, and used them, together with patient drawings, writing and poetry, to develop her ideas on end-of-life care and total pain. Saunders approached chronic pain as a 'situation' rather than an event (Saunders, 1970), requiring practitioners to be 'attentive to the body, to the family and to [the] patient's inner life' (2006: 217).

Taking her inspiration from patient narratives, Saunders argued that the constituency and temporality of pain had to be approached as a complex heterogeneity that included not only the physiological but also the social, economic and existential, so that focus shifted from the genre of disease, and from biochemistry and drugs, to treating the many symptoms of a terminal condition. In the domains of total pain, the plural constituents of pain are allowed a mysterious ecology, sometimes intra-relating and sometimes distinguishable, both substantial and withdrawn, requiring multidisciplinary, but also inventive care. And whilst recognition of total pain does not by itself ensure effective pain relief, the effort of *trying* to understand an-other's needs for care, even when one fails, remained practically and ethically significant for the content and quality of care practices (see also Mol, 2008).

In similar ways to Bourdieu's *The Weight of the World*, Saunders' work with pain often strayed into matters of the immaterial and unquantifiable: 'The spirit is more than the body which contains it' (Saunders, 1961: 396). Unlike Bourdieu, Cicely Saunders' work with death entailed recognizing irredeemable loss and the limitations of the bridging work of care in responding to different integrities, genealogies, temporalities and scales of pain. For every success story in Saunders' writing – a patient whose emotional pain is relieved by the right choice and dose of a tranquillizer – there is also often a reminder that some forms of pain cannot be explained or eased, so that in the case of emotional distress she writes 'a good deal of suffering has to be lived through' (2006: 219). The role of the care practitioner in such circumstances is marked by a quintessential passivity, and where attentiveness is not necessarily a bridge to the other 'We are not there to take away or explain, or even to understand but simply to "Watch with me". . .' (Saunders, 2006: 219). Here, responsiveness to pain and to its enigmas transfigures into a non-acting serving and standing-by of others (Waddell, 1989).

In working between the quantitative empiricism of medicine – observing, measuring, indexing, calculating, trialling – and what Alain Badiou (2002) would call a fidelity to the unknown, Saunders' work questions disciplinary boundaries. It also reinstates care as a part of human adventuring (see Greco, 2009) requiring technical skills and expertise and 'negative capability'. 'Negative capability' is the term that the poet Keats (1958 [1817]) has used to denote the capacity to tolerate incomplete understanding and mystery. Whilst not forgetting that the 'total' of total pain raises matters of a non-innocent inscription and expanded surveillance (Clark, 1999), its domains and claims are not as totalizing as its nomenclature suggests. Rather than signifying a closed system, total pain seems to point to the infinite, acknowledging that even with its openness to diverse registers of pain, painful entities can elude understanding and control. In this non-relational ontology, recognition of the puncta produced by the cryptic and withdrawn qualities of painful things suggest that phenomena can always be more (or less) than the sum of their relations.

It is difficult to find concise examples from my research that demonstrate total pain as an inventive care practice, but an event that comes close, was described by a community-based nurse Rachel (see Gunaratnam, 2008b). Shortly before I interviewed Rachel, she had spent most of the afternoon on the telephone trying to find a specialist pressure-relieving mattress for a double bed (they are most commonly available to the National Health Service for single beds). The mattress was for a couple, originally from Jamaica. The husband, in his mid-seventies, had prostate cancer that had spread throughout his body and was unable to sleep at night because of a cough. In Rachel's opinion 'The cough is his way of trying to keep himself awake because he's afraid he'll die in his sleep.' The couple were finding it difficult to talk to each other and to professionals about the progressing cancer and the husband's impending death. In the interview Rachel told me:

> My staff nurse had seen him first and had ordered a highfaluting pressure mattress. So I went to see them and said 'My colleague has ordered this for you, where do you normally sleep?' And the wife said 'Well, we've slept in the same bed for 43 years'. And I said 'Well how will you manage if we put your husband in a single bed?' 'Oh I'll sleep in a camp bed next to him.' I said 'Well at the moment things seem to be OK. If I get a double mattress would that be more preferable?' And that was what she wanted and that's what we've done. I think we will probably need to get a hospital bed and a super-duper mattress another two weeks down the line, but we've given them another 3 or 4 weeks of sleeping next to each other in bed, which I think is much more important for the moment while they build up their trust of us and cope with the loss of each other.

The three to four extra weeks of sleeping together that Rachel's act of poetic realism brought to this couple are significant both with regard to the increased valuing and pertinence of mechanical clock time for those who are dying, and in relation to an event time of togetherness that is unquantifiable. In the ontology of total pain the qualities of the mattress can be thought of as a psychic

The Sociological Review, 60:S1, pp. 108–123 (2012), DOI: 10.1111/j.1467-954X.2012.02119.x
© 2012 The Author. Editorial organisation © 2012 The Editorial Board of the Sociological Review

and material bridge and a substrate that can continue to connect and support the couple in Rachel's absence. As an affective underpinning, the significance of the mattress and its potential to relieve suffering is indivisible from its materiality; the extent to which its form and sensual qualities are themselves 'actants' in the Latourian sense, impressed by two variously suffering bodies, a cough, the physiology and metaphysics of sleep for a dying man, and suspicion of professionals.

Tracing and speculating about the overlapping layers of pain and palliation involved in Rachel's improvised use of the mattress as a care practice would be theoretically and methodologically productive (see Harman, 2009 for a lively discussion of these matters). However, radical relationality with its emphasis on the ubiquity of relations is not necessarily sensitive to the ethical imperatives of total pain or to its recognition of the withdrawn, where the sources, substance and genealogy of painful entities can be mysterious and disjunctive, whilst fracturing the present. For this reason I want to draw attention to the ways in which the mattress as a performative act of attentiveness and care is characterized by an inventive use of available resources *and* negative capability. Rachel cannot verify the sources or different knots of pain that are involved in her patient's situation. She does not know that the mattress will alleviate pain and convey her recognition of the slow losses and fears that she feels this couple are living through. There are no clinical trials or evidence base that she can draw upon. Rather, Rachel's version of total pain is created and emerges from her relationship to the couple, and out of some regard for materials and affects in their everyday lives. Such palliative care-giving works off implicated interconnections between signs and the real, it seems cognizant of how emotions can materialize by 'sticking' to certain objects (Ahmed, 2004), but it also allows painful entities a non-presentness or 'dark diachronicity' as Wyschogrod might call it (1990: 108).

In this necessarily abbreviated account are the basic tenets of total pain that at first glance seems to operate much like a flat ontology, one in which tumours as much as mattresses and coughs are recognized as contiguous, intra-acting components of pain. Yet total pain also leaves spaces for the effects of undisclosed and unfathomable entities that can defy the most bespoke titration of drugs or care-full listening, so that the 'total' of total pain operates more as a provocation for care and as a tentative placeholder for a pluralized known and unknown.

Learning to be affected

The philosophy of total pain revitalizes social science discussions of the limits of understanding pain and suffering. It also raises questions of what might be at stake in the revisions and extensions to the empirical that I have suggested that total pain implies. These questions become less abstract when applied to my ongoing teaching and collaboration with palliative care professionals. Consider what can happen in teaching when I use case stories generated from my empirical research.

The case story of Maxine describes the end-of-life care of a 63-year-old hospice patient, a retired hospital domestic who lived alone in a council house (see Gunaratnam, 2004). Maxine had talked to me in some detail, and over a period of months, about her life with her violent ex-husband. She also recounted, with incongruous wit, several incidents of racist violence on the streets of South London in the 1960s, relatively soon after she had migrated to the UK from Jamaica. In the narrating of each account Maxine was more of a heroine than a victim. In one story of a racist attack when she was seven months pregnant, Maxine described giving chase to the young perpetrators who were forced to hide in a local shop, adding *'Every time I pass that shop . . . I stand up and give a little laugh, 'cause I remember that's where they run.'*

When Maxine was admitted into the hospice for terminal care, she grew increasingly agitated. She said that she felt anxious when being lifted and touched. Some of her nurses were overly loud, and she suspected, racist: *'those girls no respect no black people'*. Maxine's nurses were not unaware of some of these anxieties and team members discussed the need to show sensitivity to Maxine's fears and 'paranoia'. In the last days of her life Maxine began to resist all routine care practices, so that her death was 'dirty' (Lawton, 2000).

In multidisciplinary teaching sessions we discuss what might be involved in Maxine's situation. If it has not been raised, and drawing from the insights of feminist and psychoanalytic scholarship, I suggest how histories of gendered and racialized violence can be implicated in Maxine's anxieties about her bodily care. In making sense of the care problematic a doctor might layer the suggestions into what she has learned from 20 years of clinical practice and from evidence-based research: paranoia, agitation and hyper-sensitivity to touch and to noise can be the consequence of drugs, biopathology, and of dying itself. A social worker may draw upon pedagogies of anti-oppressive practice (Dominelli, 2002) and diversity training, relating the case story to his experiences of counselling survivors of war and women who have been raped, for whom physical care can be traumatic.

A crucial point is that the generation of these possibilities does not simply take place through a semiotic expansion – a piling up of new symbolic categories onto existing experiential and disciplinary knowledge in order to signify with greater accuracy, a previously unthought, but ultimately generalizable real. Neither is the aim to retrieve or recover to the present a lost (explanatory) object of pain in Maxine's past. Rather, these interdisciplinary exchanges become highly focused contextualizing and specifying practices through which we can become variously sensitized (depending upon the nature of different sites of care-giving) to more qualities and registers of Maxine's pain, including those that elude us. In this process, it is attentiveness to the singularities of Maxine's situation that can produce shifts in our ontology of pain, so that the content of the experienced world expands. This process is broadly akin to what the actor

The Sociological Review, 60:S1, pp. 108–123 (2012), DOI: 10.1111/j.1467-954X.2012.02119.x

network theorist Bruno Latour calls 'articulation', a bodily practice of 'learning to be affected by differences' (2004: 210). It is a process that does not rely upon an object/subject, nature/culture split or upon common, uncontested epistemologies. For Latour, 'The more you articulate controversies, the wider the world becomes' (2004: 211).

Being affected to learn

Latour's 'learning to be affected', although firmly defined as an embodied awareness, is relevant to thinking about methodology, ethics and the role of live sociological research: how might the attentiveness of live sociology be articulated? There is a supplement that I would add to the consideration of this question. In my teaching and learning with care professionals it is apparent that we are already affected by our encounters with pain, suffering and vulnerability. At the same time there are aspects of entities and others that cannot be fully recuperated into a taught, interdisciplinary or sensual affectedness. No matter how many different perspectives, experiences and levels of analysis are brought to the interpretation of Maxine's case-studied life, no matter how questions of disciplinary knowledge production are kept in sight, there are always aspects of her experience that are singularly untranslatable. So whilst the content of our worlds have expanded through our encounters with Maxine and with each other, we cannot claim to fully understand the sources, routes, levels, temporality and meanings of Maxine's pain.

And so, within learning to be affected there is also the unintelligible and the undecidable. It is this unintelligibility – an empirical counterpart of the withdrawn in philosophies of total pain – that can become an inspiration or interpellation to the bridging work of sociological attentiveness and the improvisations of methodology. In other words there are circuits or relays of inter-dependency between learning to be affected and being affected to learn which gain traction and impetus from the things we cannot resolve, recover or connect, but which nevertheless have a status as a response (Harrison, 2007).

'Incomprehensibility', Derrida writes '. . . is not the beginning of irrationalism but the wound or inspiration which opens speech and then makes possible every logos or every rationalism' (1978: 98). There are two notions of fidelity at work here: remaining faithful to the idiom and the milieu of what is unknowable, whilst also searching for, and using every possible means by which to know it differently. I am thinking here about the commonplace but often underdescribed 'wounding' inspirations of empirical research: Bourdieu's (1999: 622) struggles with the 'infidelities' of transcribing interviews; his admission that it took him over a decade (with repeated listening to an interview recording) to better appreciate the depth of the precarious existence of two farmers whom he had known personally for a long time; and my own turn to poetry and creative writing to evoke and convey non-linearities and enigma (Gunaratnam, 2007[6]). As Graham and Thrift (2007) have also recognized despite its origins in failure and fault, in improvisation there is always the hope of a provisional responsiveness and learning:

> Improvisation allows the work of maintenance and repair to go on when things may seem bleak and it takes in a whole series of responses, from simple repetition (such as trying it again) through to attempts to improve communication so as to be clear exactly what the problem is, through disagreement over causes, through to complex theorizing, responses which are often the result of long and complex apprenticeships and other means of teaching . . . (2007: 4)

Of course we need to be careful about valorizing or embracing too readily, the unintelligible. The unknown as beyond question always risks becoming complicit with the mystifications of social and political abjection (Spivak, 1988; Butler, 2004), or of neglecting the more mundane ways in which empirical inquiry can be 'dumb', stifled by a 'dramatically poor repertoire of sympathies and antipathies' (Latour, 2004: 219). Thinking about the status of what is inaccessible, mysterious or unlocatable is to think about differential histories and scales of existence and how these histories and scales are rendered and approached – and always *in media res* – from different, and sometimes antagonistic, disciplinary perspectives. But, it is also to return to basics; to recognize that critical methodologies, as much as care, are driven by a desire (and, for some, a responsibility) to oppose unnecessary suffering 'it is precisely the radical destructibility of life that makes it a matter of care' (Hagglund, 2011: 124). The unintelligible in this regard is not so much a bounded territory or domain, an empirical no-go zone. Rather, it signifies and problematizes the underlying drive of the attentiveness of live sociology as an imperative to uncover and to do something about unnecessary suffering.

Learning from the improvisations of dying migrants and care practitioners, I am suggesting that the unintelligible in the practice of live sociology involves something more than being the opposite or absence of intelligibility. Carrying the capacity to put into motion, touch, interrupt and halt it is the very condition of future 'live' empirical activity; a site of problem-making and accounting for that is simultaneously an opening to the generation of different methodological practices, knowledge, and ways of thinking about the usefulness of what we do (see Fraser, 2009) and also what is 'sociologically unspeakable' (Gordon, 2008[1997]: 178). By way of conclusion there are two methodological points that are important to me to highlight: (1) attentiveness to a range of different materials out of which attempts at intersubjective bridging and communication can be produced, and which exceed the social, the material and the temporally linear; and (2) the cultivating of an empirical sensibility that is hospitable to the inaccessible and the non-relational.

Acknowledgements

I am grateful to the patients and care professionals who shared and continue to share their experiences with me. I would like to thank Nigel Clark, Nirmal

Puwar and the reviewer for their care-full reading and suggestions for improving the original text of this article, which is so much better as a result.

Notes

1 The events and accounts in this paper come from two separate research projects (for methodological details see Gunaratnam, 2001 and 2008b). The first, an ethnography of a London Hospice (1995–1999), generated Ibrahim's and Maxine's interviews; and the second, a study of older people from racialized minorities produced Mita and Rachel's narratives (2003–2007).
2 For Derrida, thresholds always involve the unknown, and in the case of death 'a certain *pas* [step/not]' (*Il y va d'un certain pas*) (1993: 6). The plurality of meaning in the French word *pas* as 'step' and 'not' is taken to 'mark the impossibility or impermissibility of such a step (one cannot or ought not cross)' (Calarco, 2002: 19), but it is an impossibility that also serves as an incitement to cross the impossible/impassable.
3 In Couze Venn's (2010: 148) discussion of the temporality and affective economy of narratives of spirituality, one aspect of spirituality is seen as involving 'recognition of insufficiency or incompleteness' and a waiting for unknown becomings.
4 As Sara Ahmed (2005) tells us, a lifeline involves affective and spatio-temporal orientations and investments, as well as being an expression of something that can save us. She notes that as much as a lifeline is something that is intended to save us 'we don't know what happens when we reach such a line and let ourselves live by holding on . . . We don't know what it means to follow the gift of the unexpected line that gives us the chance for new direction . . .' (2005: 18).
5 Alongside those such as Nelson Mandela, Martin Luther King Jr and Aung San Suu Kyi, Cicely Saunders was the subject of a book on courage by the former British Prime Minister Gordon Brown (2007). Of Saunders, Brown wrote '. . . in her life she did more than anyone to come to terms with the greatest mystery of all: death' (2007: 6).
6 My ongoing work with knowledge exchange has included the transformation of data into artistic forms, the collaborative development of information materials for dying people, involvement in palliative care policy development; and educational initiatives for care professionals (for examples see Gunaratnam, 2007).

References

Adkins, L., (2009a), 'Feminism after measure', *Feminist Theory*, 10 (3): 323–339.
Adkins, L., (2009b), 'Sociological futures: from clock time to event time', *Sociological Research Online*, 14 (4). Available at: http://www.socresonline.org.uk/14/4/8.html (accessed 12 November 2010).
Ahmed, S., (2004), *The Cultural Politics of Emotion*, Edinburgh: Edinburgh University Press.
Ahmed, S., (2005), *Queer Phenomenology: Orientations, Objects, Others*, Durham, NC: Duke University Press.
Back, L., (2007), *The Art of Listening*, English edn, Oxford: Berg.
Badiou, A., (2002), *Ethics: An Essay on the Understanding of Evil*, London: Verso.
Barad, K. M., (2007), *Meeting the Universe Halfway: Quantum Physics and the Entanglement of Matter and Meaning*, Durham, NC: Duke University Press.
Bar-On, D., (1999), *The Indescribable and the Undiscussable*, Budapest: Central European University Press.
Barry, A., Born, G. and Weszkalnys, G., (2008), 'Logics of interdisciplinarity', *Economy and Society*, 37 (1): 20–49.
Bourdieu, P., (1999), *The Weight of the World: Social Suffering in Contemporary Society*, 1st edn, Cambridge: Polity Press.

Brown, G., (2007), *Courage: Eight Portraits*, 1st edn, London: Bloomsbury.

Butler, J., (2004), *Precarious Life: The Power of Mourning and Violence*, London: Verso.

Calarco, M., (2002), 'On the borders of language and death – Derrida and the question of the animal', *Angelaki Journal of the Theoretical Humanities*, 7 (2): 17–25.

Clark, D., (1999), '"Total pain", disciplinary power and the body in the work of Cicely Saunders, 1958–1967', *Social Science and Medicine*, 49 (6): 727–736.

DeLanda, M., (2002), *Intensive Science and Virtual Philosophy*, London: Continuum.

Derrida, J., (1978), *Writing and Difference*, London: Routledge.

Derrida, J., (1993), *Aporias: Dying-Awaiting (One Another at) the 'Limits of Truth' (Mourir-s'attendre aux "limites de la vérité")*, Stanford, CA: Stanford University Press.

Dikeç, M., Clark, N. and Barnett, C., (2009), 'Extending hospitality: giving space, taking time', *Paragraph*, 32 (1): 1–14.

Dominelli, L., (2002), *Anti-oppressive Social Work: Theory and Practice*. New York: Palgrave.

Ekblad, S., Marttila, A. and Emilsson, M., (2000), 'Cultural challenges in end-of-life care: reflections from focus groups' interviews with hospice staff in Stockholm', *Journal of Advanced Nursing*, 31 (3): 623–630.

Fraser, M., (2009), 'Experiencing sociology', *European Journal of Social Theory*, 12 (1): 463–481.

Frost, L. and Hoggett, P., (2008), 'Human agency and social suffering', *Critical Social Policy*, 28 (4): 438–460.

Gordon, A., (2008 [1997]), *Ghostly Matters: Haunting and the Sociological Imagination*, Minnesota: University of Minnesota Press.

Graham, S. and Thrift, N., (2007), 'Out of order', *Theory, Culture and Society*, 24 (3): 1–25.

Greco, M., (2009), 'On the art of life: a vitalist reading of medical humanities', *The Sociological Review*, 56: 23–45.

Gunaratnam, Y., (2001), '"We mustn't judge people . . . but": staff dilemmas in dealing with racial harassment amongst hospice service users', *Sociology of Health and Illness*, 23 (1): 65–84.

Gunaratnam, Y., (2004), '"Bucking and kicking": race, gender and embodied resistance in health care', in P. Chamberlayne, J. Bornat and U. Apitzsch (eds), *Biographical Methods and Professional Practice: An International Perspective*, 207–219, Bristol: Policy Press.

Gunaratnam, Y., (2007), 'Where is the love? Art, aesthetics and research', *Journal of Social Work Practice*, 21 (3): 271–287.

Gunaratnam, Y., (2008a), 'Care, artistry and what might be', *Ethnicity and Inequalities in Health and Social Care*, 1 (1): 9–17.

Gunaratnam, Y., (2008b), 'From competence to vulnerability: care, ethics, and elders from racialized minorities', *Mortality: Promoting the Interdisciplinary Study of Death and Dying*, 13 (1): 24.

Hagglund, M., (2011), 'Radical atheist materialism: a critique of Meillassoux', in L. Bryant, N. Smicek and G. Harman (eds), *The Speculative Turn: Continental Materialism and Realism*, 113–129, Melbourne: re.press.

Harman, G., (2009), *Prince of Networks: Bruno Latour and Metaphysics*, Melbourne: re.press.

Harrison, P., (2007), '"How shall I say it . . . ?" Relating the nonrelational', *Environment and Planning A*, 39 (3): 590–608.

Keats, J., (1958 [1817]), 'Letter to George and Tom Keats, 21 December, 1817', in H. E. Rollins (ed.), *The Letters of J. Keats: 1814–1821*, 193, Cambridge: Cambridge University Press.

Krause, K., (2008), 'Transnational therapy networks among Ghanaians in London', *Journal of Ethnic and Migration Studies*, 34 (2): 235–251.

Latour, B., (2004), 'How to talk about the body? The normative dimension of science studies', *Body and Society*, 10 (2–3): 205–229.

Lawton, J., (2000), *The Dying Process: Patients' Experiences of Palliative Care*, London: Routledge.

Levinas, E., (1994), *Time and the Other*, Pittsburgh, PA: Duquesne University Press.

Lorimer, H., (2005), 'Cultural geography: the busyness of being "more-than-representational"', *Progress in Human Geography*, 29 (1): 83–94.

The Sociological Review, 60:S1, pp. 108–123 (2012), DOI: 10.1111/j.1467-954X.2012.02119.x

McRobbie, A., (2002), 'A mixed bag of misfortunes? Bourdieu's *Weight of the World*', *Theory, Culture and Society*, 19 (3): 129–138.

Mol, A., (2006), 'Proving or improving: on health care research as a form of self-reflection', *Qualitative Health Research*, 16 (3): 405–414.

Mol, A., (2008), *The Logic of Care: Health and the Problem of Patient Choice*, Oxford: Routledge.

Saunders, C. M., (1961), 'A patient', *Nursing Times*: 394–397.

Saunders, C. M., (1964), 'Care of patients suffering from terminal illness at St. Joseph's Hospice, Hackney, London', *Nursing Mirror*, 14: vii–x.

Saunders, C. M., (1970), 'Nature and management of terminal pain', in *Matters of Life and Death*, 15–26, London: Dartman, Longman and Todd.

Saunders, C. M., (1988), 'The evolution of the hospices', in R. Mann (ed.), *The History of the Management of Pain: From Early Principles to Present Practice.* Proceedings of a conference organized by the Section of the History of Medicine of the Royal Society of Medicine, London, 167–178, Carnforth: Parthenon Publishing.

Saunders, C. M., (2006), 'Spiritual pain', in *Cicely Saunders: Selected Writings 1958–2004*, 217–221, Oxford: Oxford University Press.

Scarry, E., (1987), *The Body in Pain: The Making and Unmaking of the World*, New York and Oxford: Oxford University Press.

Shields, R., (1996), 'Meeting or Mis-meeting? The Dialogical Challenge to Verstehen', *The Sociological Review*, 47 (2): 275–294.

Spivak, G. C., (1988), 'Can the subaltern speak?' in C. Nelson and L. Grossberg (eds), *Marxism and the Interpretation of Culture*, London: Macmillan.

Stanworth, R., (2004), *Recognizing Spiritual Needs in People Who Are Dying*, Oxford: Oxford University Press.

Turner, B. S., (2006), *Vulnerability and Human Rights*, University Park, PA: Pennsylvania State University Press.

Venn, C., (2010), 'Individuation, relationality, affect: rethinking the human in relation to the living', *Body and Society*, 16 (1): 129–161.

Waddell, M., (1989), 'Living in two worlds: psychodynamic theory and social work practice', *Free Associations*, 15: 11–35.

Warin, M. and Dennis, S., (2008), 'Telling silences: unspeakable trauma and the unremarkable practices of everyday life', *The Sociological Review*, 56: 100–116.

Weber, M., (1947), *Economy and Society: A Study in the Integration of Economic and Social Theory*, trans. M. Henderson and T. Parsons, Glencoe, IL: Free Press.

Wyschogrod, E., (1990), *Saints and Postmodernism: Revisioning Moral Philosophy*, Chicago: University of Chicago Press.

Being stuck in (live) time: the sticky sociological imagination

Emma Uprichard

Abstract: Recently, Savage and Burrows (2007) have argued that one way to invigorate sociology's 'empirical crisis' is to take advantage of live, web-based digital transactional data. This paper argues that whilst sociologists do indeed need to engage with this growing digital data deluge, there are longer-term risks involved that need to be considered. More precisely, C. Wright Mills' 'sociological imagination' is used as the basis for the kind of sociological research that one might aim for, even within the digital era. In so doing, it is suggested that current forms of engaging with transactional social data are problematic to the sociological imagination because they tend to be ahistorical and focus mainly on 'now casting'. The ahistorical nature of this genre of digital research, it is argued, necessarily restricts the possibility of developing a serious sociological imagination. In turn, it is concluded, there is a need to think beyond the digitized surfaces of the plastic present and to consider the impact that time and temporality, particularly within the digital arena, have on shaping our sociological imagination.

Keywords: ahistorical, big data, digital sociology, empirical crisis, live sociology, now casting, plastic present, sociological imagination, sticky time, transactional data

Introduction

Savage and Burrows (2007) have recently suggested that there is an impending 'empirical crisis' in British sociology. Their argument stems from the fact that in an age of 'knowing capitalism' (Thrift, 2005), digital crumbs are routinely produced through everyday online interactions, and that sociologists must engage further with these kinds of data. Their argument goes beyond injecting e-science (back) into sociology, to offer a radical rethink of what the contemporary sociologist's methodological toolbox needs to be. They point out that in the early days of the discipline, sociologists were considered to be the methodological innovators of the time, with the sample survey and the interview setting them apart from other disciplines in their ability to know the social in

The Sociological Review, 60:S1, pp. 124–138 (2012), DOI: 10.1111/j.1467-954X.2012.02120.x

exciting ways. In contrast, contemporary sociologists are seriously lagging behind, methodologically speaking that is, compared to the efforts of, say, commercial enterprises, who are far more in tune with the computational needs required to collate and explore the data deluge that is ubiquitous to modern social life.

In effect, Savage and Burrows have, albeit unintentionally, signalled a 'green light' to sociologists doing the kind of digital research in question here. To be fair, other than concluding by saying that what is needed is description, which 'seeks to link narrative, numbers, and images in ways that engage with, and critique, the kinds of routine transactional analyses that now proliferate' (2007: 896), they say very little about the specific details of empirical endeavour that they are advocating. That said, as will be spelt out further in this chapter, when we do examine empirical research that does deal directly with the kind of transactional web data that Savage and Burrows explicitly encourage us to engage with, apprehensions about what is at stake are raised. These apprehensions, it will be suggested, tap into precisely the issues that they were highlighting, namely the conduct of empirical sociological research given the data deluge that is upon us.

This article supports Savage and Burrows' (2007) main point that sociologists need to further engage with digital transactional data, but utilizes C. Wright Mills' (1959) 'sociological imagination' as a critical basis for proposing the kind of sociological research that one might aim for, even within the digital era. In so doing, it is suggested that current forms of engaging with transactional social data are problematic to the sociological imagination because they tend to be ahistorical. To be clear, this paper excludes archival digital research, which is certainly historically orientated, but focuses instead on a particular genre of emerging transactional research that is quintessentially presentist. Because this genre of digital research tends to focus on the relative 'now' – the 'plastic present' as it is referred to here – rather than pushing researchers to advance Mills' promise of the sociological imagination, this new genre of empirical research tends to be conducive to keeping people 'stuck' in their various 'series of traps'. Just as Mills argued that time, and particularly history, need to be central elements of any social study that seeks to foster the sociological imagination, so too is it argued here that transactional research needs to be further permeated in time more generally in order to go beyond the 'now' focus that tends to feature in this genre of research.

An emerging genre of ahistorical digital research

There seems to be a growing excitement and interest in an emerging genre of digital social research across the globe. In the UK, this is particularly noticeable with its key social and natural science funding bodies, the ESRC and the EPSRC, each investing in cross-disciplinary projects that develop 'new technology, innovation and skills' as a way of tackling the 'digital economy'. Savage and Burrows' (2007) paper on the 'empirical crisis' is precisely about our need to engage empirically and methodologically with 'transactional' digital data as a means of confronting the online data deluge. Whether we see it under the auspices of 'e-science', the 'digital economy', 'transactional data', 'big data' research, the point is there is an emerging genre of empirical research that is gaining greater currency across the disciplines, which typically models, explores and analyses massive Internet-based datasets. Because of the typical size of these datasets – terabytes, petabytes or larger – some have begun talking about 'big data' research (Bollier, 2010). Despite its name, it is not the size of the datasets that makes this kind of analysis particular; it is also the fact that the data are unstructured, mixed format (eg visual, text, numerical etc). Sometimes these databases result in networks (eg Twitter), sometimes less so or not at all. Data tends to be unwieldy, dynamic and noisy, and is typically produced by 'scraping' or 'crawling' the Internet, and making the most of the automated 'web crumbs', 'web logs' or 'tags', etc, which are created through individual user actions, via IP-addresses, tagging etc.

Whatever the format, though, these web crumbs usually have a time and space stamp, and indeed it is this aspect of the data that tends to be captured and exploited in some way. These 'time-space stamps' within the data deluge have become the gold nuggets from which any sociological potentiality regarding 'who', 'where' and 'what time' the web crumbs were generated is squeezed out. As Hudson-Smith *et al.* (2007: 9) point out:

> Tagging not only the type of information but where such information is produced, who uses it and at what time it is generated is fast becoming the killer application that roots information about interactivity generated across the web to systems that users can easily access and use in their own interactions with others. (Hudson-Smith *et al.*, 2007: 9)

The fact that so much information can be time-space stamped has led to an increased focus on 'real-time' methods, where streaming real-time data is harnessed as a way of capturing live trends, real time events. Research that exploits micro-blogging sites such as Twitter are excellent examples of the relative ahistorical nature that encompasses this genre of digital research (see, for example, Huberman *et al.*, 2008; Gruzd *et al.*, 2011; Cheong and Lee, 2011). CASA's Tweet-o-Meters (see http://www.casa.ucl.ac.uk/tom/) is another example; it provides a visual and dynamic display of the quantity of tweets every minute in nine cities across the world. Other examples might include efforts that go into displaying a weekend of tweets (Hudson-Smith, 2011) or even five minutes of Tweet data (Hudson-Smith *et al.*, 2007). Google 'real time' alerts are alternative examples of the kind of genre discussed here, as are the Google maps mash-ups that depict 'live crime' – events that occur in real time and can be collated and gathered as they happen. Google's Flu Trends (see http://www.google.org/flutrends/) perhaps epitomizes the genre of research in question best of all, insofar as it uses real-time searches to trace where flu outbreaks may occur, and provides therefore a real live example of the ways in which 'real-time' web data can be fed back into almost 'real-time' representations of 'now'. Readers will have their own examples in mind, since the Internet is riddled with a myriad of examples of such 'live data streams'. Increasingly, researchers are developing tools and ways of harvesting these live data sources. Like the poverty stricken scavengers who go through rubbish tips in the poorest places of the globe, the technologically savvy alchemists see their futures in data-mining the 'rubbish' that our online mundane transactions and interactions leave behind, and turning timely web data into 'gold'. The richness and power of 'real-time' or 'live' data lie in their speed, providing the 'newest', 'latest', 'most recent', 'most timely' snap-shots of 'now'. It is especially in these 'live' data mining activities, where 'time-space' stamps are increasingly collated and analysed in as close to 'real-time' as is possible, that we also see this growing 'ahistorical' genre of digital research take centre stage.

Of course, as with all research approaches, it is easy to criticize this emerging genre of digital research for lacking in this or that, and although it is true that the ahistorical nature inherent within this genre of digital research is what is being highlighted here, it seems unfair to judge it too harshly, for three main reasons. First, the world is increasingly shaped and moulded by swathes of digital information and it is therefore right and proper that contemporary social science also engages with all things digital. Secondly, the field of 'transactional social science' – if it can even be called that yet – is in its relative infancy. Social scientists are still learning and/or fine tuning their methodological and compu-tational skills and/or developing better collaborative relationships with those outside the social sciences who already possess them. Over time, improvements will be made, developments and new tools will facilitate new forms of doing and knowing. Thirdly, because of the sheer volume of data, much of the labour involved in actually trying to do anything meaningful with it necessarily goes into various data reduction techniques. Data reduction is of course a necessary part of many empirical approaches. The more data there is to deal with, the more data reduction techniques will need to be employed. As Bollier (2010: 15) points out, 'at some point, less becomes more because all you are interested in doing is to prune the [big] data, so that you can stare at the "less"'.

What this means in this case is that priorities are shifted somewhat, albeit necessarily. The onus is placed on data mining, computational power, (re)presentations or visualizations of large swathes of data at the expense of the substantive issues at hand. Indeed, McCulloch (2011) hits the nail on the head by pointing out that when data crunching becomes the focus, we are missing the point to analysing data in the first place. As he explains: 'Placing the empha-sis on data and computing technology seems to me counter-productive not only from the point of view of understanding what data have to tell us but also removes a lot of the enjoyment from doing data analysis.' He raises a genuinely difficult predicament. Big data research requires one or more processes of data reduction to make it manageable.

It is difficult to see how it would be possible to empirically engage with the digital data deluge without data reduction techniques. Indeed, one might go as far as to say that *the* key empirical issue in trying to engage with the digital data deluge is precisely one of data reduction. Which techniques are most meaningful? What information is lost and at what cost? Which data are accessed and which are not? How does data reduction advance our knowledge about types of cases? Ultimately, these questions come down to a basic sampling problem: is it better to sample and generalize? Or should we take the whole and reduce it? The answers are not trivial. Big data puts these big problems back onto the methodologist's work table.

'Timing' the (sticky) sociological imagination

To be clear, the position argued here is not that these live / real time or transactional data analyses are a problem per se. Since so much data is produced, any attempt to explore the data deluge is potentially helpful and beneficial in itself. The problem, however, is that at the moment, this genre of digital research tends to be very narrowly located in time – hence why, for the purposes of this paper, the term 'ahistorical digital research' will be used to refer broadly to a particular genre of digital social science. The term 'ahistorical' is, strictly speaking, still temporal; it is just that its time horizon is so relatively small. As Mills (1959: 165) puts it, 'A-historical studies usually tend to be static or very short-term studies of a limited milieux'. The strength of focusing on the 'now' is simultaneously this new genre's ultimate weakness. Its 'ahistoricity' is its 'Achilles heel', if you like. To sociologists, the intrinsic ahistoricity of this new genre of digital research matters a great deal. For however we choose to 'crunch' or mine our digital data deluge, as empirical sociologists engaged in the kind of research that Mills' was advocating, our work needs to go some way towards ensuring that 'the sociological imagination has its chance to make a difference in the quality of human life in our time' (Mills, 1959: 248).

It is worth returning to Mills on this last point, as he set out quite clearly the kind of critical empirical sociology that is also being advocated in this discussion. After all, any criticism about a particular genre of empirical research belies a set of assumptions about the kind of empirical research that might be otherwise preferred. Whilst avoiding a synopsis of Mills' thesis about the sociological imagination, I want to draw out three points that are specific to the argument raised here in relation to problems of the ahistorical nature of the new genre of digital research, particularly vis-à-vis this new genre's departure from Mills' vision of sociological research. First, Mills was very clear that in order to deliver the promise of the sociological imagination, which helps to free each and everyone of us from feeling trapped, it is necessary to turn to 'biography, history, society as coordinates of a well considered social study'. Indeed, it is precisely in Mills' three point hinge-pin that we see the severity of the 'fault-line' within the emerging ahistorical digital research critiqued here – a faint but visible crack that risks being serious if ignored in the long run.

The Sociological Review, 60:S1, pp. 124–138 (2012), DOI: 10.1111/j.1467-954X.2012.02120.x

This new genre of ahistorical digital research seldom does anything resembling 'biography, history and society'. This is not because it is impossible to do this digitally. In many ways, the digital lends itself to precisely the kind of multi-level, rich in context, and historically orientated research that has the potential of fulfilling the promise of the sociological imagination. Blogs, for instance, do place the individual actor at the heart of the digital ocean and also lend themselves to situating biography within society. Even there, however, 'history' is neglected, insofar as research that focuses on blogs rarely does much else other than simply describing what numerous blogs are reporting 'now', in much the same way as micro-blogging (eg Twitter) research does. Indeed, at the moment, most of the work that goes into producing anything sensible out of the masses of digital data ultimately has very little to do with 'biography', 'history' or 'society'. The cost of this omission is that this ahistorical genre of digital research tends to overlook the importance of time as 'nested'. Yet as Lewis and Weigart (1981) put it, all social acts are temporally embedded within other social acts. Indeed, they go as far as stating that 'time embeddedness' is key to understanding social action in the first place. That is to say, 'Not only are self-time structures embedded within interactional time structures, but both of these micro-level temporal structures are, in turn, embedded within the larger, macro-level temporal orders of the social institutions and of the culture' (Lewis and Weigart, 1981: 538). Mills' three coordinates of 'biography, history and society' directly tap into Lewis and Weigart's point about the importance of relating time to social action and vice versa: social action is necessarily situated in time and always and everywhere nested intricately within larger temporal orders. Therefore, to understand *any* of those coordinates – that is, biography, history or society – even in themselves, it is necessary to play close attention to their respective temporalities.

The importance of situating the empirical – digital or otherwise – within time brings us to the second point worth highlighting in Mills' work. He was vehement about the need to conduct 'historically orientated work'. He explains:

> We can examine trends in an effort to answer the question 'Where are we going?' – and that is what social scientists are often trying to do. In doing so, we are trying to study history rather than retreat into it, to pay attention to contemporary trends without being merely journalistic, to gauge the future of the trends without being merely prophetic [. . .] And we have always to balance the immediacy of the knife-edge present with the generality needed to bring out the meaning of specific trends for the period as a whole. (Mills, 1959: 170)

It seems that the balance has been completely lost, with a focus on the 'knife-edge present' winning out in this new genre of 'live' sociology. The relatively narrow time focus of these large data-mining exercises creates a genre of asynchronous snapshots, which ultimately fail to offer insights into any real historical trends.

In effect, the crux of my argument has much in common with some critiques of cross-sectional research designs. Although cross-sectional research has clear benefits with regards to costs in time and in finance, it is clearly not the design to explore trends. Of course, cross-sections over time can be used to extend the benefits to do just that, and they should be. Indeed, Li and Li (2011) are exemplary insofar as they do indeed try to go beyond the single time-point by gathering Twitter data every three minutes between two time points. This is a vast improvement to the single time points so often captured in these efforts and also signposts the potential future of this kind of real-time data-mining. Unfortunately, though, despite the immense amount of work that necessarily needs to go into extending the temporal horizon of the research design, the two time points still just provide a total time period of only 19 days. Likewise, despite collecting hourly tweets that resulted in 46,097 tweets about the Winter Olympics, Gruzd *et al.* (2011) also end up just examining three weeks of data. Whether the time span is five minutes, two weeks, one or two or six or seven months, this is hardly the 'historically orientated research' that Mills was arguing for and this is precisely the problem at the core of this new genre of ahistorical digital research. As Ito (quoted in Bollier, 2010: 19; original emphasis) aptly sums up, 'Big Data is about exactly *right now,* with no historical context that is predictive'.

That said, Mills goes on to specify something rather important about history, which brings us to the third and final point worth highlighting here:

> Periods and societies differ in respect to whether or not understanding them requires direct references to 'historical factors'. The historical nature of a given society in a given period may be such that 'the historical past' is only indirectly relevant to its understanding. [. . .] The *relevance* of history, in short, is itself subject to the principle of historical specificity. (Mills, 1959: 172–173)

Aside from the fact that Mills was attempting to distinguish 'history' from 'historical sociology', what Mills was getting at here was that the relevance of history is itself subject to sociological scrutiny and will recursively feed back into disciplinary modes of what is considered to be or not to be acceptable empirical practice. Whilst not wanting to get into that particular bone of contention, it follows that the ahistorical nature of this new genre of digital research might itself be a reflection of the 'presentist' focus that is mediated by all that is digital. Therefore, it might be concluded, the relevance of history is also eroded in this new genre of digital research. What happened last week on, say, Twitter has indeed the flavour of being 'old news'. One might indeed agree with Mills, therefore, that the relevancy of history is dependent on context. As he goes on to explain, 'Everything, to be sure, may be said always to have "come out of the past" but the meaning of that phrase – "to come out of the past" – is what is at issue' (Mills, 1959: 173).

Of course, the meanings of 'past', 'present' and 'future' are dependent on the time horizons associated with each of them. As Adam (2004) explains:

> What time is, how it is conceptualized, what it means in practice, how the parameters set by nature are transcended through the ages, what changes are wrought by the

quest for know-how and control, all these issues belong together. Collectively, they illuminate the wider picture and provide us with a basis from which to get a sense of the role of time in cultural existence in general and contemporary social life in particular. (Adam, 2004: 150)

This echoes greatly with Mead's (2002 [1932]) notion that time is fundamentally 'social' – it is always 'relational'. Mills was also all too aware of the 'social' nature of time, and of the construction of history in particular. Indeed he goes as far as saying that this feature of time's relevance – ie time's relevance as socially constructed in historical context – is likely to be positively detrimental to the sociological imagination. 'Such a retreat from history makes it impossible', he argues, 'to understand precisely the most contemporary features of this one society, which is a historical structure that we cannot hope to understand unless we are guided by the sociological principle of historical specificity' (1959: 174). Hence, however 'history' is constructed, whether it is deemed relevant or not, it is always necessary to understanding contemporary society.

Note that Mills' call for historically orientated research has much in common with the real weakness inherent in cross-sectional designs, which ultimately, Mann (2003: 57) argues, 'do not provide an explanation for their findings'. That is to say, not only do cross-sectional studies fail to provide an explanation for their findings, they cannot do so. This is the paradox of cross-sections: the only way of explaining their findings is by situating them within relevant longitudinal research and/or other methods. The same might be said for ahistorical digital research. As interesting as the findings may be, they cannot in themselves provide an explanation for their findings; longitudinal methods alongside them are necessary. As Mills (1959: 165) explains, 'Not only are our chances of becoming aware of structure increased by historical work; we cannot hope to understand any single society, even as a static affair, without the use of historical materials.' This is primarily why the new genre of ahistorical digital research is not in itself able to deliver the promise of the sociological imagination.

Some readers might protest and retort that no one has ever argued that this new genre of digital research ever could be or ever would be conducive to developing sociological imagination. However, this would be missing the point. It is not just that this genre of ahistorical digital research fails to deliver the promise, which may or may not be contested. Rather, the combined effect of the ahistorical nature *and* the fact that we are dealing with findings about the relative present means that: (a) not only are we unable to provide explanations for what is there, but (b) the findings have the potential to be immediately (re)used by those on whom the data is based in the first place. Hence, as will be suggested, it is not simply that ahistorical digital research hinders the sociological imagination, but that it also, more worryingly, makes for a 'sticky' sociological imagination, which maintains the status quo and keeps us in tighter traps in a series of recursive presents.

A 'sticky' sociological imagination?

Suggesting that the new genre of ahistorical digital research is conducive to keeping us trapped in our present(s) is perhaps a rather extreme version of possible realities. It certainly needs to be explained and justified. In effect, two main interrelated processes are involved in making this argument, the first of which concerns the recursivity of the digital with the world the digital represents, and the second concerns the nature of time itself. Both processes feedback into how we think about and act in the world and ultimately the possibilities of what it means to live in it also. As Hörning *et al.* (1999: 305) argue, 'Time unfolds in the interrelationship between people and the world; thus, practice creates and structures time, and the varying combinations of time within a social formation generate and change time structures.' And so it is with the digital in all its forms. The interrelationships between the digital and representations of the digital, structure time; vice versa, time structures those interrelationships.

A similar point is made in relation to space in Batty's (1997) concept of the 'computable city'. There, Batty (1997) sets forth some of the implications involved in modelling cities and in particular the impact real-time data collection (eg traffic flows) has on short- and longer-term decision making and subsequently the urban form of the actual city. In the 'computable city', the virtual world of data and the real city intersect and recursively and iteratively interact together in ways that are difficult to predict. As Hudson-Smith *et al.* (2007) explain:

> the virtual world and its [digital] mirror gives back to the physical world, completing the loop of recursion in strange and enticing ways. This is then the prospect: of mirror world standing astride both the real and the virtual, of information being recursed into many forms and being made available in diverse ways to people acting as avatars to people acting as themselves but in weird and wonderful environments yet to be invented. (Hudson-Smith *et al.*, 2007: 20)

Indeed, if we think of the digital as a mirror, and research on the digital as representations of that mirror, what we create is a constant recursive dynamic interaction between the world (digital or otherwise) and its representations. When dealing with real-time digital representations, the speed of the recursion is significantly accelerated. In such a scenario, it is possible to envisage a constant 'to-and-fro' between what seems to be happening, say, in real-time tweets, those observing those events, who then act upon them within seconds, minutes, hours or days, who then may or may not impact on what is 'tweeted' again, and so on and so on. This may seem like a trivial possibility, but when such real-time observations are used to police, survey, sell, etc then the recursion between real-time events and representations of real-time events becomes highly political. Moreover, in such a context, the temporal focus becomes more and more about the plasticity of the present, and transforms the relevance of other time horizons. As Hörning *et al.* argued over a decade ago:

> New technologies provoke new processes and experiences of temporal differentiation. New technologies may contribute to the reconfiguration of time, but when the plastic-

ity of time becomes an object of reflection and change, time practices may start to challenge and subvert taken-for-granted uses of technology and may lead to a transformation of the technologies themselves. (Hörning *et al.*, 1999: 305)

Governments, the military and commercial enterprises have known this for some time. The increased availability of real-time data sources increasingly means that 'to know' becomes not so much about how to predict the future, but how to predict 'now', or better still, 'to know about now before now has happened'. This being the case, this new genre of ahistorical research becomes part of the necessary processes involved in facilitating and increasingly making possible a new form of predictive research, which is focused on knowing more about the present. Bollier (2010: 20) talks about this as the rise of 'now-casting', where real-time data is used 'to describe contemporaneous activities *before* official data sources are available'. The more this happens, and the more live methods and technologies become appropriated within the public sphere (see Graham, 2010), the more the question about what it means to do and live in and with the mundanity of the present is problematized. Indeed, this set of recursions leads to a whole new set of time practices, each one differentiating alternative sets of 'presents', eg present present, past present, future present etc (see Adam, 2004). This resonates somewhat with Schutz and Luckmann's (1973) idea of persistently interacting multiple life-worlds in which the temporal frames of the 'past' and 'future' simultaneously exist in the 'present' as body rhythms, social seasons, cycles, social routines and so on. As Abbott (2001) argues:

> the 'size' of the present is something encoded at any given time into the social structure . . . Moreover, just as there are many social structures that overlap, drawing the same individuals into do zones of different intersecting structures, so too do the presents those structures imply overlap and intersect. (Abbott, 2001: 235)

As the present is embedded into structures and vice versa, the more important the present becomes. On the other hand, where the 'past' and 'future' increasingly become a matter of hours or days, and ultimately more like our present 'present', the present itself becomes more and more plastic, to be stretched, manipulated, moulded and ultimately 'casted' by those who can access more of it in the supposed 'now'.

'Now-casting' arguably turns the promise of the sociological imagination on its head. After all, whilst it is possible to argue that Mills was inflating the importance of history, the key reason for him doing so was ironically because he was all too aware of how important a role history plays in shaping the future. The conception and perception of the relevancy of history – ie 'the principle of historical specificity' – was precisely what Mills understood to be at the core of the sociological imagination. As he explains:

> Within an individual's biography and within a society's history, the social task of reason is to formulate choices, to enlarge the scope of human decisions in the making of history. The future of human affairs is not merely some set of variables to be predicted. The future is what is to be decided – within the limits, to be sure, of historical

possibility. But this possibility is not fixed; in our time the limits seem very broad indeed. (Mills, 1959: 174)

Mills is far from alone in stressing the importance of history in shaping the future. In *The World of Propensities,* for example, Popper (1990) suggests that the propensity of an event is dependent on how that event is perceived and understood; vice versa, how it is perceived and understood can change the event's propensity to occur is 'ontological and relational, and always dynamic even if the absolute probabilistic value' (1990: 17). Moreover, Popper continues:

> in our real changing world, the situation and, with it, the possibilities, and thus propensities, change all the time. They certainly may change if we, or any other organisms, *prefer* one possibility to another; or if we *discover* a possibility where we have not seen one before. Our very understanding of the world changes the conditions of the changing world; and so do our wishes, our preferences, our motivations, our hopes, our phantasies, our hypotheses, our theories. (Popper, 1990: 17; original emphasis)

The conceptions of the past and present affect the notion of the future. The 'recursivity' of 'temporal structures and dispositions' also lies at the heart of Bourdieu's (1990) concept of 'habitus'. He writes:

> The habitus is the principle of a selective perception of the indices tending to conform and reinforce it rather than transform it, a matrix generating responses adapted in advance to all objective condition identical to or homologous with the (past) conditions of its production; it adjusts itself to a probable future which it anticipates and helps to bring about because it reads it directly in the present of the presumed world, the only one it can ever know ... This disposition, always marked by its (social) conditions of acquisition and realization, tends to adjust to the objective changes of satisfying need or desire, *inclining agents to 'cut their coats according to their cloth', and so to become the accomplices of the processes that tend to make the probable a reality.* (Bourdieu, 1990: 64–65; emphasis added)

The interdependency between the past, present and future is essentially an argument I have made elsewhere (Uprichard, 2011) specifically in relation to the need for 'narratives of the future' in social research. Drawing on Mead's *Philosophy of the Present* (2002 [1932]) to develop a tentative 'philosophy of the future', I argued that the possibility of future imaginations is always and necessarily recursively shaped by narratives *of* and *in* the past and present. The point being that if we only focus on the present, or even plastic versions of the present, then we will also tend to 'cut our coats according to our present cloths', to extend Bourdieu's analogy. This is only going to make us more and more stuck in a constant series of 'presents', making the present more and more plastic, as we (re)re-negotiate the meanings of 'past' and 'future', 'history' and 'now'. When time is considered in this way, then the 'stickiness' of time and temporality also becomes apparent.

Mead (2002 [1932]: 46) refers to this 'present' recursion quite explicitly: 'We orientate ourselves not with reference to the past which was a present within which the emergent appeared, but in such a restatement of the past as condition-ing the future'. Yet if we see the digital as a mirror recursively mediating, facili-tating, catalysing and affecting action, and we inject notions of time, temporality, speed, and present into those recursive dynamics and feedback loops, then it is also possible to envisage a future of constant recursive presents, where we become stuck as we struggle to try to orientate ourselves according to redescrip-tions of the present as reconditioning the present.

Where real-time digital representations increasingly interact within shorter time spans, the temporal frames, which make up the ahistorical habitus of 'structuring structures and dispositions' to produce more 'present', are multi-plied, refracted and recursively and iteratively fed back into everyday life itself quicker than ever before. Therefore, far from speeding up the possibility of alternative emergent futures, ahistorical digital research actually has the poten-tial of doing the opposite, of slowing the present down, keeping us in an ever plastic notion of 'now', without the recourse of drawing on 'history' in the sense that Mills was encouraging. As Abbott (2001) suggests, a feature of time itself is that it is:

> highly local, in the sense that it is proper to a particular place and moment, with large inclusive presents reading beyond it topologically and temporally. Time is indexical, because of this multiplicity of overlapping presents, yet inclusive, because their rela-tions are of inclusion rather than quantity. (Abbott, 2001: 295)

Mills' sociological imagination, though, depends on 'longer term trends' (1959: 168), but the genre of ahistorical digital research that is increasingly being con-ducted just does not engage with time and temporality in the way that it could ever hope to deliver Mills' 'promise'. Yet if we are committed to the sociological imagination (Mills), or to having a say on the world of emergent propensities (Popper), or to becoming accomplices to processes that might make probable new and different realities (Bourdieu, 1990), and therefore negotiating 'pro-jected' and 'desired' possible futures (see Uprichard and Byrne, 2006), then it is also necessary to inject time and temporality routinely and mundanely into our social research practices. This applies also to rethinking the importance of time in the new genre of digital research. As Abbott (2001: 182) notes, 'serious reflec-tion about basic temporal assumptions can help us improve all our work'.

Conclusion

Like a hamster running on a wheel that can never run faster than the wheel can spin, we can never keep up with our own data production. We are always going to need to produce findings about the present faster and faster also, but we are not going to keep up (see Gleick, 1999). Of course, we will need to try to find ways to deal with that. One option might well be 'live methods' and 'real time' data collection and analysis. But is focusing on the 'now' the way to go? Is that really what we want to do? The answer to those questions as they are addressed here is a definite 'no', for fear of increasing the likelihood that we will become (more) stuck in a series of perpetual presents without any recourse to either understand our pasts or affect the future.

Thus, on the one hand, it is appropriate that the data deluge has forced a re-focus on method in sociology, especially since so much of our digital every-day life can also be tracked, monitored and measured there too. On the other hand, and this is the key point, we must not get too carried away with what we can or cannot do and in effect become distracted from what we should be doing. Just because we can, say, track and monitor millions of 'tweets' across a par-ticular time and space does not necessarily mean that this is either useful or meaningful. The quest to do more ahistorical digital work of that kind is akin to improving our success rate at hitting the bull's eye at the wrong target. At some point, we need to ask ourselves 'why' we are doing it, and more impor-tantly, what the point to sociological research is in the first place. After all, if, as C. Wright Mills has argued, part of the main aim of doing sociology is to try to develop a 'sociological imagination', then surely we need to also think beyond the digitized surfaces of the plastic present? As Abbott (2001) writes:

> The social world is constantly changing and reforming itself. To be sure, large parts of the social world reproduce themselves continually; much of it looks stable. But this is mere appearance. What transpires is reproduction, not endurance. The central reason for making this assumption is practical. It is possible to explain reproduction as a phenomenon sometimes produced by perpetual change; it is not possible to explain change as a phenomenon sometimes produced by perpetual stasis. (Abbott, 2011: 254)

This article has drawn on a lot of concepts and ideas and spun them together into a web of relative temporal gloom, where we become supposedly stuck, frozen in time in a sticky plastic present. Underpinning the entire discussion, though, has been the importance of thinking seriously about Savage and Burrows' (2007) call for a methodological engagement with the data deluge and what that might mean to the future of sociology. More poignant still, has been an explicit quest to consider time seriously within that remit. This has been done by drawing on Mills' 'sociological imagination' as a way of unpacking some of the 'time-work' that is riddled in his work and his promise to sociology more generally. In effect, the issue has been about how we 'do' time, methodologically and epistemologically, within an ever-changing world, with ever-changing biog-raphies and (re)moving histories.

If we are to understand change in and of the social world, and continue to keep alive our individual and collective imaginations of desired and projected alternatives, then there is also a need to understand how social phenomena are literally grounded in, and emergent from, multiple temporal interactions simul-taneously. As Abbott (2001: 217) argues, 'Reconstructing our full experience of time . . . requires comparison of durations'. A radical epistemological and meth-odological reconceptualization of time 'in' method is, therefore, required. Whilst each biography is relatively short, history and future of the social are not, though that they are changing may be a contingent necessary condition of us knowing about them. Understanding the ways in which biographies and societies do and do not change within those different temporal dynamics to make different histories, presents and futures is one of our greatest empirical challenges, particularly when technologies keep recreating finer-grained classifications of time itself.

Acknowledgements

This work was supported by the Economic and Social Research Council [RES-061-25-0307].

References

Abbott, A., (2001), *Time Matters: On Theory and Method*, Chicago: University of Chicago Press.
Adam, B., (2004), *Time*, Cambridge: Polity Press.
Batty, M., (1997), 'The computable city', *International Planning Studies*, 2 (2): 155–173.
Bollier, D. (2010) 'The promise and peril of big data', Washington, DC: The Aspen Institute, available at: http://www.aspeninstitute.org/sites/default/files/content/docs/pubs/The_Promise_and_Peril_of_Big_Data.pdf (accessed 15 November 2011).
Bourdieu, P., (1990), *The Logic of Practice*, Stanford, CA: Stanford University Press.
Cheong, M. and Lee, V., (2011), 'A microblogging-based approach to terrorism informatics: exploration and chronicling civilian sentiment and response to terrorism events via Twitter', *Information Systems Frontiers*, 13 (1): 45–59.
Gleick, J., (1999), *Faster: The Acceleration of Just about Everything*, London: Little, Brown and Company.
Graham, S., (2010), *Cities under Siege: The New Military Urbanism*, London: Verso.
Gruzd A., Doiron, S., and Mai, P., (2011), 'Is happiness contagious online? A case of Twitter and the 2010 Winter Olympics', *Proceedings of the 44th Hawaii International Conference on System Sciences, 2011*.
Hörning, K. H., Ahrens, D. and Gerhard, A., (1999), 'Do technologies have time? New practices of time and the transformation of communication technologies', *Time and Society*, 8 (2): 293–308.
Huberman, B., Romero, D. and Wu, F., (2008), 'Social networks that matter: Twitter under the microscope'. available at: http://ssrn.com/abstract = 1313405 (accessed 11 May 2011).
Hudson-Smith, A., (2011), 'Response', invited panel discussant, in M. Savage and R. Burrows, 'The Empirical Crisis in Sociology', paper presented at British Sociological Association annual conference 2011, Leeds.
Hudson-Smith, A., Milton, R., Dearden, D. and Batty, M., (2007), 'Virtual cities: digital mirrors into a recursive world', Working Paper 125, December, Centre for Advanced Spatial Analysis, University College London.
Lewis, J. D. and Weigart, A. J., (1981), 'The structures and meanings of social time', *Social Forces*: 432–462.
Li, Y.-M. and Li, T.-Y., (2011), 'Deriving marketing intelligence over microblogs', *Proceedings of the 44th Hawaii International Conference on System Sciences, 2011*.
Mann C., (2003), 'Observational research methods. Research design II: cohort, cross sectional, and case-control studies', *Emergency Medicine Journal*, 20 (1): 54–60.
McCulloch, A., (2011), 'Statistics and the information society', *Significance: Statistics Making Sense*, Web Exclusive April 204, available at http://www.significancemagazine.org/details/webexclusive/1048709/Statistics-and-the-Information-Society.html.

Mead, G. H., (2002 [1932]), *The Philosophy of the Present*. New York: Prometheus Books.

Mills, C. W., (1959), *The Sociological Imagination*, New York: Oxford University Press.

Popper, K., (1990), *A World of Propensities*, Bristol: Thoemmes.

Savage, M. and Burrows, R., (2007), 'The coming crisis of empirical sociology', *Sociology*, 41 (5): 885–899.

Schutz, A. and Luckmann, T., (1973), *The Structures of the Life-World*, Evanston, IL: Northwestern University Press.

Thrift, N., (2005), *Knowing Capitalism*, London: Sage.

Uprichard, E., (2011), 'Narratives of the future: complexity, time and temporality', in M. Williams and P. Vogt (eds), *The Sage Handbook of Innovation in Social Research Methods*, 103–119, London: Sage.

Uprichard, E. and Byrne, D., (2006), 'Representing complex places: a narrative approach', *Environment and Planning A*, 38 (4): 665–667.

The Sociological Review, 60:S1, pp. 124–138 (2012), DOI: 10.1111/j.1467-954X.2012.02120.x

The redistribution of methods: on intervention in digital social research, broadly conceived

Noortje Marres

Abstract: This paper contributes to debates about the implications of digital technology for social research by proposing the concept of the redistribution of methods. In the context of digitization, I argue, social research becomes *noticeably* a distributed accomplishment: online platforms, users, devices and informational practices actively contribute to the performance of digital social research. This also applies more specifically to social research methods, and this paper explores the phenomenon in relation to two specific digital methods, online network and textual analysis, arguing that sociological research stands much to gain from engaging with their distribution, both normatively and analytically speaking. I distinguish four predominant views on the redistribution of digital social methods: methods-as-usual, big methods, virtual methods and digital methods. Taking up this last notion, I propose that a redistributive understanding of social research opens up a new approach to the *re-mediation* of social methods in digital environments. I develop this argument through a discussion of two particular online research platforms: the Issue Crawler, a web-based platform for hyperlink analysis, and the Co-Word Machine, an online tool of textual analysis currently under development. Both these tools re-mediate existing social methods, and both, I argue, involve the attempt to render specific *methodology critiques* effective in the online realm, namely critiques of the authority effects implicit in citation analysis. As such, these methods offer ways for social research to intervene critically in digital social research, and more specifically, to endorse and actively pursue the re-distribution of social methods online.

Keywords: digital social research, social studies of science and technology, digital devices, online network analysis, online textual analysis, digital social methods

Introduction

As sociologists like to point out, the implications of technology for social life tend to be imagined in either highly optimistic or deeply pessimistic ways (Woolgar, 2002). Current debates about the implications of digitization for social research are no exception to this rule. The question of how digital devices,

The Sociological Review, 60:S1, pp. 139–165 (2012), DOI: 10.1111/j.1467-954X.2012.02121.x
© 2012 The Author. Editorial organisation © 2012 The Editorial Board of the Sociological Review. Published by Wiley-Blackwell Publishing Ltd, 9600 Garsington Road, Oxford OX4 2DQ, UK and 350 Main Street, Malden, MA 02148, USA

and their proliferation across social life, transform social research is generating much interest today, and, as a consequence, the question of the 'social implications of technology' is now very often posed in relation to social research itself (Back, 2010; Savage *et al.*, 2010; boyd and Crawford, 2011). As it turns out, these discussions are no less susceptible to the polarizing effects of technology on the imagination, than, say, popular debates about the implications of cloning or robotics on society. While some propose that new technologies are opening up a golden age of social research, others argue that digitization has engendered a crisis for social research, creating a situation in which we risk to lose 'the human element' from view.

Both the optimistic and the pessimistic vision of digital social research start from a similar observation: digital technologies have enabled a broad range of new practices involving the recording, analysis and visualization of social life (Fielding *et al.*, 2008). Millions of blogs document everyday life on an ongoing basis; online platforms for social networking such as Facebook generate masses of data for social analysis; and applications of 'digital analytics' make it possible for everyone with access to these tools to analyse 'social behaviour' in real time. For the optimists, this situation implies a renaissance of social research: the new technologies and practices greatly enhance the empirical and analytic capacities of social research, and they render social research newly relevant to social life (Latour *et al.*, 2012). For the pessimists, the new digital sources of social intelligence announce not so much a rejuvenation of social research, but rather pose a serious threat to established traditions and forms of sociological research (Savage and Burrows, 2007). From this vantage point, the proliferation across social life of new technologies for recording, analysing and visualizing social life masks an underlying trend of a very different nature. These technologies are leading to the privatization of social research: they enable the displacement of social research to the corporate laboratories of big IT firms.

In this paper, I would like to unsettle this opposition between the utopian and dystopian imagination of digital technology in social research. I would like to contribute to debates about the implications of digitization for social research by exploring the concept and phenomenon of the *redistribution of research*. This notion has been put forward in the social studies of science and technology (STS) to complicate our understanding of the relations between science, technology, and society (Latour, 1988; Rheinberger, 1997; see also Whatmore, 2009). It highlights that scientific research tends to involve contributions from a *broad* range of actors: researchers, research subjects, funders, providers of research materials, infrastructure builders, interested amateurs, and so on. Scientific research, according to this notion, must be understood as a *shared accomplishment* of a diverse set of actors. This idea has clear implications for digital social research: it suggests that it may be a mistake to try and locate digital social research in a single domain, be it 'the university', or 'everyday practices like blogging', or 'the private laboratories of large IT firms'. Instead, we should examine how, in the context of digitization, the roles of social research are being distributed between a range of different actors: between researchers,

The Sociological Review, 60:S1, pp. 139–165 (2012), DOI: 10.1111/j.1467-954X.2012.02121.x

research subjects, digital technologies, and so on. Moreover, the concept of redistribution directs attention to a possible implication of digitization for social research: digitization may be unsettling established divisions of labour in social research. If we use blogs in social research, does this mean that we are partly delegating the task of data collection to bloggers?

Here I would like to focus on the redistribution of a specific element in social research, namely methods. Digitization is widely said to have special implications for the role and status of social research methods in particular (Fielding *et al.*, 2008; Rogers, 2010; Adkins and Lury, 2009). Views on this matter, too, diverge: some propose that digital technology inaugurates an age of methodological innovation, as new technologies for data collection, analysis and visualization enable the further elaboration of existing methods and the development of new ones. Others are more inclined to emphasize the 'return of the same' masked by such claims to newness, proposing that the 'new' digital methods continue along the same path as the 'quantitative revolution' of the 1960s and 70s (boyd and Crawford, 2011; Uprichard *et al.*, 2008). These observations are no less pertinent than the optimistic and pessimistic diagnoses flagged above, but on the issue of method too, there seems to be potential in side-stepping the 'false choice' between an utopian and a dystopian diagnosis, and to examine instead whether and how digitization enables new ways of *distributing* methods among different agents involved in social research. Social methods, too, may be understood as a shared accomplishment, involving contributions of researchers, research subjects, technologies, and so on (Rogers, 2009). The question is how the digital inflects this circumstance.

The issue of the redistribution of methods is a slippery one, as the contributions of different agents to the enactment of methods are hard to pin down: to return to the above example, why would we call blogs agents of data collection, rather than data points in our data set? On what grounds? To prevent being paralysed by general questions like this, I will explore the redistribution of method here in a contextual and empirical way, namely by examining two online platforms for social research: Issue Crawler, a web-based application for network analysis which has been online for 10 years now, and a tool of online textual analysis that is currently under development, provisionally called The Co-Word Machine. Both of these tools adapt social research methods to the online environment, namely network and textual analysis, and more precisely, co-citation and co-word analysis.[1] And they can both be said to undertake a 'redistribution' of social research methods: these transpose onto the Web methods that have long been championed in social research and, in doing so, they come to rely on a different set of entities in the enactment of this method, such as Web crawlers and online data feeds. The translation of methods of network and textual analysis into online environments, I will emphasize, enables a form of critical intervention in digital social research: to implement these methods online is to offer a distinctive variation on more prevalent applications of methods of network and textual analysis in digital networked media. The overall aim, then, is to get a more precise sense of the space of intervention opened up by digital social methods – *of method as intervention* – online. First, however, I would like to revisit in more detail the current debate about the implications of digitization for social research.

The digitization of social life and the redistribution of social research

The ongoing debate about the implications of digital technology for social research has directed attention to three significant features of digitization. No doubt the most important one is the *proliferation of new devices, genres and formats for the documentation of social life*. The last decade has seen an explosion of digital technologies that enable people to report and comment upon social life, from photo-sharing via Flickr to the public gossip of Twitter. Such online platforms allow users to publicize their accounts of everyday life like never before, in the form of simple text or snapshots taken with mobile phones. Especially interesting about the new devices from a sociological perspective is that they enable *the routine generation of data about social life as part of social life* (Fielding *et al.*, 2008; see on this point also Marres, 2011). 'Social media' platforms, that is, embed the process of social data generation in everyday practices, whether in the form of people 'live' commenting on an event via Twitter to the smart electricity meters that record fluctuations in domestic energy use. Finally, the two previous developments cannot really be understood without considering the development of online platforms and tools for the *analysis* of digital social data.

These days, most online platforms come with 'analytics' attached: a set of tools and services facilitating the analysis of the data generated by said platforms, from blog posts to Facebook friends. In this respect, what is especially significant for social research about online platforms for 'user-generated content' is that they actively support the adaptation of these platforms for purposes of social research. An example here is Yahoo Clues, a recently launched online platform that makes data generated by the Yahoo search engine available for analysis, allowing 'you to instantly discover what's popular to a select group of searchers – by age or gender – over the past day, week or even over the past year' (see Figure 1).[2] Providing access to a searchable database of search engine queries, Yahoo Clues makes available for analysis an arguably new type of social data, in the form of millions of queries that people perform as part of everyday life. And as Yahoo Clues allows its users to break down popular queries in terms of searcher profiles (gender, age, geographic location), it enables a distinctively social form of analysis. It also provides an example of the 'relocation' of social research enabled by digitization, as it formats social analysis as a popular practice that 'anyone' might like to engage in.

Social theorists have been hard pressed to provide an integrated assessment of these various developments and their implications for social research. Some authors have sought to affirm the new popular appeal of social research, suggesting that we are today witnessing a radical expansion in the range of actors,

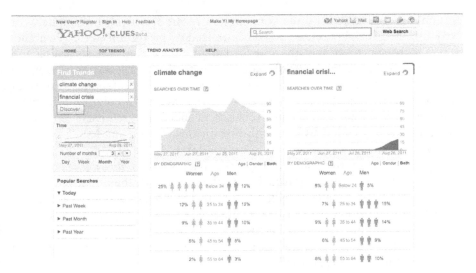

Figure 1: *Yahoo Clues: 'a new beta service that gives you a unique 'behind the scenes' look into popular trends across the millions of people who use Yahoo! to search each day' (July 2011).*

devices and settings caught up in the recording, reporting and analysis of social life. Some sociologists have been tempted to see in social media platforms a clear case of 'non-professional researchers enthusiastically engaging in the recording and reporting of social life' (my formulation). This would suggest that digitization is occasioning a revival of amateur-led social research, invoking memories of the English Mass Observation Movement, with its armies of lay people who documented scenes of everyday life in notebooks and questionnaires during the 1930s and 40s (Hubble, 2006; Savage, 2010). But others – indeed, in some cases the same authors – are more drawn to the dark side of this vision. Thus, Savage and Burrows (2007), in their influential article on 'The Coming Crisis of Empirical Sociology', prophesized that digitization signals the demise of sociology as a public form of knowledge. In their account, digitization, in spite of popular appearances, enables the *concentration* of social research capacity in a few well-resourced research centres, most notably of big IT firms. In this view, the wide popularity of online platforms for the collection, annotation and analysis of social data makes possible the displacement of social research to a few hubs of the digital economy, equipped for the central storage, processing and valuation of these data.

As has often been pointed out, the optimistic and the pessimistic diagnosis of a social phenomenon, while in some ways strictly opposed to another, may in other ways be neatly aligned (Haraway, 1991; Woolgar, 2002). As we know from the social study of consumer culture, dynamics of popularization and infrastructural concentration are by no means anti-thetical. As Celia Lury (1996, 2004) observed, popular fashion brands like Nike are marked by proliferation *and* unification, by the combination of an open-ended multiplicity of Nike-inflected social practices and a centralized orchestration of the phenomenon. To observe, then, that the spread of digital devices for the recording and analyzing social life occurs simultaneously with the concentration of control over the infrastructure that enables it is to note an all too familiar feature of post-industrial societies. It is just that, in the context of digitization, these dynamics are proving increasingly relevant to social research itself. But here I would like to argue that by concentrating on this overarching issue of the *displacement* of research capacity – to society at large, or the IT industry – we risk losing from view another, more fine-grained dynamic: the *redistribution* of social research *between* actors involved in social research. Rather than rushing to decide which sector of society will prove to be the biggest 'winner' – which will strengthen its position the most as a consequence of the digitization of social research? – we must then consider a more open-ended and complex process, namely that of the reconfiguration of the relations between the diverse set of agents caught up in social research.

The notion of the 'redistribution' of research has been put forward in STS and related fields to highlight processes of exchange *between* actors involved in social research. The notion emphasizes that the production of new knowledge and new technologies tend to involve complex interactions and transactions between a whole range of actors inside as well as outside the university, including research subjects, funding bodies, technological infrastructures, researchers, and so on. Research and innovation, then, is also a matter of the *transfer* of information, materials, and also more complex things like 'agency', between the various actors involved in research: when subjects agree to be interviewed or offer samples, when an institution allows a researcher into its archive, certain transactions occur that are critical to the production of new knowledge and/or technology. One example here is focus group research: this form of research relies on contributions from a range of actors, from research subjects, to research subject recruitment agencies and focus group moderators (Lezaun, 2007). Rather than assume that focus group research is conducted either 'in the university' or 'in the corporate sector', it therefore makes more sense to consider how this methodology enlists actors from different practices and domains, from marketing to government, activist organizations and academic research, and enables transactions among them. Indeed, social studies of focus group research have shown that the invention of the focus group in 1940s America enabled social research to take on new roles in society, among others as advisers on civic opinion (Lezaun, 2007; Grandclément and Gaglio, 2010). It also involved the development of new 'infrastructures' of social research, such as focus group research centres.

The concept of the 'redistribution of social research' has a number of implications for the debate about the consequences of digitization for social research. It suggests that some of the assumptions informing the debate about the displacement of research capacity, from the university to society, or from the public university to private industries, may be too simplistic. It suggests that the idea of the self-sufficient academy has *always* been a myth (Latour, 1988; Button, 1991; Callon *et al.*, 2009 [2001]). For a long time already, academics have not been the only or even the main protagonists of research, as other actors have historically played active roles in the production of knowledge (Latour, 1988; Law, 2004). It is just that the conventional understanding of science and innovation makes it difficult to acknowledge the contributions of 'non-scientists' as meaningful contributions to research and innovation, without problematizing the status of our knowledge. Going against this conventional understanding, the concept of the redistribution of social research defines social research as a collective undertaking, involving a diverse set of actors in a variety of roles. Processes of inquiry, from this vantage point, are best understood as *inherently* distributed among a whole range of agencies, involving active contributions from research subjects, the experimental apparatus, funders of research, and so on (Latour, 1988; Rheinberger, 1997; Law, 2009).

Once we approach social research as distributed, the question of *displacement* of research capacity – away from academia; towards popular culture or industry – no longer seems the most relevant question to ask. Rather than trying to decide in what *singular* location research capacity is today most advantageously located, we should examine what digitization means for the distribution of roles in social research *between* various actors in and outside the university. Especially important about digitization, from this vantage point, is that it may well be unsettling divisions of labour in social research. Emerging practices of online social research that seek to take advantage of the new social data made available by platforms like Facebook and Twitter provide a case in point. Digital sociology student Sam Martin, for instance, turned to Twitter to analyse the racial abuse row over the prosecution of England footballer John Terry.[3] Using various applications from Google Docs to Yahoo Pipes and the Twitter API application programming interface, Martin culled messages mentioning John Terry from Twitter over a four-day period in February 2012. Using a programme called 'TagExplorer' she produced a network map of 'topconversation-alists', which notably included 'Queens Park Ranger Captain and Footballer' Joey Barton, who was present at the pitch when the racial abuse incident occurred (see Figure 2).

This type of online research, which adapts social media applications to the purposes of social research, can be said to redistribute social research in various ways. Most notable, is its reliance on the social media platform Twitter itself: Twitter enables the ranking of twitter users according to the number of followers, tweets, and re-tweets, and in visualizing the corpus of messages using the measure of 'topconversationalists', Martin's small study arguably replicates some of the measures that are implicit in the medium under scrutiny. We should also note the various research tools and applications that allowed her to extract tweets from Twitter and visualize them, like Tageexplorer: these instruments, as well as the 'developer community' from which they sprang, here come to play a notable role in the organization of social research, and so did, arguably, the army of tweeters who in this study got a say on framing

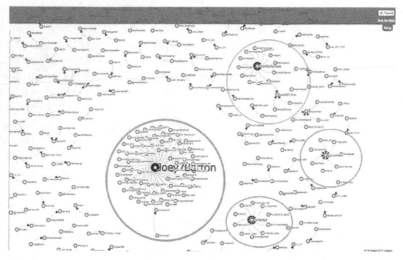

Figure 2: *Top conversationalists, the John Terry debate on Twitter, visualization using TAGSExplorer, 3–7 February 2012, by Sam Martin.*

phenomena as significant (by following some Twitter contributors rather than others).

Digital social research then enables particular redistributions of social research. Taking up digital online tools, sociologists are likely to enter into working relations with platforms, tool developers and analytic and visual devices which are operating in contexts and developed for purposes that are not necessarily those of sociology (Marres and Weltevrede, forthcoming). In examining such redistributions in digital social research, we can ask a question about the implications of digitization for social research that is at once more specific and open-ended than the question about displacement: to what extent does digitization enable *renegotiations of divisions of labour* in social research? At issue, then, is not only which institution or sector gets to define what social research is, and to occupy the 'top spot', but rather what relations between a range of different actors is enabled by particular, emerging digital social research practices. The notion of the redistribution of social research, furthermore, directs attention to *a much broader* set of actors and entities caught up in the process of the digitization of social research, including but not limited to: online platforms, users, databases, design agencies, algorithms, IT companies, digital culture commentators, information formats, social movements, and so on (see on this point also Madsen, 2012). The division of labour between users, devices and researchers in the conduct of social research, we then say, is being unsettled, contested and redefined in complex but quite specific ways.

The idea of the redistribution of social research can then provide some useful conceptual guidance, in examining the implications of digitization for social

The Sociological Review, 60:S1, pp. 139–165 (2012), DOI: 10.1111/j.1467-954X.2012.02121.x

research. It differs from the thesis of the 'displacement' of social research, high-lighted above, in at least four ways.

First, to consider the redistribution of social research is to shift attention from the *external* relations of social research to its *internal* relations. The displacement diagnosis posits a fairly strict separation between academic social science and its various outsides – industry, social life, the public. To argue that research capacity is moving away from academia to somewhere else is to accentuate the distinction between academic and other forms of social research. By contrast, a redistribution perspective highlights the contributions of actors inside and outside the university in the production of social research (Adkins and Lury, 2009; Savage *et al.*, 2010).[4] It entails a relatively loose definition of social research, to which various skills and competencies may contribute. Secondly, a redistributive understanding of social research implies a shift in perspective from *ready-made sociology* to *sociology in-the-making*. The digitization of social research, we could say, renders newly relevant a classic insight of the social studies of science and technology: our analysis of knowledge production changes radically as soon as we shift our attention from the status of social research *as a finished product*, to ongoing processes of social research (Latour, 1988).

To conjure up the spectre of the 'corporatization' or 'popularization' or 'democratization' of social research, is to build an argument that derives its normative force from a focus on outcomes. By contrast, if we focus on divisions of labour in digital social research, we explore how digitization may affect and inform the *conduct* of social research, and the normative charge of our exploration here derives from the extent to which these processes are still to a degree undecided, contested, multiple. Thirdly, and relatedly, the notion of redistribution leads us to question the distinction *between the conditions or 'context' of social research and its content*. Debates about the consequences of digitization of social research often concentrate on changes that affect the 'material base' for social research, that is, the technologies and forms of data storage on which it relies. However, of many of the features of digital social research it is actually quite hard to say whether they affect only the conditions or the substance of social research or both or neither: does Twitter research primarily signify a change of conditions in social research, as tweets can be extracted from Twitter so much faster and in quantities that are so much larger than used to be the case in popular discourse analysis (boyd and Crawford, 2011; Leavitt, 2009)? Or does the very meaning of the concept of social discourse change now that we mean by it the broadcasting of one-liners by active individuals in 'real-time' (Niederer and Van Dijck, 2010)?

Fourthly and finally, a focus on redistribution rather than displacement has implications for how we understand our own role as social researchers. That is, the practical or normative roles that we are able to envision for social research, or what we might call their 'scope of intervention', is very different depending on which of the two perspectives we adopt, displacement or redistribution. From a redistributive perspective, the principal question becomes how we may most relevantly intervene in shifting distributions of social research capacity. Here, the main point is not to paint big canvas total pictures of the unlikely future we desire for social research and the likely one that we must fend off. Rather, the question becomes where and how, given the type of redistributions of social research that are currently ongoing, we can most pertinently add a different ingredient that might change the wider mix of social research. A focus on social research *methods* appears to be especially productive in this regard.

The redistribution of social research methods: five views

Method is an important mediator of divisions of labour in social research, and this is no less the case in digital social research. The devising of new research methods, of course, has long been a strategy of choice for those attempting to establish privilege, or claim precedence or newness in science, and digital social research is no exception to this either. As in other fields, debates in social research about methodology have long been a key site and proxy for much more comprehensive controversies about the future direction of the field, with much of the 20th-century methodology contests having been dominated by the pitching of quantitative versus qualitative sociology, with the Positivismusstreit between Karl Popper and Jurgen Habermas as an illustrious example. Methods, then, offer a means to conjure up and establish particular versions of social research, and this in turn tends to involve the attempt to enforce particular divisions of labour in social research. Qualitative social research, for instance, proposes to grant much more initiative to research subjects, while much quantitative research endeavours to create a greater role for standardized tools of data collection, such as the survey, as a way to guarantee the commensurability of data.

In the area of digital social research, methods are invoked to such effects as well.[5] There have been some audacious claims about the opportunities for methodological innovation enabled by online networked media, such as the claim that changing patterns in user activity on the Web may indicate or predict real-time events, like an onslaught of the flu (Rogers, 2009; Mohebbi *et al.*, 2011). And in this context, too, qualitative and quantities methods are pitched against one another, as claims are made back and forth about the relative advantages of, for instance, digital ethnography versus large-scale online survey research (boyd and Crawford, 2011). The Internet has also been said to favour particular social methods over others, such as unobtrusive or non-interventionist methods like content analysis (Lee, 2000; Carslon and Anderson, 2007). Here I cannot do justice to these various methodology debates, but discussions about digital social research methods provide an especially useful prism through which to approach the issue of the redistribution of social research: different views on the implications of digitization for social methods imply very different understandings of what redistributions of research capacity are possible in this context, both empirically and normatively speaking. These views therefore provide a useful starting point for identifying different options in this regard. In this section, I will present some different views on the digitization of two particular methods, network and textual analysis, so as to set the stage for further discussion of the possibilities for intervention in digital social research opened up by the redistribution of methods.

It is possible to order different views on the implications of digitization for social research methods along a spectrum, which starts on one end with a minimal redistribution of research capacity and moves to a maximum redistribution on the other end. The left side of this spectrum is marked by a conservative position that is sceptical about the possibility that social methods are undergoing any significant transformation in digital environments, let alone something like a 'redistribution of methods'. This position, which might be dubbed 'methods-as-usual' can be recognized in an argument recently put forward by the eminent Chicago sociologist Andrew Abbott, who proposed that for anyone who is well versed in social research methods, the newness of the new, online media is very much overstated.[6] Abbott emphasizes that the social methodologies incorporated into digital devices like search engines, most notably network and textual analysis, are pretty standard fare, at least for trained sociologists, and has called the search engine Google 'basically a concordance machine', which matches key-words (queries) to target contexts, and which relies on 'rather routine' additional measures of network analysis, such as in-centrality, to determine the authority of sources; something which has little new to offer to sociologists who have long been familiar with such measures. This view focuses specifically on the formal metrics built into digital devices, and does not consider how these metrics are adapted to or informed by other features of digital devices, as for instance the use of 'live' data or feedback mechanisms. Indeed, it does not really consider the possibility that social research methods may be transformed by virtue of their insertion in a digital networked environment. One could accordingly say that, from this perspective, only one redistribution of research capacity has occurred, in that popular online devices now have social research methods built into them. But on the whole no real redistribution of *methods* is acknowledged: social research methods themselves are not really affected by their uptake in digital online media.

A second view differs significantly from this, and is associated with the new network science informed by mathematics, physics and computing science. This body of work is principally concerned with the opportunities that online media offer for further development of large-scale network and textual analysis, and may accordingly be called 'big methods'. It proposes that digitization has made possible new developments in the *modelling* of networks and textual worlds, and this in large part because of the very large data-sets that digital media technologies make available. The vast databases that have been built over the last decade by search engine companies, gaming industries, Internet service providers and social media platforms create opportunities to significantly expand the analytical and empirical power of network science. They enable the further development of what Duncan Watts and others (Newman *et al.*, 2007) refer to as 'the analysis of real-world network dynamics' (see also Lazer *et al.*, 2009). Contrary to methods-as-usual, this methodological programme can be said to undertake a redistribution of methods of sorts. The new network science namely favours a new set of techniques for data collection and analysis, which entail an unusual division of labour between research subjects, data collection devices, and analysts in social research. To put it somewhat crudely, the approach seeks to maximize the role of mathematical techniques, at the expense of research subjects. In their introduction to the New Network Science, Newman and Watts argue that the social data generated by digital platforms are 'more amenable to the kinds of techniques with which physicists and mathematicians are familiar', and offer a welcome substitute for survey data, and other all too 'social' types of data (Newman *et al.*, 2007).

Proposing this, the new network science reinstates a classic opposition of social research, that between subjective and objective data. Like many others, Newman *et al.* (2007) locate the opportunities that digitization offers for social research in the *type* of data that now become available for social analysis: namely transactional data, which 'record the activities and interactions of the subjects directly' and are thus routinely generated as part of social activities by digital devices, from loyalty cards to search engines (see on this point also Latour, 1998; Rogers, 2009; Savage and Burrows, 2007). Newman *et al.* (2007) give a classic positivist justification for relying on this type of data, arguing that they are much more objective and, as such, offer a welcome substitute for the 'subjective' data generated by surveys, making it possible to avoid reliance on the active contributions of erratic human subjects to data collection.[7] In their account, then, data provided by research subjects are not quite reliable data, something which in their view challenges the validity of network analysis as a whole: 'the respondent data are so contaminated by diverse interpretations of the survey instrument, along with variable recollection or even laziness, that any inferences about the corresponding social network must be regarded with scepticism' (Newman *et al.*, 2007: L-6). Paradoxically, the rise of social media like email, blogs and Facebook here makes possible the *rejection* of user-generated data for purposes of social research, and a redistribution of research capacity towards online registrational devices.

A third and fourth approach are respectively called 'virtual methods' and 'digital methods', and they can be distinguished from the former two in that they are explicitly concerned with the changing relations between social research, its devices and objects in digital online environments. These two approaches offer, however, very different accounts of these changes. The 'virtual methods' programme, developed by Christine Hine (2002, 2005) and others in the early 2000s, focused on the opportunities opened up by the transposition of qualitative social research methods into digital online environments. Its main concern was the digital transformation of *our own sociological methods*, that is, the ways in which methods like discourse analysis and ethnography were and could be transformed by their application in the new context. In focusing mostly on the fate of qualitative methods, Hine's approach to virtual methods makes the opposite manoeuvre from the new network science: it seeks to maximize the role of interpretative

The Sociological Review, 60:S1, pp. 139–165 (2012), DOI: 10.1111/j.1467-954X.2012.02121.x

subjects in social research, defining the experience of this subject as one of the principal empirical objects of virtual social research. As Hine (2002) puts it: 'ethnographers of the Internet cannot hope to understand the practices of *all* users, but through their own practices they can develop an understanding of what it is to be *a* user' (2002: 54). More generally speaking, the virtual methods approach is concerned with the *digitization* of social research methods, that is, with the translation of methodologies that sociologists define as their own into online environments (Rogers, 2010). This is to recognize a significant but limited redistribution of methods: here, the role of new entities, like web users, in the performance of social method is very much acknowledged, as everyday Internet users are seen to do things online that are similar to fieldwork (taking notes, documenting practice, checking out a strange, new social world). However, such redistributions of social method are here only explored insofar as they affect actors and agencies caught up in the sociologists' research itself: researcher, research subjects, mediating infrastructures, tools used, and so on.

In adopting this strategy, virtual methods do not address the wider issue of the general uptake of social methods in digital online environments, and the consequences of this for the shape and outlook of digital social research. It is this issue that the digital methods programme formulated by Richard Rogers and others (Rogers, 2009) explicitly takes up. This approach proposes that dominant digital devices, search engines chief among them, can be adapted for purposes of social research, and accords to these devices the capacity to inform the development of new methods of social research. Because of their large, dynamic data sets, sophisticated algorithms and feedback possibilities, search engines, Rogers argues, are able to devise forms of social analysis that were not possible before, termed 'natively digital' (see also Weltevrede, n.d.). Digital methods, then, propose that social research should take advantage of the analytic and empirical capacities that are 'embedded in online media'. These can be adapted to purposes of social research, by developing online research tools that run on top of web devices, like Google. The Googlescraper, for instance, adapts Google to conduct work frequency analysis in source sets delineated by the user.[8] This methodological programme of *repurposing* entails a particular redistribution of social research methods, namely towards *devices*: in proposing to adapt existing online devices for purposes of social research, their capacities of data collection, analysis and feedback, come to be incorporated into social and cultural research. As the Digital Methods Initiative proposes to import dominant online tools for data collection, analysis and visualization into social research – or at least parts thereof – devices that constitute the *context* of digital culture come to actively inform the content of social and cultural research.

Arguably, the Digital Methods Initiative more than any other approach discussed above seeks to come to terms with the redistribution of methods in digital environments. Recently, sociologists have recognized that online environments foster a range of tools and practices that qualify as instruments of social research, acknowledging that methods lead a 'social life' online (Savage *et al.*, 2010). But the Digital Methods Initiative proposes an empirical programme that deliberately deploys this circumstance, seeking to render it analytically useful for social research. However, in its above formulation, this approach nevertheless could be said to share a blind spot with the first two approaches already discussed above. Just as with the methods-as-usual perspective and the 'big methods' of the new network science, digital methods can be seen to bracket the issue of the *re-mediation* (Bolter and Grusin, 2000) of social methods in digital online media. As mentioned, Rogers defines the methods enabled by online digital devices as 'natively digital', proposing that they have no clear correlate in the pre- or non-digital world. In making this claim, the DMI programme statement does not really consider, or even downplays, the question of how the uptake of existing social research methods in digital environments entails a *refashioning* of these methods.[9] This question, however, seems to me all too relevant if we want to explore the type of *interventions* that social research becomes capable of in the context of the redistribution of social methods online.

The notion of the 're-mediation of methods' is especially useful, I want to propose here, in that it directs attention to the ways in which prevailing digital devices have methods built into them in which we can recognize those of social research. The foundational article in which Google founders Larry Page and Sergey Brin outlined the central idea behind the new search algorithm, Pagerank, does not only cite a famous sociologist of science, Robert Merton, but it also makes an informed critique of the limitations of sociological forms of network analysis, or as the case may be, citation analysis (Page *et al.*, 1999). Below I will further discuss the particular re-mediation of citation analysis undertaken by Google. Attending to such re-mediations of social methods in the digital context, I want to propose, brings into view a particular mode of intervention for social research itself. Insofar as predominant digital devices apply existing social methods, this may render newly relevant existing sociological *critiques* of these methods. The re-mediation of social methods in the digital context, then, opens up a space of critical intervention for engaged social research. In the remainder of this piece, I will discuss the methodological strategies involved in the development of two digital research tools along these very lines: the Issue Crawler, and an online application of co-word analysis currently under development, the Co-word machine. If we consider how these devices re-mediate social methods, we get an idea of the *digital forms of methodology critique* they enable.

Issue Crawler: from co-citation to co-link analysis

Issue Crawler is an online platform for the location, analysis and visualization of hyperlink networks on the Web. Launched in the early 2000s, Issue Crawler was intended to enable the location and analysis of 'issue networks' on the Web, as it uses hyperlink analysis to delineate sets of pages dealing with a common theme that are connected by hyperlinks (Marres and Rogers, 2008). But the tool has since been used in a variety of projects of online network analysis, including organizational networks (allowing organizations to answer questions such as 'how central are we in this area?') as well as the longitudinal study of online networks, as in the analysis of the rise of Obama and his social media campaign sites in the US democratic election network of 2008 (Borra, 2008; see Figure 3). Using the campaign sites of all democratic presidential candidates as starting points, this last study used Issue Crawler to conduct a series of scheduled crawls, which plotted the emergence of a highly ordered network on the Web, with Obama social media campaign sites dominating the entire network towards the end of the election period. Such network dynamics are arguably Web specific, insofar as the reconfiguration of material network relations can be analysed in real time. But the method on which Issue Crawler relies to demarcate hyperlink networks is based on a classic form of network analysis: co-citation analysis. As an implementation of this specific social research method, the design of Issue Crawler is informed by the context in which the platform was developed.[10]

In the late 1990s, as mentioned above, the rise of the Internet was widely interpreted as an opportunity to apply methods of citation analysis in the new medium, and to adapt this classic method for the analysis of hyperlink structures (Scharnhorst and Wouters, 2006). In this period, the rise of Google and its famous Pagerank algorithm, which relies on in-link measures to rank sources in its query return lists, made newly relevant debates about methods of citation analysis that had been developed by sociologists of science from the 1960s onwards. Larry Page's foundational article makes a specific argument about the re-mediation of citation analysis enabled by the Web, which in his view makes it possible to address *a shortcoming of this method:*

> There has been a great deal of work on academic citation analysis. Goffmann has published an interesting theory of how information flow in a scientific community is an epidemic process. [. . .] But the reason Pagerank is interesting is that there are many cases where simply citation counting does not correspond to our common sense notion of importance. For example, if a web page has a link of the Yahoo home page, it may be just one link but it is a very important one. This page should be ranked higher. Pagerank is an attempt to see how good an approximation to 'importance' can be obtained just from the link structure. (Page *et al.*, 1999)

Arguably, this issue of 'source authority' had already been discussed in citation analysis (MacRoberts and MacRoberts, 1988), and accordingly the degree to which Google's brand of hyperlink analysis contains an actual innovation can be debated. However, as methods of citation analysis were being re-invented as methods of hyperlink analysis, the question was also raised whether and how *critiques* of citation analysis transferred into the online environment. This was – in one of those stories one can tell about tools and methods – the question that Issue Crawler was made to address.

In the 1960s and 70s, sociologists had voiced concerns about citation analysis that now proved all too relevant to the methodological innovation proposed by Google. Citation analysis, it had been argued back then, enables a potentially

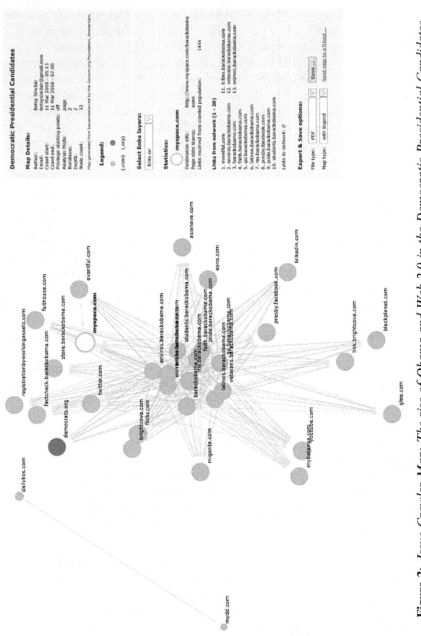

Figure 3: *Issue Crawler Map: The rise of Obama and Web 2.0 in the Democratic Presidential Candidates network, Betsy SinClair, March 2008*

perverse authority dynamic, according to which well-cited sources get cited more simply because they are already well-cited (Small, 1973; see also Callon *et al.*, 1983).[11] Any large number of citations tends to generate more of them, these now classic critiques proposed, resulting in a situation in which sources are considered authoritative simply by virtue of their authority, and accordingly processes of the valuation of knowledge are captured by social dynamics of popularity, and risk becoming divested from more substantive processes of valuation. This classic critique touched on issues of clear relevance to the new search engine algorithms, like Google's (Marres and Rogers, 2000): these algorithms, too, attributed authority to sources on the basis of the level of recognition implied by the overall number of hyperlinks they received, independent from content. In developing the methodology of Issue Crawler we then drew on this specific methodological critique of 'the authority of authority', in order to develop an alternative approach to hyperlink analysis, one that draws on co-citation analysis (Marres and Rogers, 2000).

In some respects, then, Issue Crawler simply transposed an old methodological solution into a new context. Co-citation analysis was developed in the 1960s as an alternative to the standard citation measure of the overall number of citations received. Rather than seeking to determine the overall authority of individual sources, co-citation analysis seeks to delineate clusters of relevant sources by identifying sources that are jointly linked by other sources. Applying this method to hyperlinks, Issue Crawler sought to introduce a substantive measure of relevance into hyperlink analysis. Issue Crawler deploys the method of co-link analysis in order to undercut the authority effects to which citation and network analysis are vulnerable; instead of assigning value to the overall number of links that sources receive, co-link analysis seeks to locate 'topical clusters' of sources, by identifying co-links in a thematic neighbourhood, or as we called them 'issue networks'. As is clear from the example in Figure 3, Issue Crawler has not necessarily been successful in foregrounding dynamics of relevance at the expense of dynamics of authority. Arguably, indeed, the more insightful issue networks located with Issue Crawler include a clear element of authority, though this is not always the case (Marres and Rogers (2008) discuss some exceptions).

However, it is also important to note that in transposing co-citation analysis onto the Web, Issue Crawler transformed this classic method in some important respects. Before the Web, co-citation analysis was by its very nature limited to the analysis of scientific data-bases, most notably the Science Citation Index. Even as this method sought to challenge authority dynamics, it inevitably rendered itself dependent on institutional demarcations of the relevant fields, in this case scientific fields. For this reason, co-citation could *not* include all the sources to which citations directed it: the scope of its analysis was limited to the sets of sources included in official scientific databases. The Web, by contrast, presents us with *networks* of databases, and as such, it opens up the possibility of analysing a much broader array of sources in real time, generating data-sets that are much more *heterogeneous* than those of citation analysis (Marres and Rogers, 2000; Muniesa and Tchalakov, 2009).[12]

In using co-link analysis to locate thematic networks on the Web, Issue Crawler does not only transpose a particular method into the online environment, but also a specific *methodology critique*. In advocating co-citation analysis, sociologists did not only seek to address a problem with methods of citation analysis in themselves, or with questionable citation behaviours, whereby sources mainly recognize already authoritative sources, thus aggravating the popularity effect. In the pre-digital context, critics of citation analysis specifically targeted the ways in which citation analysis *amplified* these popularity effects: their concern was that science policy would increasingly rely on these methods, as research councils took up citation measures, in their attempt to render their modes of assessment more evidence-based (Leydersdorff, 1998). Similarly, the issue with search engines is not just that, in applying measures of in-link centrality, they help to generate more authority for already authoritative sources.[13] At issue is a whole complex of behaviours: by privileging sources with a high overall in-link count, search engines encourage linking behaviours that consolidate authority dynamics, and the modification of user trajectories to a similar effect (Introna and Nissenbaum, 2000; Vaidhyanathan, 2011). In networked environments, then, it is especially obvious that *multiple* agencies have a part to play in the enactment of 'social methods'.[14] To put it differently, in the digital context social methods must clearly be defined as a *distributed* accomplishment, and our attempts to intervene critically in this context must be informed by this circumstance.

The co-word machine: from co-word analysis to online issue profiling

In questioning the dominance of authority dynamics on the Web, back in the late 1990s, and the role of devices like Google in enabling this, however, I clearly had little idea of what we were up against. In retrospect it can seem naive to expect that a methodology developed by a minoritarian movement in the sociology of science, like co-citation analysis, could be rendered effective in digital networked spaces, which were just then emerging as key hubs of the global information economy. Indeed, recent developments in this area, most notably the rise of social media platforms like Facebook and Twitter, can be taken as evidence that the medium has gone 'the other way'. Reputational dynamics, whereby things become more widely liked by virtue of being liked, have become very much the currency of online media (Onnela and Reed-Tsochas, 2010; Gerlitz and Helmond, 2012). The social network, in which actor-alliances are formed largely independent from content – and *not* the 'issue network', with its topical dynamics of the thematic clustering of sources – has become the key organizational form associated with the Internet (for the distinction between issue- and actor-network, see Marres and Rogers, 2008). However, social media platforms also highlight the limits of our earlier argument in another, less ironic sense: social media have proven that networks driven by reputational logics are very well capable of organizing content, in ways that do *not* necessarily reproduce 'the tyranny of reputation'. The rise of these platforms has been accompanied by the proliferation of tools for the analysis and visualization of substantive dynamics. Figure 4, for example, provides a word frequency analysis of action terms on Facebook, showing the relative prominence of such terms in a selection of Facebook groups.

Social media, then, have proven to be no less adaptable to the purposes of content analysis than social network analysis. Nevertheless, I think that our initial intuition still holds: online digital environments are in need of alternative measures that can provide a counter-weight to dominant popularity metrics. On closer inspection, many current instruments of online content analysis, like tag clouding, have not really attenuated authority effects. They tend to rely on versions of the 'overall citation count' too: they bring into view what (or who) is most mentioned, followed, liked and so on, in a given data set at a given moment. Tag clouds, and other online applications of textual analysis and visualization perpetuate the preoccupation with the most cited or most popular, and these instruments can arguably be said to reproduce the authority effect in another form. After the rise of social media, the question then remains how to develop alternatives to reputational measures: the question is still that of how to move beyond 'purely social' mechanics of authority, popularity or celebrity, and get to more substantive dynamics of relevance. But in this context, too, existing sociological critiques of research methods may offer a useful resource: debates about the majoritarian bias in textual analysis, and the development of alternative forms of 'discourse analysis' have been ongoing in sociology for several decades. Here I would like to single out one such alternative method, namely *co-word analysis*, as this method was explicitly developed by sociologists

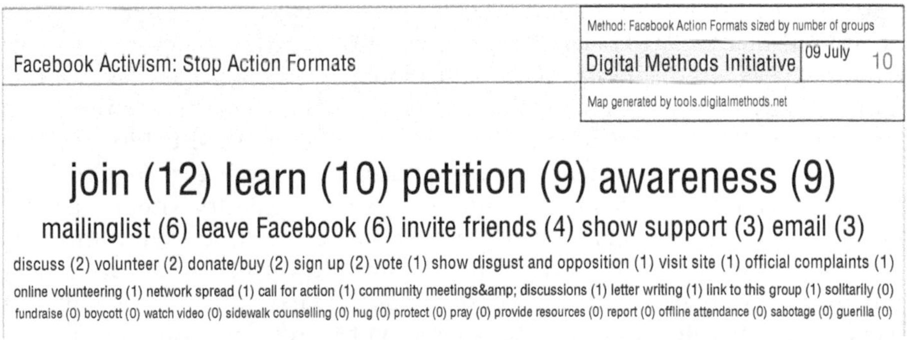

Facebook Activism: Stop Action Formats	Method: Facebook Action Formats sized by number of groups		
	Digital Methods Initiative	09 July	10
	Map generated by tools.digitalmethods.net		

join (12) learn (10) petition (9) awareness (9)
mailinglist (6) leave Facebook (6) invite friends (4) show support (3) email (3)
discuss (2) volunteer (2) donate/buy (2) sign up (2) vote (1) show disgust and opposition (1) visit site (1) official complaints (1) online volunteering (1) network spread (1) call for action (1) community meetings& discussions (1) letter writing (1) link to this group (1) solitarily (0) fundraise (0) boycott (0) watch video (0) sidewalk counselling (0) hug (0) protect (0) pray (0) provide resources (0) report (0) offline attendance (0) sabotage (0) guerilla (0)

Figure 4: *Tag cloud analysis, Facebook is for joiners*
Source: Lonneke van der Velden and Clare Lee, Project Facebook, DMI Summerschool, July 2010 (https://wiki.digitalmethods.net/Dmi/Training ProgramProjectFacebook).

of science and technology to enrich citation analysis and possibly by extension hyperlink analysis.

Co-word analysis was devised in the 1980s by the actor-network theorist Michel Callon and others as a way to expand the project of co-citation analysis. It was developed to locate 'pockets of innovation' in science, using textual analysis to locate especially active thematic clusters of sources in the scientific literature.[15] Co-word analysis did this by measuring the rise and fall of key-words, and the associations among them, in a corpus of scientific articles (Callon *et al.*, 1983; Whittaker, 1989). Analysing the keywords used to index articles in scientific databases, co-word analysis offered a way to determine which were the most 'active' key words, and word associations in the corpus. It provided a way to measure which keywords and keyword associations *varied* significantly in their mentioning and relations over a given period. In trying to determine the most 'happening' themes, this method was expressly designed to locate 'buzz' or 'live content' in the scientific literature, *but it did this without relying on popularity dynamics.* Indeed, terms that were mentioned with a constantly high frequency were automatically deleted from the set of active terms: the key indicator was not frequency of mentioning but *variation* in mentioning (and association) (Callon *et al.*, 1983).

In recent years, the method of co-word analysis has been transposed onto the Web, with various online applications deploying the methodology to visualize word associations in online data sets, such as corpi of email messages or twitter messages (Danowksi, 2009; www.infomous.com). In the online context, co-word analysis promises to offer an alternative to word frequency analysis, the method of which it seems fair to say spread like wildfire, also into the social sciences, on the back of tag clouding tools.[16] Co-word analysis determines the relevance of terms by measuring the strength and intensity of relations among them: only words that appear frequently *and* that appear together make it onto co-word maps. Co-word analysis, as mentioned, tries to purge its analysis of terms that are merely popular: it excludes terms that appear frequently but in random association with others. For this reason, co-word analysis seems to provide an alternative to the majoritarian logics of word frequency, which make a term appear larger and more visible the more often it appears. The method may help us move beyond the ranking or hit list, that most visible testimony to the tyranny of reputation, as is evidenced by the alternative visual format proposed by Callon and colleagues for co-word analysis (see Figure 5). Crucially, moreover, online co-word analysis does away with popularity without sacrificing *liveness,* or rather liveliness. Co-word analysis, too, aims to deliver the most *happening* content (see also Marres and Weltevrede, forthcoming). But it does this by deploying an alternative measure: not the safety of a large number of mentionings, but fluctuations in the presence of words and word associations is key.

Together with colleagues in Amsterdam, we are now working to develop a Co-Word Machine that deploys co-word analysis for the online location and visualization of 'issue language'. In transposing co-word analysis into the online

The Sociological Review, 60:S1, pp. 139–165 (2012), DOI: 10.1111/j.1467-954X.2012.02121.x

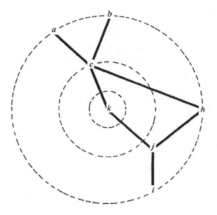

Figure 5: *Co-word visualization*
Source: Callon *et al.* (1983).

context, however, a number of issues arise which may either weaken or strengthen the analytical and critical capacities of this method, depending on how we deal with them, and how they will play out. First of all, online environments offer an opportunity which adherents of co-word analysis could only theorize in the 1980s. For Callon and his colleagues, the chief attraction of co-word analysis was its promise to help advance 'our search for the trans-disciplinary, trans-institutional problematic networks that we want to identify' (Callon *et al.*, 1983: 196) However, in the 1980s co-word analysts were frustrated in this project by the limits of the databases and genres to which they applied their method. As in the case of co-citation analysis, co-word analysis relied on scientific data-bases, and because the genre of the scientific article was so different from those current in other fields (the policy report, the newspaper article, the petition), there was no reliable way to track terms *across* discursive spheres. Online net-worked media provide a great opportunity to address this limitation, as one distinctive feature of these media is precisely the significant genre contamination across fields (which organization does not have a blog?) In this environment, co-word analysis, too, may be applied to far more *heterogeneous* data-sets (Marres and Rogers, 2000).

However, the Web also poses some serious challenges for co-word analysis, among others because of the widely divergent ways of indexing content preva-lent in the medium. In this respect at least, classic co-word analysis had it easy, as it could rely on professional indices – keywords used by institutions like the Science Citation Index to index scientific articles – to locate emergent vocabular-ies. In online media, most applications rely on self-indexing – on keywords, or tags, provided by users marking up self-generated content. This inevitably raises issues of reliability and comparability, and in this respect, digital tagging prac-tices drive home a basic but important point made by the American journalist Walter Lippmann (1997 [1922]) in his classic analysis of newspapers: any factual report is only as good as the sources from which it derives its findings (such as the National Office of Statistics). In this respect, co-word analysis certainly is *not* free of the problems associated with digital devices like tag clouding, which, as the name says, tend to rely on tags used to mark up online content, by bloggers and other users. In the case of co-word analysis as well, our results will only be as good as the classificatory practices on which we rely. We are returning, then, to the issue of the distributed accomplishment of digital methods: online textual analysis is likely to rely on the contributions of a whole host of agents, from the availability of tagging features, to the taggers who actually mark up online content, the analytical instruments used to analyse these tags, visualization modules, and so on. In order to intervene relevantly in online social research, we do well to recognize such assemblages of users, devices and informational practices, as the relevant unit of 'methodological innovation' in social research.

Conclusion

In online environments, the distributed nature of social research is especially hard to deny. User behaviours, information formats and digital devices that are embedded in the medium are likely to leave an imprint on social analysis. Something that applies to other research practices too is then rendered explicit in online social research: here, social research is *noticeably* marked by informational practices and devices not of its own making, from the analytic measures built into online platforms (eg numbers of links, number of mentionings, follower counts), to the visual forms embedded in visualization modules (the tag cloud). Online social research is visibly a distributed accomplishment. This circumstance, I have argued, does not only pose problems for social research but also offers opportunities for the development of social research methods. Digitization enables a broadening of the agencies playing an active role in the enactment of social methods, broadly conceived: in this context, a wide range of actors including platform users and analytic devices like search engines come to play a part in the collection, analysis and presentation of social data. And this redistribution of methods in digital social research opens up a space of intervention for social research.

Social methods, I have argued, are a key instrument with which wider divisions of roles in social research are being curated in online environments. Prominent digital devices like Google and Twitter and Facebook, and the users and developers enrolled by them, today actively inform the enactment of social methods online. The types of data platforms make available, the measures and formats on which they rely in communicating this data (rankings, follower counts and clouds), and the wider informational practices in which they are taken up (Facebook members visualizing the network of their Facebook friends): all of these elements inform the performance of 'social methods' in digital networked environments. The contours of these 'methodological spaces online' are not necessarily easy to determine, as platform settings change, and users change their allegiance to a new device. However, these assembled devices, settings and actors open up a particular space of intervention in digital social research: if specific digital social methods are a distributed accomplishment – such as the 'overall citation count' that is materialized in Google and other platforms – then sociological research may seek to intervene in the relations among entities that sustain these methods, by proposing alternative methods and distributions thereof. Web-based applications of co-link analysis and co-word analysis, the Issue Crawler and the Co-word machine currently under development, aim to do just this. In so doing, they extend some of the long-standing normative projects of sociological research into digital environments, such as the commitment to methods that privilege substantive dynamics of relevance over purely social or reputational ones, or what we could call 'post-social methods'.

As noted, there is a strong tradition in social research of seeking to bracket the effects of the methods deployed by 'the social actors themselves': many social researchers have become experts in devising tricks that make it possible to ignore the active contribution of research subjects to the organization of data and the framing of methods. But digital networked environments provide opportunities to explore different possible approaches to the distributed nature of social research and its methods. As online social research forces us to acknowledge the contributions of digital devices, practices and subjects, to the enactment of social research, it can be taken as an invitation to move beyond 'proprietary' concepts of methods, that is, beyond the entrenched use of method as a way to monopolize the representation of a given field or aspect of social reality. A redistributive approach to social research redefines methods as involving the combination and coordination of diverse competencies: classification, visual design, automated analysis, and so on. Behind debates about the unreliability of data generated by research subjects, and the 'mess' of self-indexed online content, there lies a debate about the redistribution of methods between researchers, devices, information and users, in online environments. Which is also to say, the debate about the digitization of social methods is perhaps most productively approached as a debate about *participatory* research methods.

Acknowledgements

I would like to thank Les Back, Erik Borra, Sabine Niederer, Nirmal Puwar, Richard Rogers, Emma Uprichard and Esther Weltevrede for their comments on earlier versions of this article.

Notes

1 Both of these methods have been central to the development of actor-network theory and in focusing on the re-mediation of these methods, I am also exploring how online research

tools translate methods of actor-network theory into networked digital media. In doing so, I will join others in arguing that digitization offers opportunities for a generalization of this sociological research programme (Latour, 1998; Law, 2008; Savage, 2010; Latour *et al.*, 2012).

2 'New Yahoo! Clues Launches', posted 29 June 2011, http://www.ysearchblog.com/2011/06/29/new-yahoo-clues-launches/

3 See http://twitterabused.com/2012/02/09/visualising-twitter-networks-john-terry-captaincy-controversy/

4 The notion of the redistribution of social research in the digital context is both inspired by and deviates from the idea of the double social life of methods proposed by Savage *et al.* (2010). Whereas the latter proposes that social research methods are both deployed in social science and in society at large – as for instance 'the survey' – the idea of the redistribution of research directs our attention to shifting relations *between* agencies inside and outside the university.

5 One redistributive issue requires special attention: digital social research entails a reshuffling of roles between human and technical elements, and as such it raises the question of which delegations of roles to new actors or devices are exactly occurring, and what their implications are for the analytic and empirical capacities of social and cultural research (Niederer and van Dijck, 2010; see also Bach and Stark, 2005).

6 Andrew Abbott, 'Googles of the Past: Do Keywords Really Matter?', lecture, Department of Sociology, Goldsmiths, 15 March 2011.

7 They note: 'For most of the past fifty years, the collection of network data has been confined to the field of social network analysis, in which data have to be collected through survey instruments that not only are onerous to administer, but also suffer from the inaccurate or subjective responses of subjects. People, it turns out, are not good at remembering who their friends are, and the definition of a 'friend' is often quite ambiguous in the first place' (Newman *et al.*, 2007: L-5).

8 https://tools.issuecrawler.net/beta/scrapeGoogle/

9 This notion of re-mediation was put forward by Bolter and Grusin (2000) in an effort to shift the debate about digital culture beyond yes/no exchange which pitched two sterile positions against one another: either new media merely offered old culture in a new jacket, or they enabled the invention of radically new forms of culture. Rejecting both positions, Bolter and Grusin proposed to focus instead on how older cultural forms underwent a process of *refashioning* in new media. I am proposing here that this notion can be usefully adapted to make sense of the digital social research methods.

10 Issue Crawler was developed between 1999 and 2002 by the govcom.org foundation in Amsterdam, which is directed by Richard Rogers and of which the author was a founding member. www.govcom.org.

11 This dynamic is in some ways similar to a classic sociological problematic, discussed by Tocqueville, of 'the tyranny of reputation'. According to this wider dynamic, ideas gain influence for the reason of being well regarded, a circular dynamic in which substantive considerations of the ideas in question do not necessarily enter.

12 In some sense, online hyperlink analysis enabled a move beyond the database. In this respect, the technique of crawling the Web allows for a renewed engagement with a classic sociological concern of actor-network theory: the issue of the pre-ordering of data, as what prevents sociology from engaging with heterogeneous ontologies.

13 Issue Crawler also engages with issues which in retrospect we can designate as issues of public sociology: its methodology concentrates on a publically accessible metric, hyperlinks, and the Issue Crawler archive of all located networks, dating back to 2001, is available to all users.

14 Issue Crawler also seeks to put this situation to positive effect. The quality of its network maps depends on the knowledge implied in the hyperlinks that it analyses: Issue Crawler can only provide us with 'telling networks', if sources in the network link intelligently, ie if they identify issue-protoganists and alliances among them by way of hyperlinks.

15 More specifically, co-word analysis was developed as a way to deal with the problem that co-link analysis reproduced a reputational logic in spite of itself. This problematics is all too relevant

in relation to Issue Crawler: this platform too can be said to reproduce popularity and authority effects, for various reasons: because of its demarcationist approach, because of hyperlinking reproducing authority effects, and because platform users want to know 'who is the most popular source'. In this respect, the reproduction of reputational dynamics by Issue Crawler is itself partly a social effect, ie it is a consequence of the distributed nature of digital social research: the effect can partly be traced back to 'reputational linkers', and the research agendas of the users of Issue Crawler.

16 There are a number of related tools for visualizing word frequency analysis, like the Dorling visualization, and one of my favourites, the Bubble line.

References

Adkins, L. and Lury, C., (2009), 'Introduction to special issue "What is the empirical?"', *European Journal of Social Theory*, 12: 5–20.

Bach, J. and Stark, S., (2005), 'Recombinant technology and the new geography of association', in R. Latham and S. Sassen (eds), *Digital Formations: IT and the New Global Realm*, 37–53, Princeton, NJ: Princeton University Press.

Back, L., (2010), 'Broken devices and new opportunities': re-imagining the tools of qualitative research', NCRM Working Paper Series, 08/10.

Bolter, J. and Grusin, R., (2000), *Remediation: Understanding New Media*, Cambridge: MIT Press.

Borra, E., (2008), 'The web as anticipatory medium, blogpost', http://erikborra.net/blog/2008/12/the-web-as-an-anticipatory-medium/#more-709.

boyd, d. and Crawford, K., (2011), 'Six provocations for big data', paper presented at Oxford Internet Institute's *A Decade in Internet Time: Symposium on the Dynamics of the Internet and Society*, 1–17.

Button, G., (1991), 'Introduction', in G. Button (ed.), *Ethnomethodology and the Human Sciences: A Foundational Reconstruction*, 1–9, Cambridge: Cambridge University Press.

Callon, M., Courtial, J., Turner W. and Bauin, S., (1983), 'From translations to problematic networks: an introduction to co-word analysis', *Social Science Information*, 22: 191–235.

Callon, M., Lascoumes, P. and Barthe, Y., (2009 [2001]), *Acting in an Uncertain World: An Essay on Technical Democracy*, Cambridge: MIT Press.

Carlson, S. and Anderson, B., (2007), 'What are data? The many kinds of data and their implications for data re-use', *Journal of Computer-Mediated Communication*, 12 (2), http://jcmc.indiana.edu/vol12/issue2/carlson.html

Danowski, J., (2009), 'Network analysis of message content', in K. Krippendorff and K. Bock (eds), *The Content Analysis Reader*, 421–430, Thousand Oaks, CA: Sage Publications.

Fielding, N., Lee, R. and Blank, G., (2008), 'The Internet as research medium: an editorial introduction to *The Sage Handbook of Online Research Methods*', in N. Fielding, R. Lee and G. Blank (eds), *The Sage Handbook of Online Research Methods*, 3–20, London: Sage.

Gerlitz, C. and Helmond, A., (2012), 'The like economy: social buttons and the data-intensive Web', *New Media and Society*, forthcoming.

Grandclément, C. and Gaglio, G., (2010), 'Convoking the consumer in person: the focus group effect', in D. Zwick and J. Cayla (eds), *Inside Marketing: Practices, Ideologies, Devices*, Oxford and Cambridge, MA: Oxford University Press, http://dx.doi.org/10.1093/acprof:oso/9780199576746.003.0005

Haraway, D., (1991), 'Cybermanifesto: science, technology and socialist-feminism in the late 20th century', in *Cyborgs, Simians and Women: The Reinvention of Nature*, 149–182, New York: Routledge.

Hine, C., (2002), *Virtual Ethnography*, London: Sage.

Hine, C. (ed.), (2005), *Virtual Methods: Issues in Social Research on the Internet*, Oxford: Berg.

Hubble, N., (2006), *Mass Observation and Everyday Life: Culture, History, Theory*, Basingstoke: Palgrave Macmillan.

Introna, L. and Nissenbaum, H., (2000), 'Shaping the Web: why the politics of search engines matters', *The Information Society*, 16 (3): 1–17.

Latour, B., (1988), *The Pasteurization of France*, trans. A. Sheridan and J. Law, Cambridge, MA: Harvard University Press.

Latour, B., (1998), 'Thought experiments in social science: from the social contract to virtual society', *1st Virtual Society? Annual Public Lecture*, http://www.artefaktum.hu/it/Latour.htm

Latour, B., (2005), *Reassembling the Social: An Introduction to Actor-network-theory*, Oxford: Oxford University Press.

Latour, B., Jensen, P., Venturini, T. and Boullier, D., (2012), 'The whole is always smaller than its parts: a digital test of Gabriel Tarde's Monads', *The British Journal of Sociology*, forthcoming.

Law, J., (2004), *After Method: Mess in Social Science Research*, London and New York: Routledge.

Law, J., (2008), 'On STS and sociology', *The Sociological Review*, 56 (4): 623–649.

Law, J., (2009), 'Assembling the world by survey: performativity and politics', *Cultural Sociology*, 3 (2): 239–256.

Lazer, D., Pentland, A., Adamic, L., Aral, S., Barabási, A., Brewer, D., Christakis, N., Contractor, N., Fowler, J., Gutmann, M., Jebara, T., King, G., Macy, M., Roy, D. and Van Alstyne, M., (2009), 'Computational social science', *Science*, 6 February, 5915 (323): 721–723.

Leavitt, A. (ed.), (2009), 'The Iranian election on Twitter: the first eighteen days', *Web Ecology Project*, http://www.webecologyproject.org/2009/06/iran-election-on-twitter/ (5 March 2011).

Lee, R. M., (2000), *Unobtrusive Methods in Social Research*, Buckingham: Open University Press.

Leydersdorff, L., (1998), 'Theories of citation?', *Scientometrics*, 43 (1): 5–25.

Lezaun, J., (2007), 'A market of opinions: The political epistemology of focus groups', *Sociological Review*, 55: 130–151.

Lippmann, W., (1997 [1922]), *Public Opinion*, New York: Free Press Paperbacks, Simon & Schuster.

Lury, C., (1996), *Consumer Culture*. Cambridge: Polity Press.

Lury, C., (2004), *Brands: The Logos of the Global Cultural Economy*, New York and London: Routledge.

MacRoberts, M. H. and MacRoberts, B. R., (1988), 'Problems of citation analysis: a critical review', *Journal of the American Society for Information Science*, 40 (5): 342–349.

Madsen, A. K., (2012), 'Web visions as controversy lenses', in A. Carusi, A. Sissel Hoel and T. Webmoor (eds), Special Issue on Computational Picturing, *Interdisciplinary Science Reviews*, 37 (1).

Marres, N., (2011), 'The cost of involvement: everyday carbon accounting and the materialization of participation', *Economy and Society*, 40 (4): 510–533.

Marres, N., (2012), 'The experiment in living', in C. Lury and N. Wakeford (eds), *Inventive Methods: The Happening of the Social*, 76–95, London: Routledge.

Marres, N. and R. Rogers (2000), 'Depluralising the Web and repluralising public debate: the case of the GM food debate on the Web', in R. Rogers (ed.), *Preferred Placement: Knowledge Politics on the Web*, 113–135, Maastricht: Jan van Eyck Editions.

Marres, N. and Rogers, R., (2008), 'Subsuming the ground: how local realities of the Ferghana Valley, the Narmada Dams, and the BTC pipeline are put to use on the Web', *Economy and Society*, 37 (2): 251–281.

Marres, N. and Weltevrede. E., (forthcoming), 'Scraping the social? Issues in real-time research', *Journal of Cultural Economy*.

Mohebbi, M., Vanderkam, D., Kodysh, J., Schonberger, R., Choi, H. and Kumar, S., (2011), 'Google Correlate Whitepaper', http://correlate.googlelabs.com/whitepaper.pdf

Muniesa, F. and Tchalakov, I., (2009), 'What do you think a simulation is, anyway? A topological approach to cultural dynamics', Working Paper, http://www.atacd.net/

Newman, M., Barabási, A. and Watts, D., (2007), *The Structure and Dynamics of Networks*, Princeton, NJ: Princeton University Press.

Niederer, S. and Van Dijck, J., (2010), 'Wisdom of the crowd or technicity of content? Wikipedia as a sociotechnical system', *New Media and Society*, 12 (8): 1368–1387.

Onnela, J.-P. and Reed-Tsochas, F., (2010), 'Spontaneous emergence of social influence in online systems', *Proceedings of the National Academy of Sciences*, 107 (43): 18375–18380.

Page, L., Brin, S., Motwani, R., and Winograd, T., (1999), 'The PageRank Citation Ranking: bringing order to the Web. Technical Report', Stanford InfoLab. http://ilpubs.stanford.edu:8090/422/

Rheinberger, H.-J., (1997), *Toward a History of Epistemic Things: Synthesizing Proteins in the Test Tube*, Stanford, CA: Stanford University Press.

Rogers, R., (2009), *The End of the Virtual: Digital Methods*, Amsterdam: Amsterdam University Press.

Rogers, R., (2010), 'Internet research: the question of method', *Journal of Information Technology and Politics*, 7 (2/3): 241–260.

Savage, M., (2010), *Identities and Social Change in Britain since 1940: The Politics of Method*, Oxford: Oxford University Press.

Savage, M. and Burrows, R., (2007), 'The coming crisis of empirical sociology', *Sociology*, (41): 885–899.

Savage, M., Law, J. and Ruppert, E., (2010), 'The double social life of methods', CRESC Working Paper Series. No. 95, http://www.cresc.ac.uk/our-research/cross-theme-research/social-life-of-methods

Scharnhorst, A. and Wouters, P., (2006), 'Web indicators – a new generation of S&T indicators?' *Cybermetrics*, 10 (1).

Small, H., (1973), 'Co-citation in the scientific literature: a new measure of the relationship between two documents', *Journal of the American Society for Information Science*, 24 (4): 265–269.

Uprichard, E., Burrows, R. and Byrne, D., (2008), 'SPSS as an "inscription device": from causality to description?', *The Sociological Review*, 56 (4): 606–622.

Vaidhyanathan, S., (2011), *The Googlization of Everything (And Why We Should Worry)*, Berkeley, CA: University of California Press.

Weltevrede, E., (n.d.), 'Studying society, not Google: repurposing Google for social and cultural research', Department of Media Studies, University of Amsterdam, ms.

Whatmore, S. J., (2009), 'Mapping knowledge controversies: science, democracy and the redistribution of expertise', *Progress in Human Geography*, 33 (5): 587–598.

Whittaker, J., (1989), 'Creativity and conformity in science: titles, keywords, and co-word analysis,' *Social Science in Science*, 19: 473–496.

Woolgar, S., (2002), 'Introduction: five rules of virtuality', in S. Woolgar (ed.), *Virtual Society? Technology, Cyberbole, Reality*, Oxford: Oxford University Press.

De-signing the object of sociology: toward an 'idiotic' methodology

Mike Michael

Abstract: This paper outlines a version of 'live sociology' that enacts and engages with the openness and processuality of events. This is initially explored through a focus on everyday objects that, in their relationality, 'misbehave', potentially challenging standard sociological framings. Drawing on the work of Isabelle Stengers, it is suggested that such objects can be understood as 'idiotic' – possessed of an incommensurability that enables social scientists to 'slow down' and reflect upon 'what is busily being done' (not least by the social scientists themselves). This responsiveness to the idiot object is then contrasted to the proactive idiocy of Speculative Design. Here, artefacts – probes and prototypes – are designed to have oblique and ambiguous functions that allow both their users and designers to open up what is at stake in particular events. Examples taken from past and current research are used to illustrate how speculative designs can open up what 'the neighbourhood' and 'energy demand reduction' can be. The paper ends with a discussion of a possible 'idiotic methodology' and its implications for the conceptual and practical doings of social scientific research.

Keywords: design, event, idiot, methodology, process, sociology

Introduction

This paper begins to sketch out a way of doing sociology that is alive to the processes by which society is made, by which those bits of society known as sociology are made, and by which sociology makes society. In many ways, there is nothing new in such a proposal – after all, there are many authors who have addressed one or more of these processes. However, the present paper also aims to develop a particular version of 'doing a sociology that is alive' – a live sociology. Approaching this motif from a Deleuzian perspective, 'live-ness' can be seen to take on at least two connotations. In Ansell Pearson's (1999) reading of Deleuze and Guattari, life does not simply proceed in a linear fashion whereby one species evolves from another, branching out to form Darwin's famous tree

The Sociological Review, 60:S1, pp. 166–183 (2012), DOI: 10.1111/j.1467-954X.2012.02122.x
© 2012 The Author. Editorial organisation © 2012 The Editorial Board of the Sociological Review. Published by Wiley-Blackwell Publishing Ltd, 9600 Garsington Road, Oxford OX4 2DQ, UK and 350 Main Street, Malden, MA 02148, USA

of life. There is also another mode whereby genetic material moves transversally, across species, generating monstrous, entangled becomings. So, on the one hand, a 'live sociology' can imply incremental, directional change in society, in the discipline, and in the discipline's enactment of the social. In this case, live sociology can be said to proceed through the depiction of, and response to, social change, and the critical accretion of theoretical and empirical 'knowledge'. On the other hand, live sociology can point to a much more chaotic, unexpected and 'involutionary' relation to other disciplines and to society. In this case, live sociology is sensitive to, and indeed actively seeks out, that which is empirically and practically nonsensical – what will later be called 'idiotic'. In the process, sociology potentially undergoes, and promotes, creative transformation. It is the latter version of 'live sociology' that is explored here.[1]

This project is developed through a consideration of the role of the object in society and sociology. In part this is a pragmatic move: it makes the analysis more manageable. In part this is opportunistic: recent studies of the object are particularly fertile in facilitating the perspective developed here. In part this is accidental: it is prompted by a chance encounter with a rather different disciplinary treatment of the object and its relation to the social, namely 'speculative design'.

On the subject of objects, it is commonplace to see them as an integral part of society. In the social sciences, they have been studied in very many ways. Objects have been, for instance, tied to processes of consumption, of production, of attachment, of identity, of exchange, of knowledge, of civilization, of representation, of corporealization, of spatialization and temporalization to list but a few of the most obvious. At the risk of over-generalization, objects have by and large been treated as inert matter: stuff which, while it has had a central part to play in the mediation of social relations, has nevertheless largely stood in contrast to the subject.

Objects as 'objects of study' have taken on a renewed significance in the last twenty or so years not least with the increasing prominence of science and technology studies (STS) and the rise of such approaches as 'material culture studies'. Along the way, the object has come to be regarded, by some, as altogether more lively and heterogeneous. In the case of STS, it might be seen as a black hole or an actant – each of these signalling the object's complex, relational and emergent character. Precursors to such formulations can be found in the anti-bifurcatory, processual philosophies of Serres (quasi-subjects), Deleuze and Guattari (assemblages), and especially Whitehead (societies, the concrescence of prehensions).

The present paper draws on this tradition to develop an argument that the object is not only an 'object of study', complex and variegated though this undoubtedly is, but can also be a part of the empirical 'process of engagement'. By this it is meant that objects can be a component of the ontology of empirical study. Over and above their role as tools (eg questionnaires, digital recorders, paper and pen, computers etc) objects contribute to the process of making the events that constitute 'society', including those aspects of society commonly

known as 'sociological research'. To be sure this is a convoluted formulation
which will, hopefully, become clearer as some of the terms (eg event, process)
are unpacked, and supplementary concepts (eg idiot, becoming-with) are introduced. Suffice it to say for the moment that objects serve in the 'making' of
social events (including sociological empirical events such as interviews, focus
groups, ethnograpies, etc), and this process of making is incomplete, that is,
open and emergent. In any case, the aim here is to contribute to a live sociology
that, in engaging with objects (and events) that are seen to be relational, emergent and open, enacts itself and society as relational, emergent and open. On
this score, then, the present paper is not concerned with the methodological
demarcation of sociological facts or social problems, but with 'matters of
process'.

In what follows, after a brief overview of some of the more recent approaches
to the object, the main theoretical underpinnings of the present paper will be
laid out. Science and technology studies, especially recent variants of actor-
network theory, will be central here, though also key will be the work of Whitehead, Deleuze and Guattari, and Stengers. What will emerge is a version of the
object that is processual, emergent, relational and open but also, in principle at
least, 'idiotic' – possessed of an incommensurable difference that enables us to
'slow down' and reflect on 'what we (as social scientists) are busy doing'. This
is illustrated with an example of empirical research that went badly wrong, and
the role of objects in this. The paper then moves on to argue that the idiotic
properties of objects can be fruitfully mobilized in the doing of research. On
this score, the paper draws on a different discipline – speculative design – to
show how a 'proactive idiocy' can be operationalized partly through designed
artefacts. The paper ends with an exploration of the implications of taking on
this approach (distilled in the term 'idiotic' methodology) for the conceptual
and practical doings of social scientific research.

Objects and things

Amongst recent writings on the role of objects in society, a number of terms
have been developed to access the ways in which objects – in their material and
semiotic complexity – interact with humans. A sample of such terms might
include pre- and proscriptions (Akrich and Latour, 1992), sociality (Knorr-
Cetina, 1997), affordances (Ingold, 1993), propensities (Miller, 2005), or enact-
ments (Mol, 2002). Often associated with these modes of interaction are also a
series of terms which aim to access alternative units of analysis that encompass
humans-and-nonhumans-together. Again, a not especially representative survey
could list: hybrids (Latour, 1999), monsters (Law, 1991), cyborgs, black holes
(Haraway, 1991, 1994), ontologies (Mol, 2002), co(a)gents (Michael, 2000) and
the more-than-human (Whatmore, 2006).

These concepts of heterogeneity serve to evoke the constitutive mixing of the
social and material, the human and non-human, the subject and object: they

also presuppose an exchange between these entities such that each is partly comprised of its opposite. Thus Michel Serres (eg 1982) writes of quasi-objects and quasi-subjects, and Bruno Latour has put it thus:

> We are never faced with objects or social relations, we are faced with chains which are associations of humans (H) and nonhumans (NH). No-one has ever seen a social relation by itself . . . nor a technical relation . . . Instead we are always faced with chains which look like this H-NH-H-NH-H-NH . . . (1991: 110).

How do we empirically engage these relationalities between humans and objects? The answer to this depends in large part on the quality of those relationalities. In some cases, where the objects are relatively novel (say new information or biomedical technologies) then one could conduct ethnographic study of how these come to be 'domesticated' (Silverstone and Hirsch, 1992; Lie and Sorensen, 1996), or, where these technologies are more controversial, of how they emerge with their publics as political issues (Marres, 2007; Latour, 2005). Here, the general analytic strategy is one of tracing the processes by which the unfamiliar object comes to be rendered familiar. However, and in some ways more profoundly, the social world is, of course, profusely inhabited by objects that are familiar to the point of invisibility. In this instance, what is required is the development of a sensibility that, in one way or another, renders what is familiar in everyday life unfamiliar (eg Highmore, 2002; Gardiner, 2000). In some cases, this might be precipitated when the objects themselves 'go wrong' or misbehave – as when door-closers discriminate against the elderly and the young (Latour, 1992), or walking boots turn out to be excruciatingly painful (Michael, 2000). In other cases, this might entail particular sorts of close observation such as autobiographical reflection (Highmore, 2011), or attention to the experiences of others (Akrich, 1992). In the process, these sensibilities enable the analysis of the mundane role of objects: how they go about their business in the reproduction of everyday life.

However, what these objects are – what their ontology is – rests on the sorts of events of which they are a part. The different characteristics or 'qualities' of objects depend on their embeddedness within particular events. That is to say, objects emerge from the specific combination (Whitehead would say 'concrescence') of specific social and material components (Whitehead would say 'prehensions') in specific events or actual occasions (Whitehead, 1929, 1933; Halewood, 2011). Accordingly, there are no objects whose substance pre-exists their qualities: there is no abstracted car that is yellow, or is cold, or is broken; there is a yellow car, a cold car, a broken car. Or if we insist on an abstracted car, it is specifically abstracted by a philosopher or an engineer or a designer.

The event in which an object emerges can be conceptualized as taking, broadly speaking, two different forms. Drawing on Motamedi Fraser (Fraser, 2010) excellent discussion of the event in Whitehead and Deleuze, she notes that in contrast to Whitehead, Deleuze's version of the event is a moment where its component entities rather than simply 'being together' also 'become together'. In what we can call the 'eventuation' of an object – the making of an event in which an object emerges – the constitutive elements do not simply 'interact' with one another while retaining their identity, but change in the process of that interaction (or to use a different terminology, intra-action, see Barad, 2007). As such, this version of the event can be characterized by a mutual changing.

As noted above, in much social science, the study of objects considers their role in the reproduction of social situations. They are instrumental in making events. However, also as noted, sometimes objects 'misbehave': they do things they are not supposed to. This can facilitate insight into the workings of the everyday. For instance, in a 'disastrous interview episode' (see Michael, 2004), a cassette tape recorder placed on the floor between the interviewer and interviewee was dragged away by the latter's cat to the point where none of the interview (such as it was) could be recorded. The initial insight this episode yielded into the everyday-ness of the social scientific interview was that a whole array of entities had to be disciplined in order for the interview to be possible. Objects and human and non-human animals, and the relations between them, must be made orderly if the (social scientifically) desired event – the interview and the production of social scientific data – is to take place. And yet, these constituent entities also changed in their relations to one another: minimally, the cat became playful, the recorder became a plaything. There was, a becoming-with in this particular event where cat and tape recorder co-emerged.

However, this becoming-with of the tape-recorder object also gives us pause to reflect on the interview event. Is it an interview event any longer? In the work of Isabelle Stengers (2005), we have the resources to operationalize such reflection. Her figure of the idiot – which she adapts from Deleuze – is particularly helpful. It is a 'conceptual character' who 'resists the consensual way in which the situation is presented and in which emergencies mobilize thought or action' (2005: 994). Here, Stengers is thinking of what she calls 'cosmopolitical' events where politics embraces the human and non-human, but also, in part thanks to the idiot, where such events might proceed more carefully and slowly. This is because the idiot, as a figure that refuses to enter such events, whose responses are nonsensical in the context of those events as normally understood, can also serve to challenge their meaning. Stengers writes: 'the idiot can neither reply nor discuss the issue . . . (the idiot) does not know . . . the idiot demands that we slow down, that we don't consider ourselves authorized to believe we possess the meaning of what we know' (2005: 995). As such, the task becomes one of how 'we bestow efficacy upon the murmurings of the idiot, the "there is something more important" that is so easy to forget because it "cannot be taken into account", because the idiot neither objects nor proposes anything that "counts"' (2005: 1001). By attending to the nonsensicalness, we become open to a dramatic redefinition of the meaning of the event.

To be sure there are other figures we might draw upon – the fool, the jester, or the trickster, for example. However, these figures might best be regarded as primarily oppositional – turning events 'on their head' does not radically undermine the meaning of those events, and indeed can serve in their re-enactment.[2] In contrast, the etymology of the idiot – as the private individual who has no interest in the demos, that is, politics – suggests a figure whose (non-)actions are so incommensurable with those (political) events that it chaotically disrupts the orthodox interpretation of those events.[3]

In the case of the social scientific interview event, the tape recorder has become idiotic in that it 'misbehaves': it has, in its guise as a plaything, mutely 'refused' to enter into the event of the interview. But, paying it proper attention – by practising a listener's art as Les Back (2007) would call it – we can also begin to query this interpretation of the event: this is not a disastrous interview episode (an oppositional view), but an event of a cat-become-playful playing with its new found tape recorder-become-plaything. The idiot allows us to slow down – to take time to question our own assumptions about the event and to reinterpret it. The idiotic object affords an opportunity to engage in a process of, as Motamedi Fraser (Fraser, 2010) puts it, 'inventive problem making'. Accordingly, the 'disastrous interview episode' becomes not only a playful event enacted with non-human animals, but an occasion for inventively rethinking the 'social' and 'social data' in relation to the non-human.

In sum, the object can be regarded, through its various (intra-)relations, as something that is in process, becoming-with and, crucially, idiotic.[4] As such, it can resource a radical rethinking of the meaning of social and social scientific events. Yet, thus far our relation to the idiotic object has been a reactive one. As analysts we are simply *responsive* to the waywardness of objects. Moments of evident idiocy and spontaneous becoming-with serve as opportunities for doing a particular sort of analytic work. That is to say, the emergence of idiotic objects occasions a radical rethinking of the events in which they emerged.

However, notice that this 'occasion of radical rethinking' is itself an event – a becoming-with the event that is studied and the data that are analysed. What this points to is the radical openness of the event (DeLanda, 2002): events, as argued above, are processual. They open out onto a 'virtuality', and the idiot has allowed us to get a particular grasp of this. Specifically, in the case of the 'disastrous interview episode' the idiotic tape recorder illuminated the role of (the disciplining of) animals in the making of social data. In the process, we have become a different sort of analyst, not of the topic of the interview (which was on the risks of radiation) but of the part played by the non-human in social ordering. The suggestion here is that it might be possible to approach this openness or virtuality through a practice of *proactive idiocy*. Thus, we might pose the question: is it possible to invent objects which have this property of idiocy (and becoming-with-ness) as a novel way of engaging with the processuality or openness of a specific social event? In the next sections, I will explore this question by drawing on the practices and processes of 'speculative design'.

Critical and speculative design

Design as a discipline is routinely represented as oriented toward both objects and the future. It is concerned with the making of stuff that will shape the future for the 'better' (though this better future takes divergent forms – see Papanek, 1984). In contrast to such standard forms of product-oriented design, there are versions of design that are less interested in the making of objects that fulfil specific functions or meet particular needs or ends. To set the scene, I begin with a brief discussion of critical design because it has been crucial in opening up the potential of design to rethink its relation to the object. It also serves in highlighting what is peculiar about speculative design, which, it will be claimed, produces 'idiotic' artefacts.

Critical design, typically identified with the interaction designers Anthony Dunne and Fiona Raby (eg Dunne and Raby, 2001; Dunne, 2005), aims critically to address the possible futures entailed by contemporary technological developments. As such, the aim is to design 'prototypes' whose function is to enable a critical engagement with such futures. While the methods of critical design might draw on art practice, there is nevertheless a distinction insofar as critical design must navigate between the extremes of contemporary art (shocking, highly personal) and the normalities and normativities of functional design. For instance, in the 2009 'What if . . .' exhibition at the Dublin Science Gallery curated by Dunne and Raby, the aim was to present 'people with hypothetical products, services and systems from alternative futures . . . [that] probe our beliefs and values, challenge our assumptions and encourage us to imagine how what we call "reality" could be different. They help us see that the way things are now is just one possibility, and not necessarily the best one'.[5] In response to the question 'WHAT IF . . . Robots were designed from an emotional point of view?' Dunne and Raby themselves contributed nervous or needy robots that raised such questions as 'What new interdependencies and relationships might emerge in relation to different levels of robot intelligence and capability: intimate, subservient, dependent, equal'?[6]

Key here is the oppositional stance that underpins the design of these robots: a predominant future of emotionless robots is countered by the designs. In the idiotic terms set out above, the encounter with these objects does not necessarily yield a 'becoming together' in part because the objects are grounded in a particular critique: it is hard to see how these might yield 'inventive problem making' when the 'problem' is so clearly staked out. In addition, these critical designs are eventuated in an exhibition space that also serves to delimit the range of possible meanings that they might carry. The upshot is that for all the apparent strangeness of these designs they are unlikely to serve as idiots that prompt 'inventive problem making'. For this we turn to speculative design.

Speculative design is associated particularly with the work of Bill Gaver (eg Sengers and Gaver, 2006; Gaver *et al.*, 2008) and, like critical design, produces objects that are obliquely functional in order to provoke reflection on the complex roles of new technology (in the case of Gaver, this also means emerging computational capacities such as ubiquitous computing). However, for speculative design, the designs' obliqueness is not set critically against a particular sociotechnical future. This is because the designs partly emerge from an initial engagement with the public – an engagement that is itself oblique. This initial

The Sociological Review, 60:S1, pp. 166–183 (2012), DOI: 10.1111/j.1467-954X.2012.02122.x
© 2012 The Author. Editorial organisation © 2012 The Editorial Board of the Sociological Review

engagement through such techniques as 'cultural probes' generates a series of disparate materials that through the design process yield prototypes which are then implemented (installed in users' homes, for instance) and subsequently 'ethnographically' studied.

Probe

In a recent reflection on cultural probes, latterly shortened to probes, Kirsten Boehner, William Gaver and Andy Boucher (in press) describe them in terms that place them at odds with typical social scientific methods. Thus, rather than addressing 'what is', probes are oriented to 'what might be' (and as such they echo the engagement with the emergent and the virtual mentioned above); rather than producing a coherent and generalizable account of a particular setting or situation, probes are used to develop singular and fragmented understandings; rather than aiming for faithful interpretations (even if these are presented with heavy doses of modesty and reflexivity as is routinely the case for qualitative sociological methods), probes celebrate idiosyncrasy, risk and uncertainty in the interpretations of both the designers and the participants in the design process (Gaver *et al.*, 2004; Sengers and Gaver, 2006).

So, what are probes? In brief, they are items, often gathered together in small packages, that are sent to volunteers (typically recruited through small advertisements in local newspapers). The items set seemingly peculiar tasks. For instance, the packet might contain a disposable camera that has been customized with instructions that ask the volunteer to take a photograph of something seen from their kitchen window or of the spiritual centre of their home. Or there might be a 'listening glass' – an ordinary drinking glass with instructions to press against the wall in order listen to unusual sounds around the house. This is packaged with a marker pen which can be used to record details about the noise directly onto the glass. Or there might be a 'telephone jotter pad' that encourages volunteers to doodle in it, or respond to various images or questions contained in it, while doing other things (such as answering the telephone). Importantly, the designers are clear that there is nothing compulsory about the use of the probes: volunteers can use them if, as and when they felt the urge. Living with the probes for about a month, volunteers are asked to mail the individual items back to the designers at their own discretion.

As Boehner *et al.* (in press) elaborate, the probes are part of a speculative design process that is less concerned with developing instrumental or utilitarian devices than objects that enable playfulness and exploration, and that precipitate new thinking about technology. This is not necessarily a comfortable process because the aim is to throw up the peculiar, the unexpected, the troublesome, the incommensurable. In the terminology of this paper, the probes proactively seek the 'idiotic'. This window on the 'idiotic' is reinforced by virtue of the array of responses that flow back with the return of the different probe items. The result is a process in which otherwise unthought design routes become exposed – or, to rephrase it, 'inventive problem making' becomes available.

How are the probes derived? Usually, the designers will discuss at length the potential participants and settings, attempting to derive a series of questions that address the range and complexity of participants' views of the target setting (eg the home) or activity (eg energy demand reduction). The outcome is a tightly considered array of themes such as community, connection, responsibility, nature, information. The probes are designed around a particular aesthetic (eg bright, cheerful) and a sense of the balance of the items (some are serious, some playful, some professional, some amateurish). Overarching all of this is the requirement that the probes probe: they must be sufficiently provocative, novel, entertaining, open, inviting to prompt answers that are unexpected, expressive and creative.

Once the probe items (not all of which are successful – some are simply not used by the participants) are returned, how is the material processed? Given that the subsequent design objects are meant to embody uncertainty, opaqueness, playfulness, multiple interpretability then the returned material is treated accordingly. It is not regarded as 'information' but as a prompt to intuition, multiplicity, uncertainty (just as the probes were meant to prompt such responses in the volunteers). Some material is sidelined, some enters the foreground, some is met with ambivalence.

This piecemeal appropriation of the returned material suggests a relationship to the empirical that is very different to that typically found in social science. In contrast to typical modes of social scientific analysis which seek out patterns, the material from the prototypes is mobilized in intuitive, open, uncertain ways in relation to the emerging design of prototypes. It can be likened to a process of de- and re-territorialization (Deleuze and Guattari, 1988) in which idiotic responses (to the idiotic probes) come to the fore to prompt the emergence of new idiotic ideas that will affect the designers and enter into their designs.

One is tempted to say that this 'idiotic sensibility *cum* sensitivity to the idiot' that is bound up with the emerging design object reflects what we might call 'corporeal' or 'sensory' or 'affective' scholarship. Here, the term scholarship echoes Mick Billig's (1988) use: the idiosyncratic, wayward but serious, accumulated knowledge of the scholar whose peculiar engagement with history enables them to provide fresh insights (not least into the operations of ideology and rhetoric). Reference to the affective, sensory and corporeal serves to connote the embodiedness of this scholarship. Over and above the recourse to design history and principles, there is also a set of tacit skills, aesthetic sensibilities, complex intuitions that come into play. In other words, there is a 'feel' for, or put differently, a non-representational theorization of (Thrift, 2008), what in the probe returns can count as productively idiotic. As such, the probe material is mobilized through a dialogue with its future design objects that entails ongoing mutual shaping of both: there is a becoming-with.

Now, this becoming-with extends to the dialogic relation between designers and participants (Boehner *et al.*, in press). After all, probes are designed to be open to volunteers' eccentricities while also complex and multiple in their interpretability. Beyond this, the probes are meant to resource, in a productively

The Sociological Review, 60:S1, pp. 166–183 (2012), DOI: 10.1111/j.1467-954X.2012.02122.x

fragmented way, another object – the prototype – which will subsequently be deployed with volunteers. Here, we get glimpses of the ways in which the probes serve as a sort of mediator (which according to Latour, 1999, is something that mediates relations in unreliable and contingent ways) between designer and participant who, in the process, become-with one another or, phrased otherwise, are each other's idiots.

From a social scientific perspective, the tacit model behind this entire process is one in which the world is open, inventive, ambiguous, complex, emergent, relational. If that were not the case there would be no point in designing and giving probes or prototypes to participants. The value for a social scientist is that these speculative design techniques neither aspire to yield more or less accurate representations of the social world nor aim to establish particular relations between various variables however 'soft' these might be.[7] Rather they concern 'matters of process' – they are not about problems or facts, but about the process of emergence of new relations which, potentially at least, can reconfigure what the very 'fact' or 'problem' might be. This rather gnomic formulation and its implication for sociological methodology will be elaborated below. However, before that, the discussion will turn to the deployment and ethnographic study of the speculative prototypes.

Prototype

The eventual outcome of the use of the probe material described above is a prototype or a range of prototypes: these are highly finished design objects that have the characteristics of openness, playfulness, provocation, uncertainty and so on. Over the course of various projects, Gaver and his collaborators have developed such objects as: the drift table, the photostroller, the history tablecloth, the prayer companion or the key table. Each of these, in their own peculiar ways, invites not only multiple interpretations by their users, but also, in part because of their complex and ambiguous semiotic and material composition, emergent and unforeseen orderings and disorderings. Novel relations amongst participants (humans and non-human) and between participants and prototypes develop that are often at odds with the designers' own initial expectations.[8]

For present purposes I will focus on what Gaver *et al.* (2008) call 'threshold devices' which entail gathering information from the home's environs to generate new and surprising views on the domestic situation. These devices look out from the home, collecting particular forms of information from its surroundings in order to suggest novel ways in which the home is connected to and situated within its wider physical and social environment. As such, these devices were designed to serve as means or resources through which inhabitants are invited to contemplate how the home emerges out of, and mediates, where it is, and what and who is around it: in other words, these devices encourage exploration of the home as it is at once bounded and blurred. The aim is to access these homely engagements in their richness and complexity, which might well incorporate interpretations that span the utilitarian, the emotional and the aesthetic.[9]

Of the three devices Gaver *et al.* (2008) report on – the 'video window', the 'plane tracker' and the 'local barometer', for ease of exposition I will discuss only the last.[10] The local barometer was made up of six brightly coloured devices, each with a small screen across which texts and images scrolled. These images and texts were selected from Loot.com, an online classified advertisement site. The selection process was determined by local wind speed and direction measured by a commercially available anemometer mounted to the outside of the home. As such, advertisements were taken from areas upwind of the home, and were closer or further away depending on the strength of the wind. The idea informing the design of the local barometer was that it could inspire people to think about the social, economic and cultural complexities of their environs: for example, ads might be seen to reflect, or contradict, the reputation of different neighbourhoods.

The local barometer was deployed for around a month with a volunteer, R, who lived in, and worked from, a small apartment in London. After the six devices were positioned around R's home, R's time with the barometer was studied through ethnographic methods. Over the course of the month, R was visited several times by one of the design team (visits lasted approximately half a day, about 30 hours in all). The main materials collected took the form of field notes (of observations of R's use of the device, informal interviews) and photographs.

Through the local barometer a wide range of advertised items 'blew' into R's home, including: antiques, books, furniture, musical instruments, property, toys, vehicles. R's initial interpretation of the barometer was that it was another unwelcome medium for marketing or advertising, and he was generally resistant to using it. He became more attentive to the devices after noticing items that were of special interest to him (eg having been a musician, he was taken with the image of a collectable guitar). His interpretative stance began to shift: rather than to intrusive advertisements, the devices introduced him to ironic 'gifts' or 'surprises' that prompted a range of strong emotional responses (the guitar prompted attachment, a sports car provoked dislike and distrust). But further, the barometer began to interact with his historical sense of the local area, sometimes reinforcing it, sometimes undermining it. Some items were seen to be indicative of the particular neighbourhoods from which they were advertised, while others sat uneasily with his understanding of the character of their neighbourhood. Over and above this, and much to the surprise of the designers, R began to use the devices as a means to attending to local weather conditions: he began to read the weather according to the types of advertisements and the neighbourhoods from which they were blown.

In sum, we can say that the local barometer, as a speculative prototype, served to render open and unravel, but also reconfigure, some of the complexity of, put crudely, the relations between commerce and aesthetics, neighbourhoods and reputation, and nature and culture. Put another way, the perceived 'function' of, and the practical engagement with, the barometer drifted (at the very least) across the commercial, the demographic, the personal, the political and the meteorological. The idiocy of the local barometer 'lures' R into an event in which there is a sequence of 'becoming-withs' between R and the barometer.

Accordingly, the local barometer also idiotically generates the opportunity for some 'inventive problem-making'. We have hinted at how this might occur for R: not only are apprehensions of particular neighbourhoods deterritorialized, but we can see how, for example, the idea of a neighbourhood itself becomes problematized – perhaps tending toward something like a shifting mélange of weather, people, wealth, artefacts, electromagnetic waves, etc. Further, the barometer also inventively problematizes our own sociological – or more broadly, analytic – eventuations: what are the complex, piecemeal combinations and concatenations of categories such as class, status, nature, technology, place, consumption, aesthetics, identity and so on? Finally, speculative design can itself be portrayed as sociology's idiot: it enacts a way of engaging with the (social) world that, in principle at least, affords the opportunity for inventive problem-making within sociological practice. It is this last prospect that the next section addresses.

Conclusion: toward an 'idiotic' methodology

What lessons do the ethos and practice of speculative design hold for sociology and its methodologies? Given that ethos and practice, and the general analytic of this paper, this is, arguably, precisely the wrong question to pose. Rather, at stake is the mutual 'becoming-with' of these disciplines. In contrast to the juxtaposition of speculative design and sociology, we begin from a more topological grounding: what are the common byways along which they travel? Where are the junctures at which they touch? How can the engagements between these be rendered open, multiple, uncertain, playful?

Needless to say, there already exist points of partial crossover. In the sociological tradition of action research, objects regularly feature in the collaborations between social scientists and communities (see Reason and Bradbury, 2001a, for a range of examples; also Lewin, 1946; Bargal, 2006). While action research takes many forms, it can be broadly defined as 'social research carried out by a team that encompasses professional action researchers and the members of an organization, community or network ('stakeholders') who are seeking to improve the participants' situation' (Greenwood and Levin, 2007: 3). This finds echoes in the tradition of participatory design where objects emerge out of close collaborations between designers and users (eg Muller, 2008). In both cases objects are part of a process whereby experts and lay people, working together, come to identify particular problems and open up routes to solutions. Clearly, then, these objects,[11] insofar as they are solution-oriented, do not have designed into them the sort of idiocy found in speculative prototypes.[12]

Nevertheless, drawing on the problem-orientation and collaborative ethos of action research and participatory design traditions, and combining this with the openness, uncertainty and playfulness of speculative design, we can tentatively propose 'ludic action research'. In broad outline, ludic action research would draw on the following range of 'sensibilities'. If action researchers together with participants aim to identify social problems and propose and implement possible solutions to those problems, ludic action research would seek to open up possibilities. Most relevantly in the present context, this could be done by introducing into particular situations (domestic, workplace, public) artefacts that embody openness, ambiguity, playfulness. These can take the form of probes – a medium (or rather mediator) by which participants' apprehensions can be collected. For example, in a current research project 'Sustainability Invention and Energy Demand Reduction: Co-Designing Communities and Practice',[13] participants are asked to document on a map the aesthetics of energy in different parts of their home (the sound of energy in the hallway, the smell of energy in the living room, etc). This oblique – that is, idiotic – means of gathering 'data' is a way of inviting the participants playfully to engage not with the closed problem of reducing energy demand, but with the open prospect of re-imagining their relation to energy. This probe is designed as a prompt to play and as such is characterized by emergence and contingency, exploration and provisionality (Gaver, 2009). Instead of seeking out solutions to such questions as 'how do we change energy consumption behaviour?', the probe facilitates the open prospect of re-imagining one's very relation to energy, of inventing new problems (What 'is' energy in the home? What sort of individual and collective body is enacted through energy use? Can there be a 'unit' of energy that incorporates experience?).

As is well known, there are numerous means of deriving patterns from sociological data sets (eg Mason, 1996; Silverman, 1993). However, the probe 'data' that will be returned will be treated idiotically in order to enable 'inventive problem-making'. This will mean they will be used in a piecemeal, playful, unsystematic, open way to develop idiotic prototypes (yet to be determined!). These prototypes will subsequently be installed in a setting (yet to be determined!) to eventuate more idiotic participant responses, that is to say, more 'inventive problem-making'. As such, ludic action research is a processual 'collaboration' between 'experts' (designers, social scientists) and 'participants' that would generate events where the idiocy of objects (in this case a map and subsequent prototypes) eventuates something like a process of serial 'inventive problem-making'. The aim here is to circumvent the standard and not especially successful perspectives on energy demand reduction (see, for example, Shove *et al.*, in press) by redefining the parameters of the problem.

The probe and the prototype reflect speculative design's ethos of inventing artefacts whose openness prompts unexpected relationalities (for the home, the neighbourhood or energy consumption, for example). This might be reframed as a form of 'de-signing', in the sense of loosening, or 'ambiguating', the significations that contribute to the eventuation of objects. There are precedents for this sort of de-signing in sociological accounts, perhaps most notably in the guise of de Certeau's (1984) 'idle walker'. This figure moves through a panoptically surveilled society tricksterishly, evading, albeit momentarily, the strictures (and particular productivities) of disciplinary grids (see Michael, 2006). In other words, idle walkers are contingently heedless to the meanings that are inscribed into the objects that comprise their environment. This suggests that, in principle at least, any object can be 'de-signed', rendered idiotic.[14]

On the surface, there is a contrast to be drawn here. On the one side, in the sociological case, the process of de-signing takes place through re-ordering the event (eg idle walking) out of which the ambiguous object emerges. On the other side, for speculative design, the probe or prototype is deployed to de-sign the relations through which it might emerge (eg those relations that make up the home of which the prototype is becoming a part). On the one hand the event deterritorializes to allow a new 'thing' to emerge; on the other, the object deterritorializes to allow new events to emerge.

However, this contrast misses the mark. After all, as sketched above, the probes fed playful, designerly events that yielded playful, open prototypes that fed open relationalities for their users. These events were documented in a way that did not seek patterns but odd specificities, specificities that might resource inventive problem-making for both users and designers. The local barometer opens a space of strange encounters between, say meteorology and demography that hints at an alternative way of categorizing the world (eg in terms of natu-recultures and the sort of politics these might imply). In this trajectory where event and object interweave we get a glimpse of the processuality of the idiot. But also, we get a sense of the potential mutuality of idiocy. The actions and reactions of participants can be just as idiotic for the researchers: it is those actions and reactions that escape analytic patterning or theoretical sense-making that can engender becoming-with and inventive problem-making within the research process itself.

Above, mention was made of 'collaboration' between researchers and participants, but over and above the usual, explicit forms of interaction that makes research 'do-able' (eg arranging meeting times, having ethics forms filled, exchanging ideas, explicit learning from one another etc), there is also a subterranean form of 'sociality' being enacted, what we might call the mutual idiocy between researcher and participant. This can be likened to a non-dialogical conversation where mirrored incommensurability nevertheless triggers affects, reactions and responses which mediate a parallel inventive problem-making (see Horst and Michael, 2011): for both the participants and researchers this might entail a re-imagining of home, energy or neighbourhood.

To be sure, the foregoing is rather programmatic and abstracted: at best, it is an initial sketch for what has been called an 'idiotic' methodology. Inhabited by a series of intra-related terms such as ludic action research, de-sign, becoming-with, the idiot and mutual idiocy, and inventive problem-making, the aim has been to set a particular scene for the development of practical, processual, open methods. Underpinning this suggestion of 'idiotic' methodology is the view that social events are ontologically open, in-process, emergent. This openness is also a marker of the 'liveness' of social events: 'idiotic' methodology is simply meant to afford a point of access to such openness and liveness, and hopefully, along the way, make some small contribution to the larger project of a live sociology.[15]

Acknowledgements

The author would like to thank Les Back, Mariam Motamedi Fraser and Nirmal Puwar for their uncommonly helpful comments on this paper. The paper could not have been written without the long-term engagement with, and support of, a number of designers, notably Andy Boucher, Jennifer Gabrys, Bill Gaver, Tobie Kerridge, Liliana Ovalle and Alex Wilkie. Part of this paper is derived from work carried out under the research project 'Sustainability Invention and Energy Demand Reduction: Co-designing Communities and Practice' funded by the ESRC/EPSRC Energy and Communities Collaborative Venture, Grant Number: RES-628-25-0043.

Notes

1 This differs somewhat from Abbott's (2001) chaotic, that is fractal, version of disciplinary change in that the emphasis here is less on repeating patterns and more on dramatic disjuncture. It should also be noted that this contrast between the two versions of live sociology are ideal typical. As Deleuze and Guattari (1988) made clear, the linear, branching, 'root-like' (territorializing) model of life, and promiscuous, topological, 'rhizomic' (deterritorializing) model are thoroughly and necessarily interwoven. The same applies no less to the relation between a sociology that undergoes progressive, linear development and a sociology that changes abruptly in unexpected directions.

2 There is much that can be said about the relation of the present perspective to critique. For instance, the present paper could be aligned with Latour's (2004) claims about the exhaustion of critique. Suffice it to say, and this point is reiterated in the discussion of critical design, critique does not well accommodate the possibility of a co-emergence of researcher-and-researched: the problem is pre-figured in critique, rather than inventively emergent. In the case of critical theory (eg Geuss,1981), for example, this pre-figuration might refer to a utopia (transcendental critique) or a standard of non-contradiction (immanent critique).

3 For a different rendering of the idiot that stresses its malleability and manipulability, see Lezaun and Soneryd (2007).

4 It can also be thought of as 'thingly' in the sense that Rheinberger (1997) uses the term 'epistemic things' to contrast with 'technical objects'. If the latter are stabilized components within the context of an experimental system, epistemic things – the objects of scientific study – physical structures, chemical reactions, biological functions – 'present themselves in a characteristic irreducible vagueness . . . [because they] . . . embody what one does not yet know' (1997: 28). For a more cultural studies version of 'thingliness', see Highmore (2011). For a philosophical perspective that stresses the vitality of the material object, see Bennett (2010).

5 http://www.dunneandraby.co.uk/content/projects/512/0 – accessed 12 March 2011.

6 http://www.sciencegallery.com/emorobotsSG – accessed 12 March 2011.

7 One can also attach this discussion to the issue of 'surprise' that can accompany social scientific analysis. One of the great pleasures of such work is 'seeing' the pattern in the data. In the case of speculative design, the pleasure lies less in this 'solving' of the riddle of, or in this 'discovery' of a hermeneutic handle on, data (a mode of territorializing, though often this is knowingly contingent). Rather, it is associated with an active proliferation of possible design trajectories.

Having noted this, the next stage is to reduce these to yield a single designed object, the prototype.

8 Details of the specifications and unexpected interpretations of these and other speculative design objects can be found at: http://www.gold.ac.uk/interaction/public/ – accessed 12 March 2011.

9 These devices can again be linked to Thrift's non-representational theory but this time to its focus on play and experiment for the sake of 'seeing what will happen . . . [of letting] the event sing you [as 'experimenter']' (Thrift, 2008: 12).

10 Michael and Gaver (2009) have addressed these devices in terms of their 'poetical' qualities and their relation to issues of 'dwelling' in and 'caring' for the environment reconceived as techno-culture or natureculture. While this analysis is partly echoed here, the primary concern is with the implications of the deployment of these devices for social scientific methodology.

11 While the focus here is on objects, solutions take many forms including systems, programmes, sociotechnical arrangements, resources and so on.

12 Having noted this, these collaborative endeavours can certainly possess elements of contingency and uncertainty. This is because they can be situated as part of broader social projects: in the case of Action Research, this might include, for instance, the re-enchantment of the world (see Reason and Bradbury, 2001b), and for participatory designers this might include social democracy (eg Gregory, 2003).

13 For details see www.ecdc.ac.uk (last accessed 24 May 2011).

14 While not elaborated here, this can also be linked up to the procedures and proposals of the Situationists.

15 However, lest this paper end on too triumphalist a note, there is also good reason to treat idiotic methodology and ludic action research circumspectly. The emphasis on creativity and play is not something that can be promoted without some consideration of its emergence elsewhere, not least in business and managerial training practice. Thrift (2005) suggests that techniques of inculcating inventiveness and creativity reflect a new managerial subject position that is able to adapt to the chronic emergency that faces capital. Ludic action research, while it might not directly feed into the (re)production of capitalism is not immune from negative outcomes. There is nothing in this processually oriented methodology that can preclude, for example, the eventual emergence of a more profligate consumption of energy or a more prejudiced view of neighbour-hoods. In the end, ludic action research does not directly address problems but opens up the possibility of creatively re-inventing those problems, and as with any process of invention, things can go wrong.

References

Abbot, A., (2001), *The Chaos of Disciplines*, Chicago: University of Chicago Press.

Akrich, M., (1992), 'The de-scription of technical objects', in W. E. Bijker and J. Law (eds), *Shaping Technology/Building Society*, 205–224, Cambridge, MA: MIT Press.

Akrich, M. and Latour, B., (1992), 'A summary of a Convenient Vocabulary for the Semiotics of Human and Nonhuman Assemblies', in W. E. Bijker and J. Law (eds), *Shaping Technology/Building Society*, 259–263, Cambridge, MA: MIT Press.

Ansell Pearson, K., (1999), *Germinal Life*, London: Routledge.

Back, L., (2007), *The Art of Listening*, Oxford: Berg.

Barad, K., (2007), *Meeting the Universe Halfway*, Durham, NC: Duke University Press.

Bargal, D., (2006), 'Personal and intellectual influences leading to Lewin's paradigm of action research: towards the 60th anniversary of Lewin's "Action research and minority problems" (1946)', *Action Research*, 4: 367–388.

Bennett, J., (2010), *Vibrant Matter*, Durham, NC: Duke University Press.

Billig, M., (1988), 'Methodology and scholarship in understanding ideological explanation', in C. Antaki (ed.), *Analysing Everyday Explanation*, London: Sage.

Boehner, K., Gaver, W. and Boucher, A., (in press), 'Probes', in C. Lury and N. Wakeford (eds), *Inventive Methods: The Happening of the Social*, London: Routledge.

De Certeau, M., (1984), *The Practice of Everyday Life*, Berkeley, CA: University of California Press.

DeLanda, M., (2002), *Intensive Science and Virtual Philosophy*, London: Continuum.

Deleuze, G. and Guattari, F., (1988), *A Thousand Plateaus: Capitalism and Schizophrenia*. London: Athlone Press.

Dunne, A., (2005), *Hertzian Tales: Electronic Products, Aesthetic Experience, and Critical Design*, Cambridge MA: MIT Press.

Dunne, A. and Raby, F., (2001), *Design Noir: The Secret Life of Electronic Objects*, London/Basel: August/Birkhauser.

Fraser, M., (2010), 'Facts, ethics and event', in C. Bruun Jensen and K. Rödje (eds), *Deleuzian Intersections in Science, Technology and Anthropology*, 57–82. New York: Berghahn Press.

Gardiner, M., (2000), *Critiques of Everyday Life*, London and New York: Routledge.

Gaver, W., (2009), 'Designing for Homo Ludens, still', in T. Binder, J. Löwgren and L. Malmborg (eds), *(Re)searching the Digital Bauhaus*, 163–178, London: Springer.

Gaver, W., Boucher, A., Law, A., Pennington, S., Bowers, J., Beaver, J., Humble, J., Kerridge, T., Villar, N., and Wilkie, A., (2008), 'Threshold devices: looking out from the home', in *Proceedings of the 26th Annual SIGCHI Conference on Human Factors in Computing Systems, Florence, Italy*, 1429–1438, New York: ACM Press.

Gaver, W., Boucher, A., Pennington, S., and Walker, B., (2004), 'Cultural probes and the value of uncertainty', *interactions*, 11 (5): 53–56.

Geuss, R., (1981), *The Idea of a Critical Theory*, Cambridge: Cambridge University Press.

Greenwood, D. J. and Levin, M., (2007), *Introduction to Action Research*, 2nd edn, Thousand Oaks, CA: Sage.

Gregory, J., (2003), 'Scandinavian Approaches to Participatory Design', *International Journal of Engineering Education*, 19: 62–74.

Halewood, M., (2011), *Alfred North Whitehead and Social Theory: The Body, Abstraction, Process*, London: Anthem Press.

Haraway, D., (1991), *Simians, Cyborgs and Nature*, London: Free Association Books.

Haraway, D., (1994), 'A game of cat's cradle: science studies, feminist theory, cultural studies', *Configurations*, 2: 59–71.

Highmore, B., (2002), *Everyday Life and Cultural Theory: An Introduction*, London: Routledge.

Highmore, B., (2011), *Ordinary Lives: Studies in Everyday Life*, Oxford and New York: Routledge.

Horst, M. and Michael, M., (2011), 'On the shoulders of idiots: Rethinking science communication as "event" ', *Science as Culture*, 20: 283–306.

Ingold, T., (1993), 'The temporality of the landscape', *World Archeology*, 25: 152–174.

Knorr Cetina, K. D., (1997), 'Sociality with objects: social relations in postsocial knowledge societies', *Theory, Culture and Society*, 14 (4): 1–30.

Latour, B., (1991), 'Technology is society made durable', in J. Law (ed.), *A Sociology of Monsters*, 103–131. London: Routledge.

Latour, B., (1992), 'Where are the missing masses? A sociology of a few mundane artifacts', in W. E. Bijker and J. Law (eds), *Shaping Technology/Building Society*, 225–258, Cambridge, MA: MIT Press.

Latour, B., (1999), *Pandora's Hope: Essays on the Reality of Science Studies*, Cambridge, MA: Harvard University Press.

Latour, B., (2004), 'Why has critique run out of steam? From matters of fact to matters of concern', *Critical Inquiry*, 30: 225–248.

Latour, B., (2005), 'From realpolitik to dingpolitik – or how to make things public', in B. Latour and P. Weibel (eds), *Making Things Public: Atmospheres of Democracy*, 14–41, Cambridge, MA: MIT Press.

Law, J., (1991), 'Introduction: monsters, machines and sociotechnical relations', in J. Law (ed.), *A Sociology of Monsters*, 1–23, London: Routledge.

The Sociological Review, 60:S1, pp. 166–183 (2012), DOI: 10.1111/j.1467-954X.2012.02122.x
© 2012 The Author. Editorial organisation © 2012 The Editorial Board of the Sociological Review

Lewin, K., (1946), 'Action research and minority problems', *Journal of Social Issues*, 2: 34–46.

Lezaun, J. and Soneryd, L., (2007), 'Consulting citizens: technologies of elicitation and the mobility of publics', *Public Understanding of Science*, 16: 279–297.

Lie, M. and Sorensen, K. H. (eds), (1996), *Making Technology our Own? Domesticating Technologies into Everyday Life*, Oslo: Scandinavian University Press.

Marres, N., (2007), 'The issues deserve more credit: pragmatist contributions to the study of public involvement in controversy', *Social Studies of Science*, 37: 759–780.

Mason, J., (1996), *Qualitative Researching*, London, Sage.

Michael, M., (2000), *Reconnecting Culture, Technology and Nature: From Society to Heterogeneity*, London: Routledge.

Michael, M., (2004), 'On making data social: heterogeneity in sociological practice', *Qualitative Research*, 4 (1): 5–23.

Michael, M., (2006), *Technoscience and Everyday Life*, Maidenhead: Open University Press/ McGraw-Hill.

Michael, M. and Gaver, W., (2009), 'Home beyond home: Dwelling with threshold devices', *Space and Culture*, 12: 359–370.

Miller, D., (2005), 'Introduction', in S. Küchler, and D. Miller (eds), *Clothing as Material Culture*, 1–19. Oxford: Berg.

Mol, A., (2002), *The Body Multiple: Ontology in Medical Practice*, Durham, NC: Duke University Press.

Muller, M. J., (2008), 'Participatory design: the third space in HCI', in J. Jacko and A. Sears (eds), *Handbook of HCI*, Mahway, NJ: Erlbaum. Available at: http://domino.research.ibm.com/cam-bridge/research.nsf/0/56844f3de38f806285256aaf005a45ab/$FILE/muller%20Chapter%20v1-2.pdf (accessed 23 March 2011).

Papanek, V., (1984), *Design for the Real World*, 2nd edn, London: Thames and Hudson.

Reason, P. and Bradbury, H. (eds), (2001a), *Handbook of Action Research*, London: Sage.

Reason, P. and Bradbury, H., (2001b), 'Introduction: inquiry and participation in search of a world worthy of human aspiration', in P. Reason and H. Bradbury (eds), *Handbook of Action Research*, 1–14. London: Sage.

Rheinberger, H-J., (1997), *Toward a History of Epistemic Things: Synthesizing Proteins in the Test Tube*, Palo Alto, CA: Stanford University Press.

Sengers, P. and Gaver, W., (2006), 'Staying open to interpretation: Engaging multiple meanings in design and evaluation', *Proceedings of the 6th Conference on Designing Interactive Systems, University Park, PA*, 99–108, New York: ACM Press.

Serres, M., (1982), *The Parasite*, Baltimore, MD: John Hopkins University Press.

Shove, E., Pantzar, M. and Watson, M., (in press), *The Dynamics of Social Practice*, London: Sage.

Silverman, D., (1993), *Interpreting Qualitative Data: Methods for Analysing Talk, Text and Interaction*, London: Sage.

Silverstone, R. and Hirsch, E. (eds), (1992), *Consuming Technologies*, London: Routledge.

Stengers, I., (2005), 'The cosmopolitical proposal', in B. Latour and P. Webel (eds), *Making Things Public*, 994–1003, Cambridge, MA: MIT Press.

Thrift, N., (2005), *Knowing Capitalism*, London: Sage.

Thrift, N., (2008), *Non-representational Theory*, London: Routledge.

Whatmore, S., (2006), 'Materialist returns: practising cultural geography in and for a more-than-human world', *Cultural Geographies*, 13 (4): 600–609.

Whitehead, A. N., (1929), *Process and Reality: An Essay in Cosmology*, New York: The Free Press.

Whitehead, A. N., (1933), *Adventures of Ideas*, Cambridge: Cambridge University Press.

Going live: towards an amphibious sociology

Celia Lury

Abstract: In this paper, I outline one strand in a genealogy of 'liveness', exploring the role of media in its emergence as a privileged spatio-temporal organization of experience. In order to consider the opportunities afforded by current developments in 'live methods' I then explore some of the implications for sociology of not simply studying practices of mediation but of inhabiting media, of being *in medias res*. Here I propose an amphibious sociology, for the potential it offers sociology to deploy methods reflexively in more than one medium, contrasting the methods of making distributive middles to the methods of establishing measures of representativeness, and exploring the opportunities and pitfalls of participation, or being in the middle.

Keywords: mediation, middles, participation, liveness and methods

Introduction: a frog's eye view

The preliminary call for papers for this Special Issue outlined a manifesto for 'live' methods. It described its aims in relation to the construction of 'a laboratory for the practice of a sociological imagination': 'The aim is to make social research responsive to social life, to bring it alive'. A live sociology was described as 'operating with mobile and volatile notions of space, experiment, mapping and a keen eye to how methods embedded in specific instruments offer up new ways for thinking of intervention'. This paper seeks to contribute to this project, but it starts by outlining some of the historical circumstances in which 'liveness' emerges.[1]

To do this, let me introduce in outline Orit Halpern's account of the historical relationship between communication science, neuro-science and design emerging in the second half of the 20th century (Halpern, forthcoming). Halpern starts her discussion by quoting extracts from 'What the frog's eye tells the frog's brain', an article by a group of cybernetically informed neuro-scientists describing their study of an isolated optic nerve of a frog: 'A frog hunts on land by vision. He escapes enemies mainly by seeing them. . . . The frog does not seem to see or, at any rate, is not concerned with the detail of stationary parts of the

The Sociological Review, 60:S1, pp. 184–197 (2012), DOI: 10.1111/j.1467-954X.2012.02123.x
© 2012 The Author. Editorial organisation © 2012 The Editorial Board of the Sociological Review. Published by Wiley-Blackwell Publishing Ltd, 9600 Garsington Road, Oxford OX4 2DQ, UK and 350 Main Street, Malden, MA 02148, USA

world around him. He will starve to death surrounded by food if it is not moving' (Lettvin *et al.*, 1959: 230). Halpern draws special attention to two features of this account: 'the mobility of vision and the capacity of vision to act (or hunt)'.[2] The title of the piece suggests, she says, an eye autonomously speaking to the brain: an eye capable of cognition. Informed by theories of information, the authors of the article claim that their innovation is to model vision in terms of communication and feedback, refusing to treat it as a series of discrete separate mechanisms (a causal chain of stimulus-response behaviour), imagining instead a continuous sensing built as a communication channel emerging from the relationship between that being seen and the seer. Halpern says:

> This experiment, even at first glance, appeared to replace a desire to ontologically describe what the physiology of the eye *is* and what the discrete and causal nature of the stimulus and response *were*, with a new focus on patterning the *process* of interaction between the eye and the world as a communication channel. This shift from objects to patterns, perhaps from ontological descriptions of the essence of an object to an epistemology focused on the relations or interactions between objects, has historical significance for making visible [a] history of visuality and politics. (forthcoming)

Her argument is that the emerging post-war neuro-sciences did not understand the image as a representation being received by the eye, transmitted through nerves and then translated upon arrival in the brain, but rather redefined vision as encompassing the entire relationship structuring the act of seeing. In this redefinition, ontology and epistemology were collapsed into each other in an approach that focused on method, process and feedback. In this collapse, the act of processing information and the act of analysing it became the same, and the possibility emerged that this decontextualized seeing process could be rebuilt in other locations. Halpern's analysis thus signals the importance of changes in how the relations between sensing and knowing were reconfigured in the second half of the 20th century by highlighting transformations in the workings of both representation and temporality, and the changes in relations between epistemology and ontology that ensued. Indeed, she also suggests that these transformations, linked as they were to issues of autonomy and survival, need to be understood in relation to contemporary concerns with security, information and biopolitics. It is these transformations, I suggest, that underpin the current interest in live methods.

To explore this claim a bit further, consider how vision was being 'rebuilt' in other locations in this period. Take, for example, television. As William Uricchio observes, 'The idea of the medium, invoked in terms like "television" and the German word for television, "Fernsehen," was about the extension of vision in real time' (2005: 232). Similarly, Samuel Weber observes that while the word itself literally describes the transport of vision, something other than the transport or transmission of the image of a fixed object is involved. He says,

> Television takes place in at least three places at once: 1. In the place (or places) where the image and sound are 'recorded'; 2. In the place (or places) where those images

and sounds are received; and 3. In the place (or places) in between, through which those images and sounds are transmitted.

> The unity of television as a medium of presentation thus involves a simultaneity that is highly ambivalent. It overcomes spatial distance but only by splitting the unity of place and with it the unity of everything that defines its identity with respect to place: events, bodies, subjects. (1996: 117)

In this view, television is organized not as the transport of images but as an active channel of communication; the objects of television – programmes, series, advertisements, trailers and so on – emerge in a 'built' organization of vision through the coordination of method, process and feedback. This is famously described by Raymond Williams as 'The replacement of a programme series of timed sequential units by a flow series of differently related units in which the timing, though real, is undeclared, and in which the real internal organization is something other than the declared organization' (1974: 87).

Weber further argues that television does not simply bring existing spaces into relation with each other, but makes a new kind of space, in which the identity (of subjects and objects) is no longer defined in relation to unity.[3] This is because television confounds the points of reference that allow the subject's determination of a single unity, of what is near and what is far, what is connected and what is disconnected. In their place, it organizes an active surface of coordinatization. (Tele)vision is here a channel, endowed with capacities to act, to see, in a space that is not given, but is brought into existence continuously and simultaneously with the objects it 'sees' or produces. Indeed, it is the continual re-making of relations in a surface of coordinatization – that is, the undeclared but 'real, internal organization' of which Williams speaks – that produces television's distinctive spatio-temporal characteristic, namely, 'liveness' (Williams, 1974 and many others).[4] Of course, the liveness of television does not only mean simultaneity of broadcast and event, though it can mean that; it also refers to the simulation of a shared present, created in processes of method, process and feedback. It thus has multiple modes and genres, including 'live' or event broadcasting, reality TV, and 'breaking' news, alongside the programmed simultaneity of collective viewing, and an aesthetics of immediacy and co-presence.

And television is not the only medium that has a space or surface of cognition, calculation and communication that may be described in terms of liveness. To give only one of many obvious contemporary examples, in April 2009, two researchers from Google research published a paper titled 'Predicting the present with Google Trends' (Varian and Choi, 2009). Varian and Choi argue that Google Trends data, based on query indices, may be used to estimate the 'current' level of economic activity in given industries, including for example, 'Motor vehicles and parts and New Housing Starts'. They indicate that a possible use of such data is to identify 'turning points in the data'. 'Simple autoregressive models do remarkably well in extrapolating smooth trends; however, by their very nature, it is difficult for such models to describe cases where the direction changes.

Perhaps Google Trends data can help in such cases'. In March 2010 two web scientists from HP's Palo Alto lab published a paper showing how the chatter on Twitter could be used to forecast box-office revenue for movies. They analysed 2.89 million tweets by 1.3 million users referring to 24 different movies released over a period of three months. They discovered that the rate at which movie tweets are generated could be used to build an effective model for predicting box-office revenue. They also found that predictions derived in this way are 'consistently more accurate than those produced by . . . Hollywood Stock Exchange, the gold standard in the industry' (Asur and Huberman, 2009). Since these reports emerged, a variety of other agencies and individuals – for example, Asda Pulse of the Nation – have begun to develop real-time web-based analytics as a way of understanding 'current activity' or the present, as we used to call it.[5]

The mediation of sociology

One implication of this brief and incomplete account of the rise of 'liveness' is that a reconsideration of the significance of mediation is necessary for sociology. Most fundamentally, it suggests that it is important for sociology to take seriously the notion of media as the environment in which the liveness (or not) of its methods now takes place. This might include drawing on the writings of Peter Sloterdijk (2009) among others. Sloterdijk argues that a technical relation to the media is emerging from the last century with increasing clarity. Writing with bravura, he describes the first use of poison gas in warfare as the event that marks 'the introduction of the environment into the battle between adversaries' (2009: 13). Now, he suggests, it is in relation to an environment – not in terms of point to point communication – that not only war, but also business and politics are conducted. He observes: 'Shakespeare prophetically articulated the principle of this relation to the environment in Shylock's line: "You take my life/When you take the means whereby I live" ' (2009: 14).

As the example of poison gas suggests, in Sloterdijk's view, the term medium refers not only to television and other media of communication, but also to the physical mediums of air, water and earth, as well as calculative infrastructures such as the gridding of time and space, the proliferation of registers, filing and listing systems, the making and remaking of categories, the identification of populations or multitudes, the transformation of urban space,[6] and the invention of logistics (Thrift, 2004). As numerous commentators have observed, software is now so substantially integrated into the dynamics of contemporary culture and society that it is routinely involved in the reformulation of processes, ideas, institutions and cultural objects. Such developments contribute to what Sloterdijk describes as air-conditioning, or the creation of atmospheres, the making active or operational of the 'environment', powered by abstractions, calculations and extensions of movement, of tracking, tracing and tagging, of reiteration, looping and folding. For Nigel Thrift (2004), this is the creation not of a space of movement but a movement-space, a dynamic or live space that is the product of artificial, paratextual forces, which form a new calculative back-ground, a pre-personal, post-social substrate of correlations, encounters and unconsidered anticipations, in which the partial actualization of superpositions bring new 'awhereness' into the world.

Such awhereness, I suggest, is one response to the condition of liveness, a condition that is consequent on the socio-technical mediation of 'life'. But, more than this, the argument I am proposing here suggests that liveness is itself but one specific form of the mediation of life.[7] To describe the nature of this speci-ficity and its implications for methods I need now to delve further into the social organization of liveness, and in particular the role of indices or indicators.[8] The suggestion I want to put forward is that the realm of the indexical is being vastly extended through the development of diverse, iterative and automatic informa-tion processing systems, supported by many different kinds of sensory memory systems (Thrift, 2008). In short, the expanded role of the indexical is what informs the particular form of life – liveness – currently being brought into existence.

Liveness

To develop this argument it is helpful to consider the understanding of indices put forward by C. S. Peirce (1931–35). For Peirce, indices are one of a three-part typology of signs – the others being icons and symbols; they use some physical or existential continuity with their objects to direct attention to that object. This capacity draws on the two components that are necessarily part of any act of signifying for Peirce: the sign-object relation and the sign-interpretant relation. The indexical act of signifying, he says, consists of a sign that signifies its object by using some physical or existential continuity (this is the sign-object relation), and generates a further sign to signify that object (this is, the sign-interpretant relation). It is thus what he calls a two-place relation. That the interpretant need not be a person but can be another sign is obviously significant in relation to the proliferation of the automated systems mentioned above,[9] and the possibility of an extended role for indices in inter-linking diverse systems, but what is also important is that, in the dynamic spaces of liveness, indexical continuity need no longer operate only extensively (in terms of nearness or farness) but may also take place intensively, that is, in the n-place relations of auto-spatialization.[10]

Consider what is involved here by way of a discussion of the relations between indices and symbols. A number of writers, from a range of different disciplines, have proposed that the importance of symbolic culture across societ-ies arises because symbols allow humans to ignore most of a vast web of word-object and object-object indexical associations by using the short-cut of symbol-symbol relations to make and mark a specific associative path. Symbols, in this view, are powerful because of their virtual character, because they are shared, and because – in systems such as language – they are exterior to the individual human mind (Lenoir, 2008). They are also powerful because of their capacity to introduce movement – or life – into culture, through their use in metaphors. So for example in his analysis of symbols that 'stand for themselves' Roy Wagner (1986) understands metaphor as a fundamental trope, and posits that metaphor is one of the principal sources of, not liveness, but *liveliness*, in any and all cultures.

For Wagner, liveliness is a consequence of the ways in which metaphor is formed not by indicating things, or by referencing them, but by setting pointers or reference points in relation with one another in such a way that the relation is innovative upon the original order of reference:

> Thus we may say that [a metaphor] 'embodies' or 'images' its object, figuring sympa-thetically by becoming itself that which it references. . . . Such a construct is interest-ing, and relevant to anyone's concerns, only insofar as it touches upon – converts inverts, reverts, subverts, perverts – and as it relates to, conventional points of refer-ence. (1986: 6)

The metaphor as self-referential coordinate (symbols that stand for them-selves in the phrase that Wagner uses as the title of the book) introduces relativity within coordinate systems, and within culture; metaphorical expressions within a symbolic culture are relative to, innovative upon, and ambiguous with regard to one another. A culture founded upon these relations is, Wagner says, lively.

The suggestion here, however, is that while the 'life-likeness' of culture is not new, the emergence of liveness (rather than or as well as liveliness) is a conse-quence of a shift in how the tropic relations of culture described by Wagner are made, unmade and remade in relations between symbols and indices, including in the methods of social (and natural) science. The use of indices in social and natural scientific methods has of course historically been supported in various ways, by complex sets of social relations and technologies, often enabling their objects – scientific facts – to travel great distances in stable form (Latour, 1987). Indeed, such support has been what made objectivity in natural and social science possible, as numerous historians and sociologists have made clear. But, to speak in very general terms, it has typically required the use of indices in ways that enabled them to make references in relation to objects as if they were indifferent to those objects. The mobility or liveness of today's indices, in con-trast, is precisely to do with the development of an active or technical relation to a dynamic environment as described by Sloterdijk. In this relation, the useful-ness of one of the most important capacities of indices – to point, to indicate 'here' – a usefulness for making culture that has been limited by the stabilized fixity of the coordinates of the relations they have been used to enact, is being expanded as liveness by the introduction of dynamic feedback loops.

In the middle

What implications does this account of the role of indices have for the doing of methods in the social sciences?[11] Perhaps the most important is that methods need no longer be implemented as if from what is sometimes described as a bird's eye view (that is from above or outside that which is seen), but, rather, with a frog's eye, that is, in or as the work of a medium, or, *in medias res*.[12] Importantly, this shift – towards what I call an amphibious sociology – involves a very particular understanding of middle. In a discussion of the work of Walter Benjamin, Peter Fenves argues that a 'pure middle' would be one whose middleness is no longer defined with respect to determinable end points; rather it is an infinite and infinitely divisible space. As in Weber's discussion of the simultaneity of television, in which unity is destroyed, Fenves claims that,

> Nothing can withstand this space [that of the pure middle] *intact*: infinite indivisibility is the 'law' of this space, which, however, cannot be posited as a law, since this division is never governed by an identifiable rule. The 'law' of this space, the rule by which its infinite divisibility is articulated, must likewise be infinitely co-divisible: in German, *mit-teilbar*, which is to say, 'communicable.' (2001: 255)

Clearly, this is an abstract understanding of middle, but the introduction of the principles of such abstraction into social life by way of active indices and the work of mediation is precisely what is of interest here.

Indeed, I want to suggest that a fantasy pure middle of infinite divisibility may be seen as one of the animating dynamics of contemporary mediation. Such a claim may make more sense if a Luhmannian understanding of mediation as, not a unity, but the operation of the difference of medium/form is used (Luhmann, 1992). So, for example, Elena Esposito (2004) draws on Luhmann's formulation as follows: 'on both sides of the distinction medium/form there are elements that in the medium are coupled loosely, and are coupled more tightly in the form – like, for instance, grains of sand in a beach that have no connection to one another and therefore are fit to receive the form left by a footprint or like light rays making objects visible'. In short, following Luhmann she is suggesting that if a medium is understood not as a unity but as the difference medium/form, then the organization of that difference in terms of, for example, the functions of search and retrieve, will enable the tracks of some forms of life to be made visible and not others.

These divisible or 'distributive' middles of mediation may be contrasted with the middles of representation, such as the representative measures of central tendencies that are well established in social science (eg mean, mode, median etc) as well as measures of spread (eg range, standard deviation etc).[13] In contrast to such centralizing measures, in an amphibious sociology, with a frog's eye view, there can be no single centre but only a middle, or rather many middles to be worked in, worked up and worked out. In these middles, in the work of distributive middles or mediation, the absoluteness of the distinction between data and analysis is called into doubt. Indeed, the suggestion being made here is that this distinction was previously upheld only through a carefully established (but also usually taken-for-granted) use of the index and the stabilizing, centralizing statistical techniques of representativeness. In such uses, the capacity of the index to individualize was fixed, located in a particular place and time, in order that it could provide the fixed coordinates in relation to which the centre, depth and liveliness of a whole or unified culture could be established. In the dynamic spaces of liveness, however, indices can – and are – being put to new uses founded on the manipulation of the capacity for dynamic, two-way signifying relations to make distributive middles, that is, to continually make available the possibility of changing relations between an individualized entity and the population, history, context or environment of which it is a part.

In these uses, data are shifting indicators, indices of actualization, of a process of individuation, the isolation or divisibility of some specific thing. They are forward as well as backward looking, markers of the multiple composite durations – simultaneity, immediacy, real-time, the contemporary – that comprise liveness. As such, they may be seen to contribute to a rather different version of structuralism to that described by, for example, Levi-Strauss (1973 [1955]), for whom generative structural transformation is driven by ahistorical relational differentiation. In the dynamic spaces brought to life in the activity of indices as described here, transformations are, by contrast, historically generated in the sense that the relational principles of differentiation (of medium/form) may themselves change as circuits or channels, rather than as structures.

Indeed, this possibility is what Latour finds already described in the work of Gabriel Tarde: as Latour represents Tarde, 'the very heart of social phenomena is quantifiable because individual monads are constantly evaluating one another in simultaneous attempts to expand and to stabilize their worlds' (Latour, 2010: 4). Latour's conclusion is that the aim for sociology should be to:

find ways to gather the individual 'he' and 'she' without *losing out on* the specific ways in which they are able to mingle, in a standard, in a code, in a bundle of customs, in a scientific discipline, in a technology – but never in some overarching society. The challenge is to try to obtain their aggregation without either shifting our attention at any point to a whole, or changing modes of inquiry. (2010: 4–5)

The implication here then is that methods of liveness cannot work from or find a centre since there is no single whole in relation to which a centre might be found. Instead, live methods must be satisfied with an engagement with relations and with parts, with differentiation, and be involved in making middles, in dividing without end(s), in mingling, bundling and coming together. The objects of such methods – being live – are without unity, un-whole-some; put another way, they are partial un-divisible, distributed and distributing.

Taking part

But this formulation of live methods in terms of partiality introduces a new set of methodological concerns, those to do with objectivity and subjectivity, and the problems of the presumed circularity or self-referentiality of the circuits or channels of mediation.[14] In relation to social science, this concern is sometimes presented in terms of a contrast between reflection and reflexivity, in which reflection is an uncritical doubling of the object by the subject (or researcher), while reflexivity is an operation that involves the subject in considering the ground of the object, and the relation between subject and object. In some formulations in philosophy of social science, this contrast is formulated as a binary opposition: on the one hand, the collapse of the object-subject distinction in reflection and on the other, its reinstatement as reflexivity. In relation to live methods, there is however an alternative to be found – in the middle – that is neither the erasure of the difference between subject and object that comes from the absolute feedback of reflection (sometimes allied with narcissism) nor its absolute re-establishment as reflexivity (sometimes allied with scepticism). This alternative, middle, position is one in which, while the (critical) subject is always in relation to an (epistemic) object, this is a relation that is never stable, is always being continually re-established.[15] This might be described as a situation of perpetual animation.

This situation is crucially shaped, however, by the involvement of many actors, who are also, variously, in the middle. Of course the involvement of multiple actors in the conduct of social research is not new in itself, but there is currently an ongoing redistribution that appears to be challenging established relations between social research in the academy, business and public and everyday life. The historical importance of the links between (cultural and political) representation and (epistemological) representativeness for methods of social research have been well documented by Desorisières, who argues that the significance and efficacy of, for example, statistical information was created in a state-supported network 'of stabilized connections, of routinized equivalences, and words to describe them. . . . It is precisely this language that provides the reference points and the common meaning in relation to which the actors [of the public sphere] can qualify and express their reactions' (1998: 333). That this network is being tested by the contemporary redistribution – or mediation – of expertise and authority in methods of social research is thus not surprisingly one of the issues at stake in recent discussions of a public sociology (Burawoy, 2005; Back, 2007).[16] It is also at issue in any consideration of the potential of live methods.

The suggestion here, however, is that, rather than representativeness, it is the nature and characteristics of partiality – of the taking part, or participation – or partisanship (Latour and Weibel, 2005; Rogers and Marres, 2002) that will be the crucial issue in relation to the use of live methods. This involves not only questions of who has access to getting involved but also how that involvement or participation happens, and who is held accountable and how for what happens. At the same time the essentially recursive or automatic character of mediation is becoming more and more important. For example, while the relations between categories and scales of valuation have always been dynamic (Guyer, 2004), sociology has often sought to cleanse the data it employs of categorical instability in order to produce continuity (Uprichard, forthcoming). An alternative approach, however, may be found in the use of indices as markers of the edge between an epistemic object or thing and a dynamic space of problem-solving (Rheinberger, 1997), as epistemology and ontology are, as Halpern observes from the frog's eye view, collapsed in an approach that enables categories and scales to be mutually adjusted to a problem that itself only emerges through the continuous application of method, process and feedback.

To explore the dimensions of the issues at stake let me give some examples. First, to return to the case of television: a number of commentators observe that the last twenty to thirty years have seen a clear shift from broadcasting as an activity associated with the maintenance of the public sphere to narrowcasting via the organization of metadata to support adaptive agent-based mediations of individual tastes. As Uricchio puts it, there has been a transformation in 'the viewer-television interface – and particularly the notion of flow – that has slowly transformed from programming-centered, to active audience-centered, to adaptive agent-centered' (2005: 256). Then take the Internet. Consider, for example, the opportunities for participation offered by the social buttons, counters and access to the Open Graph provided to a user of Facebook. They enable the individual to filter the content of the web through the activities of their own 'likes' or recommendations *and* that of their contacts (Gerlitz and Helmond, unpublished paper). This is a powerful use of middles by live algorithmic methods. However, while the filter can be modified by the user to create a variety of differently scaled assemblages through the manipulation of profiles, users are only given partial – and temporary – access to the 'likes' they themselves generate, and there is no general ranking of content available within the platform based on Facebook's specific engagement measures such as 'likes'. In short, the organization of participation – even when it is enabled as a dynamic process – may result in highly uneven positions of access and control to problem-setting and problem-solving.

Consider also the findings of a study of the forms of participation on the Internet that have emerged over the last ten years. In the context of observing that publics – unlike organizations – exist only when they are addressed as such, that is, that publics are temporally and discursively constituted by constant attention and circulation of discourse about specific issues (Warner, 2002), Fish *et al.* (2011) identify a number of salient characteristics of contemporary forms of participation. These include the findings that: participation nearly always employs both a 'formal social enterprise' and an 'organized public'; the formal enterprise and public are typically engaged in some structural and temporal relationship to one another; and that forms of participation are divided up into tasks and goals, and relate to the resource that is created through participation. Such findings are significant. As they observe:

> many contemporary endeavors no longer draw a distinction between the deliberative and critical function of a public sphere and the action orientation of organizations, but instead seek ways to express political discontent or solve social problems through direct action. Social entrepreneurialism and Free Software/Free Culture movements starkly represent aspects of this change. Though the terms public and organization (like 'community' and 'network') seem more appropriate to some projects or groups

than others, they remain too vague to help understand variation and similarity across them all, and fail to indicate what might be occurring, or at stake, in the promotion (or critique) of participation. (2011: 5)

What such examples suggest is that there is more than one way of being in a middle, as well as more than one middle. Or put differently, the issue of participation is central not only to an emerging media economy of cumulative interaction (Bateson, 1987) but also to the liveness of sociology.

Stuck in the middle?

So, what are the implications for sociology of working in the middle, *in medias res*? Is 'going live' going to lead, unavoidably, to a position of compromise, of complicity with media? In some ways the argument put forward here is, yes, but only in the sense that sociology is always *in medias res*. In other ways, the answer is no: rather than seeing live methods in terms of a compromise between the two ends of reflection or reflexivity, or as failing in its ability to identify a centre (to be representative), the argument put forward here is that live methods must involve operating the middle or middles in the interests of parts rather than of wholes. And it is in this respect that I have put forward the notion of amphibious sociology. Etymologically, the term derives from amphi- meaning 'both sides' and -bios meaning 'life'. The term was initially used for all kinds of combined natures (not quite fish, not quite reptiles), but is now used to refer to animals that live both on the land and in the water, that is, live in two media. The proposal for an amphibious sociology arises from the belief that the recognition that we live in (at least) two media will facilitate an understanding of the work of mediation, and with this, the significance of the operation of the difference medium/form for sociology.

And while there may be no law adequate to the pure middle to guide the social researcher, this does not mean that the middle is a muddle or a mess, or, of course, that it is politically neutral. Rather, as Elena Esposito (2004) says, the distinction medium/form may be applied in sociology to many different problems, including – perhaps especially – those cases 'where one wants to show how a specific modality of contingency is produced and how it is controlled through special forms'. Amphibious sociology is put forward here as a way to insist upon the importance of recognizing that liveness is necessarily a question of specific forms of life and not others, and that it is and always has been linked to issues of autonomy, security and biopolitics from which it cannot be disentangled. It suggests that the challenge today is to learn how to take part(s), to operate the middles of liveness in such a way that the specific modality of contingency that such forms of control bring into existence are made available for many kinds of occupation, organization and association: that is, to make of liveness methods that might support more than 'bare life' (Agamben, 1998).

Notes

1 Les Back, Robert Zimmer and I are currently coordinating an ESRC-funded NCRM research network, 'Real-time research' that seeks to address this issue. This paper draws on discussions with them, and with Lisa Adkins (with whom I have been working on a series of projects relating to the empirical), and with Luciana Parisi and Tiziana Terranova (with whom I have been working up a related notion of a-liveness in an exploration of the becoming topological of culture (Lury *et al.*, forthcoming)). I would like to acknowledge the contributions of all these people to the ideas presented here and thank them for sharing their ideas.

2 It is interesting to substitute 'vision' with 'method' here: 'the mobility of method and the capacity of method to act'.

3 Williams himself seems to hold onto a notion of wholeness if not of unity: 'It is evident that what is now called 'an evening's viewing' is in some ways planned, by providers and then by viewers, *as a whole*; that it is in any event planned in discernible sequences which in this sense override particular programme units' (1974: 93).

4 It is interesting to consider the parallels between social research methods and the historical emergence and development of specific media. As Les Back (unpublished paper) observes, until the late 20th century ethnographic research was set within a field framed by a particular sequence and set of time frames, that is, initial encounter, immersion and fieldwork, note taking, leaving the field and writing up often from afar. Ethnographies were written within 'the ethnographic present' that provided accounts of culture as if captured like timeless snapshots. Like photography they relied on a notion of indexicality to organize representation as 'this will have been'. This version of ethnographic representation and authority was critically transformed as ethnographers reflected on the implication of their own writing in the making of ethnographic texts. Today the growth of connectivity poses a further challenge for researchers because the separation between 'the field' and the place of analysis and interpretation no longer holds. The ethnographic present is expanding, resulting in the proliferation of ethnographic accounts that destabilize the relationship between 'the field' and the time and place of ethnography.

5 Natural and social scientists have also begun to develop a diverse range of methods for the analysis of web-based data sets, including network analysis, digital methods and mathematical dynamics.

6 One example is described by Larry Busbea in his account of experiments in urban space in France in the second half of the twentieth century (2007), specifically the spatial urbanism and mobile architecture of the 1960s which comprised architectural design, artistic production, and engineering experimentation. Busbea argues that what characterizes this period is an exploration of the way in which non-material structures begin to be perceived as active within social space: réseau, nappe, trame, tissu and combinatoire were the key concepts. He describes this new culture of relational space as topological.

7 As Elena Esposito observes, 'while on the one hand a medium cannot be observed immediately and is apprehended indirectly in the forms through which it exists, . . . [on the other] these forms themselves would not exist without the corresponding medium'. http://www.helsinki.fi/science/commens/terms/index2.html

8 This approach draws on the recognition that 'social organization is necessarily "present" in [a] description, . . . description depends upon it though it does not explicate it. This organization is already "in" the description' (Smith, 1981: 336, quoted in Uprichard, forthcoming).

9 Other features of the index described by Peirce also relevant to an understanding of their significance in spaces of liveness include the fact that indices have their characteristics independently of interpretation; as Peirce puts it, 'an index is a real thing or fact which is a sign of its objects quite regardless of its being interpreted as a sign'. Peirce also claims that indices assert nothing; that is, while they indicate or show things they do not describe, they do not have meanings. Moreover, indices do not resemble, nor do they share any law-like relations with their objects.

10 This is a term taken from the work of philosopher Gilles Châtelet (2006) who observes a renewal of the notion of indexation in what he describes as graphic reason. In 'classical' mathematical

calculation, he argues, a set of indices was neutral: indexation remained external to the development of calculation. Indices were operated as if notation was completely indifferent to that which it noted. In 'contemporary' calculation, he proposes however, notation is becoming concrete: indexation is no longer determined by an external 'set' (of numbers or data) but by a process of deformation in a surface that is itself in motion. Indexation is no longer reduced to the external evaluation of a collection or set, he says, but becomes 'the protagonist of an experiment which secretes its own overflow' (2006: 40).

11 It is worth pointing out that one of the authors of the article discussed by Halpern, Herbert Maturana, went on to produce a series of publications that have come to be influential in many branches of social science.

12 In an account of the history of programmability, Wendy Hui Kyong Chun (2010) proposes that software cultures are best known through involvement, indeed, can hardly be known from the outside.

13 I am grateful to Emma Uprichard for her observation that these kinds of 'where' and 'what' measures are fundamental to the constitution of sample and population.

14 As Elena Esposito observes, this is not a problem specific to a mediated sociology, since sociological research always involves 'investigating a category of object – communication – to which the research itself belongs', although all too often it 'takes as an object distinctions that depend on communication itself' (Esposito, 2004: 14).

15 In his analysis of the 20th century's technical relation to the environment, Sloterdijk refers to what he calls 'an acceleration in "explication" ', by which he means 'the revealing-inclusion of the background givens underlying manifest operations' (2009: 9).

16 As Ruppert and Savage (forthcoming) among others suggest, the emerging politics of methods is likely to be tightly linked to the formation of constituencies of informational gatekeepers, organizers, and interpreters who may be only loosely or not at all attached to formal organizations and companies.

References

Agamben, G., (1998), *Homo Sacer: Sovereign Power and Bare Life*, Stanford, CA: Stanford University Press.

Asur, S. and Huberman, B. A., (2009), 'Predicting the future with social media', available at: arxiv.org/abs/1003.5699v1

Back, L., (2007), *The Art of Listening*, Oxford: Berg.

Bateson, G., (1987), *Steps to an Ecology of Mind*, San Francisco: Chandler.

Burawoy, M., (2005), 'For public sociology', *American Sociological Review*, 70 (1): 4–28.

Busbea, L., (2007), *Topologies: The Urban Utopia in France, 1960–1970*, Cambridge, MA: MIT Press.

Chatêlet, G., (2006), 'Interlacing the singularity, the diagram and the metaphor', in S. Duffy (ed.), *Virtual Mathematics: The Logic of Difference*, 31–45. Manchester: Clinamen Press.

Chun, W. Hui Kyong, (2010), *Programmed Visions*, Cambridge, MA: MIT Press.

Desorisières, A., (1998), *The Politics of Large Numbers: A History of Statistical Reasoning*, trans. C. Naish, Cambridge, MA: Harvard University Press.

Esposito, E., (2004), 'The arts of contingency', *Critical Inquiry*, 31 (1): 7–25.

Fenves, P., (2001), *Arresting Language: From Leibniz to Benjamin*, Stanford, CA: Stanford University Press.

Fish, A., Murillo, L. F. R., Nguyen, L., Panofsky, A. and Kelty, C. M., (2011), 'Birds of the Internet', *Journal of Cultural Economy*, 4 (2): 157–187.

Gerlitz, C. and Helmond, A., 'The like economy – social buttons and the data-intensive web', unpublished paper.

Guyer, J., (2004), *Marginal Gains: Monetary Transactions in Atlantic Africa*, Chicago: University of Chicago Press.

The Sociological Review, 60:S1, pp. 184–197 (2012), DOI: 10.1111/j.1467-954X.2012.02123.x

Halpern, O., (forthcoming), *The Eye of Time: Histories of Representation, Perception, and Archiving in Cybernetic Thought*, Cambridge, MA: MIT Press.

Latour, B., (1987), *Science in Action*, Cambridge, MA: Harvard University Press.

Latour, B., (2000), 'On the partial existence of existing and nonexisting objects', in Lorraine Dalston (ed.), *Biographies of Scientific Objects*, 247–269, Chicago and London: University of Chicago Press.

Latour, B., (2010), 'Tarde's idea of quantification', in M. Candea (ed.), *The Social after Gabriel Tarde: Debates and Assessments*, 145–162, Abingdon: Routledge.

Latour, B. and Weibel, P., (2005), *Making Things Public: Atmospheres of Democracy*, Cambridge, MA: MIT Press.

Lenoir, T., (2008), 'Foreword: Machinic Bodies, Ghosts and Para-Selves: Confronting the Singularity with Brian Rotman', in B. Rotman, *Becoming Beside Ourselves: The Alphabet, Ghosts and Distributed Being*, Durham, NC: Duke University Press.

Lettvin, J. Y., Maturana, H. R., McCulloch, W. S. and Pitts, W. H., (1959), 'What the frog's eye tells the frog's brain', *Proceedings of the IRE*, 47 (11): 1940–1959. Re-published in W. S. McCulloch, (1965) *Embodiments of Mind*, Cambridge, MA: MIT Press: 230–255.

Levi-Strauss, C., (1973 [1955]), *Tristes Tropiques*, New York: Atheneum.

Luhmann, N., (1992), 'The form of writing', *Stanford Literature Review*, 9: 25–42.

Lury, C., Parisi, L. and Terranova, T., (forthcoming), 'The becoming topological of culture', *Theory Culture and Society*, Double Special Issue, forthcoming.

Peirce, C. S., (1931–35), *Collected Papers of Charles Sanders Peirce*, Vols. 1–6, ed. C. Hartsorhen and P. Weiss, Cambridge, MA: Harvard University Press.

Rheinberger, H-J., (1997), *Toward a History of Epistemic Things*, Stanford, CA: Stanford University Press.

Rogers, R. and Marres, N., (2002), 'French scandals on the Web, and on the streets: stretching the limits of reported reality', *Asian Journal of Social Science*, 30 (2): 339–353.

Ruppert, E. and Savage, M., (forthcoming), 'Transactional politics', in L. Adkins and C. Lury (eds), *Measure and Value*, Sociological Review Special Issue.

Sloterdijk, P., (2009), *Terror from the Air*, Los Angeles: Semiotext(e).

Thrift, N., (2004), 'Movement-space: the changing domain of thinking resulting from the development of new kinds of spatial awareness', *Economy and Society*, 33 (4): 582–604.

Thrift, N., (2008), *Non-Representational Theory: Space, Politics, Affect*, London: Routledge.

Uprichard, E., (forthcoming), 'Dirty data: Longitudinal classification systems – York Food Retail Outlets', in L. Adkins and C. Lury (eds), *Measure and Value*, Sociological Review Special Issue.

Uricchio, W., (2005), 'Television's next generation: technology /interface culture / flow', in L. Spigel and J. Olsson (eds), *Television after TV: Essays on a Medium in Transition*, Durham, NC: Duke University Press.

Varian, H. and Choi, H., (2009), 'Predicting the present with Google Trends', available at: googleresearch.blogspot.com/20

Wagner, R., (1986), *Symbols that Stand for Themselves*, Chicago and London: Chicago University Press.

Warner, M., (2002), *Publics and Counterpublics*, Cambridge, MA: Zone Books.

Weber, S., (1996), *Mass Mediauras: Form, Technics, Media*, Stanford, CA: Stanford University Press.

Williams, R., (1974), *Television: Technology as Cultural Form*, London: Fontana.

Notes on contributors

Les Back is Professor of Sociology at Goldsmiths, University of London. His work attempts to create a sensuous or live sociology committed to new modes of sociological writing and representation. His books include: *Cultural Sociology: An Introduction* with Andy Bennett, Laura Desfor Edles, Margaret Gibson, David Inglis, Ronald Jacobs and Ian Woodward (Wiley-Blackwell, 2012); *The Art of Listening* (Berg, 2007), *Auditory Cultures Reader* with Michael Bull (Berg, 2003), *Out of Whiteness* with Vron Ware (University of Chicago Press, 2002); *The Changing Face of Football: Racism and Multiculture in the English Soccer*, with Tim Crabbe and John Solomos (Berg, 2001); and *New Ethnicities and Urban Culture: Racisms and Multiculture in Young Lives* (University College Press, 1996). In 2011 he published a free online book called Academic Diary (http://www.academic-diary.co.uk/) that argues for the values of scholarship and teaching. He also writes journalism and has made documentary films. e-mail: l.back@gold.ac.uk

Mariam Motamedi Fraser is a senior lecturer at Goldsmiths, University of London. She is currently working on a Reader on stories and storying in sociology and social theory. She is also exploring the pedagogical challenges posed by Islamic studies in higher education. Her previous research focused on a 'family' of concepts – facts, values, ethics, process and event – which she explored most thoroughly in relation to sociology and science, but also in relation to other fields including art and music. She has since become engaged in the question of the limits (or not) of sociological method and critique. Her publications include: 'Making music matter', *Theory, Culture and Society* (2005), 22 (1): 173–189; *Intimacy in Research*, co-edited with Nirmal Puwar, special issue of *History of Human Sciences* (2008), 21 (4); 'Experiencing sociology', *European Journal of Sociology* (2009), 12 (1): 63–81; and 'Facts, ethics and event' in C. B. Jensen and K. Rödje, eds, *Deleuzian Intersections* (Berghahn Books, 2010). e-mail: m.motamedi-fraser@gold.ac.uk

Yasmin Gunaratnam teaches in the Sociology Department at Goldsmiths, University of London on research methods, culture and gender. Her research is

The Sociological Review, 60:S1, pp. 198–201 (2012), DOI: 10.1111/j.1467-954X.2012.02124.x
Editorial organisation © 2012 The Editorial Board of the Sociological Review. Published by Wiley-Blackwell Publishing Ltd, 9600 Garsington Road, Oxford OX4 2DQ, UK and 350 Main Street, Malden, MA 02148, USA

interested in understanding life's threshold moments and transitions, including more recent work on the materiality of race and climate change. Yasmin has a specialist interest in narrative and stories. She is author of *Researching Race and Ethnicity* (Sage, 2003) and has jointly edited *Narratives and Stories in Health Care* with David Oliviere (Oxford University Press, 2009). Yasmin is currently writing a book of creative non-fiction *Mortal Cartographies* (to be published by Bloomsbury Academic) which brings together her work on dying migrants and intercultural care. She is interested in developing new forms of sociological writing and has published short stories as well as poems. Yasmin has spent an extensive amount of time working as a freelance researcher and community activist. She is a member of the editorial collective of the journal *Feminist Review*. e-mail: y.gunaratnam@gold.ac.uk

Celia Lury is Director of Centre for Interdisciplinary Methodologies (CIM) at the University of Warwick. The Centre is designed to explore the role of inter-disciplinary methods in the making of collaborative experimental spaces. She is co-editor of *Inventive Methods* (Routledge, 2012) with Nina Wakeford and of *Measure and Value* (Wiley-Blackwell, 2011) with Lisa Adkins, as well as a Special Issue on 'What is the empirical?' (2009) in the *European Journal of Social Theory*. Other publications include the edited collection (with Mariam Fraser and Sarah Kember) on *Inventive Life: Approaches to the New Vitalism* (Sage, 2006), as well as the jointly authored book on *The Global Culture Industry: The Mediation of Things* with Scott Lash (Polity, 2007) and the monograph *Brands: The Logos of the Global Economy* (Routledge, 2004). e-mail: c.lury@warwick.ac.uk

Noortje Marres is a lecturer in sociology and Co-Director of the Centre for the Study of Invention and Social Process (CSISP) at Goldsmiths, University of London. She also convenes the MA/MSc Digital Sociology. Noortje was part of the team that developed Issuecrawler, an online platform for the location, analysis and visualisation of issue networks. Her first book, *Material Participation* (Palgrave, 2012), examines the role of devices, objects and everyday settings in organizing public engagement. With Javier Lezaun she co-edited a Special Section on 'Materials and Devices of the Public' for the journal *Economy and Society*. e-mail: n.marres@gold.ac.uk

Mike Michael is Professor of Sociology at the University of Sydney. His inter-ests include the relation of everyday life to technoscience, and biotechnological and biomedical innovation and culture. Current research projects include an examination of the ethical aspects of HIV pre-exposure prophylaxis (with Marsha Rosengarten), and the interdisciplinary exploration of energy demand reduction through sociological and speculative design techniques (with Bill Gaver and Jennifer Gabrys). Amongst recent publications are *Techno-science and Everyday Life* (Open University Press, 2006) and (with Lynda Birke and Arnie Arluke) *The Sacrifice: How Scientific Experiments Transform*

Animals and People (Purdue University Press, 2007). e-mail: mike.michael@
sydney.edu.au

Nirmal Puwar is a senior lecturer in sociology at Goldsmiths, University of
London. Her work draws on multiple methods from inter-disciplinary sources
to consider the encounters of bodies and space. She has coordinated a number
of research projects on politics, space and inventive methods. She is keen to
initiate and build on a form of creative and critical public sociology to be considered 'Curating Sociology'. She is Director of the Methods Lab http://www.
gold.ac.uk/methods-lab/ She is the author of *Space Invaders: Race, Gender and
Bodies out of Place* (Berg, 2003) and has co-edited a number of collections
including: *South Asian Women in the Diaspora* (2003) with Parvati Raghuram;
'Post-Colonial Bourdieu' for *The Sociological Review* (2009); 'Intimacy in
Research' in *The History of the Human Sciences* (2008) with Mariam Fraser;
'Noise of the Past' for *Senses and Society* (2011) with Sanjay Sharma; as well
as ten issues of the international journal *Feminist Review*, including Issue 100.
e-mail: n.puwar@gold.ac.uk

Sanjay Sharma is a senior lecturer in the Department of Sociology and Communications, School of Social Sciences, Brunel University, UK. He has published widely in the areas of critical multiculturalism and radical pedagogy. This
work interrogates the problem of difference and alterity, and questions the
efficacy of contemporary 'race' work in the fields of media/cultural studies and
sociology which principally operate in the arena of identity and representation.
His recent work includes exploring the technologies and materialities of race in
digital spaces. He has authored the monograph, *Multicultural Encounters* (Palgrave, 2006), and is a founding editor of the online, open access *darkmatter*
Journal (http://www.darkmatter101.org). e-mail: sanjay.sharma@brunel.ac.uk

Alberto Toscano is senior lecturer in the Department of Sociology, Goldsmiths,
University of London. He is the author of *Fanaticism: On the Uses of an Idea*
(Verso, 2010), and *The Theatre of Production: Philosophy and Individuation
between Kant and Deleuze* (Palgrave, 2006). He is also an editor of the journal
Historical Materialism. He has published widely in the field of social theory and
philosophy; Marx and Marxisms; theories of 'real abstraction' and value in
capitalism; anarchism and communism; political subjectivity; revolt, revolution,
and social change; the politics and sociology of religion (fanaticism, messianism,
political theology); Italian workerism (operaismo) and autonomism; cognitive
capitalism and immaterial labour; biopolitics; imperialism and empire; economic sociology; contemporary French and Italian thought; the politics of art
and the aesthetics of the economy. e-mail: a.toscano@gold.ac.uk

Emma Uprichard is an associate professor at the Centre for Interdisciplinary
Methodologies, University of Warwick. She is particularly interested in the
methodological challenge of applying complexity theory to the study of patterns

The Sociological Review, 60:S1, pp. 198–201 (2012), DOI: 10.1111/j.1467-954X.2012.02124.x
Editorial organisation © 2012 The Editorial Board of the Sociological Review

of change and continuity in the social world. She has substantive research interests in: methods and methodology, cities and urban regions, time and temporality, children and childhood, and food. She has edited a four-set volume, with David Byrne, on *Cluster Analysis* (Sage, 2012). She is currently PI on the ESRC grant, 'Food Matters: A Sociological Case Study of Food and Eating across the Life Course in York c. 1945–2010'. e-mail: e.uprichard@gold.ac.uk

Index

The Sociological Review, 60:S1, pp. 202–206 (2012), DOI: 10.1111/1467-954X.12000
Editorial organisation © 2012 The Editorial Board of the Sociological Review

The Sociological Review, 60:S1, pp. 202–206 (2012), DOI: 10.1111/1467-954X.12000
Editorial organisation © 2012 The Editorial Board of the Sociological Review